Contemporary Social Issues

Series Editor: George Ritzer, University of Maryland

The Wilding of America
How Greed and Violence Are Eroding Our Nation's Character

Charles Derber

Boston College

St. Martin's Press

New York

Manager, publishing services: Emily Berleth
Packaging project editor: Kalea Chapman
Production supervisor: Joe Ford
Art director: Lucy Krikorian
Cover design: Rod Hernandez
Cover photo: Comstock, Inc.

Manufactured in the United States of America.

0 9 8
f e d c

For information, write:
Worth Publishers
33 Irving Place
New York, NY 10003

www.worthpublishers.com

ISBN: 0-312-13290-5 (softcover)
ISBN: 0-312-14069-X (hardcover)

Acknowledgments
Acknowledgments and copyrights appear at the back of the book on page 168, which
constitutes an extension of the copyright page.

Library of Congress Cataloging-in-Publication Data

Derber, Charles.
    The wilding of America : how greed and violence are eroding our
nation's character / Charles Derber.
        p. cm. -- (Contemporary social issues)
    ISBN 0-312-14069-X
    1. Violence--United States. 2. Violent crimes--United States.
3. Wealth--Moral and ethical aspects--United States. 4. United
States--Social conditions--1980-   I. Title. II. Series
Contemporary social issues (New York, N.Y.)
HN90.V5D47   1996
303.6'0973--dc20   95-36301
                                                             CIP

Contents

Foreword

As we move toward the close of the twentieth century, we confront a seemingly endless array of pressing social issues: crime, urban decay, inequality, ecological threats, rampant consumerism, war, AIDS, inadequate health care, national and personal debt, and many more. Although such problems are regularly dealt with in newspapers, magazines, and trade books and on radio and television, such popular treatment has severe limitations. By examining these issues systematically through the lens of sociology, we can gain greater insight into them and be better able to deal with them. It is to this end that St. Martin's Press has created this series on contemporary social issues.

Each book in the series will cast a new and distinctive light on a familiar social issue, while challenging the conventional view, which may obscure as much as it clarifies. Phenomena that seem disparate and unrelated will be shown to have many commonalities and to reflect a major, but largely unrecognized, trend within the larger society. Or a systematic comparative investigation will demonstrate the existence of social causes or consequences that are overlooked by other types of analysis. In uncovering such realities the books in this series will be much more than intellectual exercises; they will have powerful practical implications for our lives and for the structure of society.

At another level, this series will fill a void in book publishing. There is certainly no shortage of academic titles, but those books tend to be introductory texts for undergraduates or advanced monographs for professional scholars. Missing are broadly accessible, issue-oriented books appropriate for all students (and for general readers). The books in this series will occupy that niche somewhere between popular trade books and monographs. Like trade books, they will deal with important and interesting social issues, be well written, and as jargon free as possible. However, they will be more rigorous than trade books in meeting academic standards for writing and research. Although they are not textbooks, they will often explore topics covered in basic textbooks and therefore will be easily integrated into the curriculum of sociology and other disciplines.

Each of the books in the St. Martin's series "Contemporary Social Issues" is a new and distinctive piece of work. I believe that students, serious general readers, and professors will all find the books to be informative, interesting, thought provoking, and exciting.

George Ritzer

Preface

In 1992, I went to New York City to talk about "wilding" on WABC, the flagship radio station of ABC. The station invited me shortly after the brutal Central Park gang-rape of a jogger—the event that led the media to coin the term wilding. Although I hoped to educate New Yorkers, it turned out that the Big Apple still had a few things to teach me about my subject.

As I was waiting in the studio for my turn, I heard my talk-show host, Bob Grant, talk about the city's graffiti problem and raise one possible solution: cutting off the hands of the young offenders. I sensed I had some differences with this tough hombre, but I realized why he had invited me down. He and his callers were obsessed with the disintegration of the city and young wilders running loose on the street.

I soon learned why, in a very personal way. The day after my conversation with Grant, I drove down at noon to a conference on the lower West Side of Manhattan. After about an hour, I had a premonition that I had better check my car, probably a residue of my conversation with Grant. I walked quickly back to the street and could hardly believe my eyes. My new Honda Accord was sitting only on its naked brake drums—tires, rims, and lug nuts all stripped. In the wink of an eye, my car had been transformed into one of those abandoned vehicles one sees in deserted areas of the South Bronx, except that the windows were not broken or the inside looted.

It was early Saturday afternoon with lots of people around. In a state of disbelief, I ran up to two policemen, who had just arrived at the corner to write up an unrelated accident. They told me to wait, and in the next fifteen minutes, I watched a parade of people drive up to my car, stop, get out, and survey my vehicle. I quickly recognized that they were interested in finishing the job: the radio, the carburetor, anything to sell.

While I pleaded with the police to help me tow the car to a garage before it was picked clean, they shrugged their shoulders and told me they could not tow it unless I had committed a crime in it. I was lucky enough to find a garage, a tow truck, and a tire shop. The tire-shop proprietor, who told me his own car had disappeared from in front of his house in the Bronx, sounded just like Bob Grant and his callers. He wanted to know if my home state of Massachusetts had a death penalty. When I mentioned I was a teacher, he said he figured kids today were becoming a generation of criminals and needed a moral education more than technical skills. As I drove off, he waved and yelled out, "Please help us raise a better generation."

His plea helps to define the mission of this book. As we move closer to 2000, the national crises of violence and greed that motivated my desire to write this book have deepened. Americans, although deluged with stories of crime and corruption, are not making the connections necessary to explain the real nature of the wilding problem or what might solve it.

The media publicize sensational street violence and personal crimes that sell tabloids or TV advertising. But wilding, as viewed by a sociologist, involves multiple forms of violence, including that perpetrated in the corporate suites as well as on the streets. Only a few media stories, such as the 1992 *US News and World Report* cover story on health-care fraud entitled "White Collar Wilding," suggest that the criminals in the corporate boardrooms and on the street share elements of the same greed and the same dream.

Street wilding and white-collar wilding are racing out of control at the same time, reflecting new contradictions between today's American Dream and American prospects for success. Americans pursue divisive and increasingly unattainable goals which cannot meet our deepest needs for respect, love, and justice. As the Dream simultaneously beckons and recedes, the price of failure is frustration and rage; the price of success, too often, is inner emptiness and a debilitating fear of those left behind. Deepening inequalities, rising tides of social frustration, and corrosive moral decay threaten the bonds of community and the very survival of the social fabric.

For the citizen, this is frightening, but for the sociologist the fear inspires a sense of burning intellectual mission. The impending sense of social breakdown raises a central question: What makes community—and society itself—possible at all? This is the core problem of sociology, one with special urgency for our highly individualistic and competitive capitalist societies, but it is not a problem for sociologists alone.

The metaphor of societal illness that the wilding epidemic evokes points to the need for all of us to become practitioners of the art of social healing. This book offers one diagnosis of our weakened but still resilient collective condition. My hope is that the cure cannot long resist an awakened community brave enough to look deeply at its shared pathologies and empowered with the insights of the sociological imagination.

Acknowledgments

I am grateful to many friends and colleagues whose excitement about this book helped it come to fruition. David Karp's enthusiasm at early stages nourished my own belief in the project, and his continuing close reading of the manuscript helped me improve the book at every stage. Morrie Schwartz spurred me on with his insights and always generous emotional support. I thank Noam Chomsky, Jonathan Kozol, Howard Zinn, Robert Reich, Robert Coles, Philip Slather, and Alvin Poussaint for reading the manuscript and responding to it. I am also grateful to my colleagues Ritchie Lowry, Severyn Bruyn, David Horton Smith, Mike Malec, and Paul Gray for helpful suggestions, and especially to John Williamson and S. M. (Mike) Miller for their support and many useful ideas.

George Ritzer gave me strong encouragement to write this new St. Martin's edition and made many helpful suggestions. Debra Osnowitz's intellectual clarity and expert editorial skills strengthened the new chapters for this edition. Phyllis Fisher made her own expert editorial contributions to Chapter Seven.

Fiona McCrae, my editor at Faber and Faber, offered support and insights that made the first edition of this work possible. Sabra Scribner and Barbara Anderson, my editors at St. Martin's, championed this book with the enthusiasm and skill that every author desires. Scribner's assistant, Elizabeth Bast, a sociologist, gave me valuable theoretical suggestions.

Ann Cordilia helped me believe that I should take the risk of the new endeavor that this book represented. Ted Sasson, Jonathan White, and Janine Berkowitz, who also creatively compiled the index, demonstrated that students would be excited and challenged by this book. Eunice Doherty's irrepressible enthusiasm convinced me that the book could inform and inspire people in many walks of life. Brenda Pepe, Maureen Eldredge, and Roberta Negrin offered indispensable office support.

I owe much to my parents, who nurtured the concern for society that animates this book. And also to Elena Kolesnikova, who heroically endured the obsessions of an author about his work. She contributed ideas, helped me overcome my doubts, and nourished me all along the way.

I dedicate this book:
    To Elena—*For rekindling my faith in America and in myself*
    To My Father, Milton Derber—*For standing by me from the beginning*
        and never letting me down
    and To Morrie Schwartz—*For giving me the gift of his life-sustaining*
        unconditional love to the very end

1

The Good Man Fills His Own Stomach: All-American Crimes and Misdemeanors

The readings of history and anthropology . . . give us no reason to believe that societies have built-in self preservative systems.

—Margaret Mead

WILDING IN BLACK AND WHITE

On April 19, 1989, in New York City, a group of teenagers aged 14 to 16 went into Central Park. It was a clear night and not too cold, at least not too cold to discourage hardy joggers from getting their exercise. The teenagers dispersed into small bands and began targeting victims for some mischief. One group of six youths came upon a young woman jogging alone past a grove of sycamore trees. They cornered her in a gully and began to have some "fun."

That fun would capture headlines around the world. Using rocks, knives, and a metal pipe, they attacked her. Some pinned her down while others beat and raped her. One defendant, Kharey Wise, aged 17, told police that he held the jogger's legs while a friend repeatedly cut her with a knife. They then smashed her with a rock and punched her face, Wise said, until she "stopped moving." After half an hour, she had lost three-quarters of her blood and was unconscious. The group left her for dead.[1]

What most captured public attention were the spirits of the assaulters during and after their crime. According to 15-year-old Kevin Richardson, one of the participants, "Everyone laughed and was leaping around." One youth was quoted by police as saying, "It was fun . . . something to do." Asked if they felt pretty good about what they had done, Richardson said

"Yes." Police reported a sense of "smugness" and "no remorse" among the youths.[2]

From this event, a new word was born: *wilding*. According to press reports, it was the term the youths themselves used to describe their behavior—and it seemed appropriate. The savagery of the crime, which left the victim brain-damaged and in a coma for weeks, evoked the image of a predatory lion in the bush mangling its helpless prey. Equally shocking was the blasé attitude of the attackers. It had been no big deal, a source of temporary gratification and amusement. They were "mindless marauders seeking a thrill," said Judge Thomas B. Galligan of Manhattan, who sentenced three of the teenagers to a maximum term of five to ten years, charging them with turning Central Park into a "torture chamber." These were youths who seemed stripped of the emotional veneer of civilized humans, creatures of a wilderness where anything goes.[3]

The story of wilding quickly became tied to the race and class of the predators and their prey. The youths were black and from the inner city, although from stable working families. The victim was white, with degrees from Wellesley and Yale, and a wealthy 28-year-old investment banker at Salomon Brothers, one of the great houses of Wall Street.

To white middle-class Americans, wilding symbolized something real and terrifying about life in the United States at the turn of the decade. Things were falling apart, at least in the hearts of America's major cities. Most suburbanites did not feel their own neighborhoods had become wild, but they could not imagine walking into Central Park at night. Drugs, crime, and unemployment had made the inner city wild.

The fear of wilding became fear of the Other: those locked outside of the American Dream. They had not yet invaded the world most Americans felt part of, but they menaced it. The Central Park attack made the threat real, and it unleashed fear among the general population and a backlash of rage among politicians and other public figures. Mayor Koch called for the death penalty. Donald Trump took out ads in four newspapers, writing "I want to hate these murderers . . . I want them to be afraid." Trump told Newsweek that he "had gotten hundreds and hundreds of letters of support."[4]

Six months later, a second remarkably vicious crime grabbed people's attention all over the country. On October 23, 1989, Charles and Carol Stuart left a birthing class at Boston's Brigham and Women's Hospital, walked to their car parked in the adjoining Mission Hill neighborhood, and got in. Within minutes, Carol Stuart, eight months pregnant, was dead, shot point-blank in the head. Her husband, a stunned nation would learn from police accounts two months later, was her assassin. He had allegedly killed her to collect hundreds of thousands of dollars in life insurance money and open a restaurant. Opening a restaurant, Americans everywhere learned, had long been Chuck Stuart's American Dream.

Many white middle-class Americans seemed to instinctively believe Stuart's story when he told police that a black gunman shot him and his wife, leaving Carol Stuart dead and Stuart himself with a severe bullet wound in the abdomen. When Stuart's brother Matthew went to the police to tell them of Chuck's involvement, and when Charles Stuart subsequently apparently committed suicide by jumping off the Tobin Bridge into the river bearing his name, some of the threads connecting his crime to the horrible rape in Central Park began to emerge. Stuart had duped a whole nation by playing on the fear of the wild Other. Aware of the vivid images of gangs of black youths rampaging through dark city streets, Stuart brilliantly concocted a story that would resonate with white Americans' deepest anxieties. Dr. Alvin Poussaint, Harvard professor and advisor to Bill Cosby, said, "Stuart had all the ingredients. . . . [H]e gave blacks a killer image and put himself in the role of a model, an ideal Camelot type that white people could identify with."[5]

Chuck Stuart's crime became a national obsession. A 21-year-old Oklahoman visiting Boston told a *Boston Globe* reporter, "You wouldn't believe the attention this is getting back home. It's all anyone can talk about. I've taken more pictures of this fur shop and Stuart's house than any of the stuff you're supposed to take pictures of in Boston."[6] The quiet Stuart block in Reading had become what the *Globe* called a "macabre mecca," with hundreds of cars, full of the curious and the perplexed, parked or passing by. One reason may have been that white middle Americans everywhere had an uncomfortable sense that, as the nineties emerged, the Stuart case was telling them something about themselves. Stuart, after all, was living the American Dream and reaping its benefits—a tall, dark, athletic man with roots in working-class Revere making over one hundred thousand dollars a year selling fur coats, married to a lovely, adoring wife, and living the good life in suburban Reading complete with swimming pool. Had the American Dream itself, by the late 1980s, become the progenitor of a kind of wilding? Was it possible that not only the inner cities of America but its comfortable suburbs were becoming wild places? Could "white wilding" be as serious a problem as the "black wilding" publicized in the mass media? Was America at the turn of the decade becoming a wilding society?

To answer these questions we have to look far beyond such exceptional events as the Central Park rape and the Stuart murder. We shall see that there are many less extreme forms of wilding, including a wide range of antisocial acts that are neither criminal nor physically violent. Wilding includes the ordinary as well as the extraordinary, may be profit-oriented or pleasure-seeking, and can infect corporations and governments as well as individuals of every race, class, and gender.

THE MOUNTAIN PEOPLE: A WILDING CULTURE

Between 1964 and 1967, anthropologist Colin Turnbull lived among the people of Uganda known as the Ik, an unfortunate people expelled by an uncaring government from their traditional hunting lands to extremely barren mountainous areas. In 1972, Turnbull published a haunting book about his experiences that left no doubt that a whole society can embrace wilding as a way of life.[7]

When Turnbull first came to the Ik, he met Atum, a sprightly, barefoot old man with a sweet smile, who helped guide Turnbull to remote Ik villages. Atum warned Turnbull right away that everyone would ask for food. Although many would indeed be hungry, he said, most could fend for themselves, and their pleas should not be trusted; Turnbull, Atum stressed, should on no account give them anything. But before he left that day, Atum mentioned that his own wife was severely ill and desperately needed food and medicine. On reaching his village, Atum told Turnbull his wife was too sick to come out. Later, Turnbull heard exchanges between Atum and his sick wife, and moans of her suffering. The moans were wrenching, and when Atum pleaded for help, Turnbull gave him food and some aspirin.

Some weeks later, Atum had stepped up his requests for food and medicine, saying his wife was getting sicker. Turnbull was now seriously concerned, urging Atum to get her to a hospital. Atum refused, saying "she wasn't that sick." Shortly thereafter, Atum's brother-in-law came to Turnbull and told him that Atum was selling the medicine that Turnbull had been giving him for his wife. Turnbull, not terribly surprised, said that "that was too bad for his wife." The brother-in-law, enjoying the joke enormously, finally explained that Atum's wife "had been dead for weeks," and that Atum had "buried her inside the compound so you wouldn't know." No wonder Atum had not wanted his wife to go to the hospital, Turnbull thought to himself: "She was worth far more to him dead than alive."[8]

Startling to Turnbull was not only the immense glee the brother-in-law seemed to take in the "joke" inflicted on his dying sister, but the utter lack of embarrassment Atum showed when confronted with his lie. Atum shrugged it off, showing no remorse whatsoever, saying he had simply forgotten to tell Turnbull. That his little business enterprise may have led to his wife's death was the last thing on Atum's mind. This was one of the first of many events that made Turnbull wonder whether there was any limit to what an Ik would do to get food and money.

Some time later, Turnbull came across Lomeja, an Ik man he had met much earlier. Lomeja had been shot during an attack by neighboring tribesmen and was lying in a pool of his own blood, apparently dying from two bullet wounds in the stomach. Still alive and conscious, Lomeja looked up at Turnbull and asked for some tea. Shaken, Turnbull returned to his Land Rover and filled a big, new, yellow enamel mug. When he returned, Lomeja's wife was bending over her husband. She was trying to "fold him up" in the dead position although he was not yet dead, and started shrieking at Turnbull to leave Lomeja alone because he was already dead. Lomeja found the strength to resist his wife's premature efforts to bury him and was trying to push her aside. Turnbull managed to get the cup of tea to Lomeja, who was still strong enough to reach out for it and sip it. Suddenly, Turnbull heard a loud giggle and saw Lomeja's sister, Kimat. Attracted by all the yelling, she had "seen that lovely new, bright yellow enamel mug of hot, sweet tea, had snatched it from her brother's face and made off with it, proud and joyful. She not only had the tea, she also had the mug. She drank as she ran, laughing and delighted at herself."[9]

Turnbull came to describe the Ik as "the loveless people." Each Ik valued only his or her own survival, and regarded everyone else as a competitor for food. Ik life had become a grim process of trying to find enough food to stay alive each day. The hunt consumed all of their resources, leaving virtually no reserve for feelings of any kind, nor for any moral scruples that might interfere with filling their stomachs. As Margaret Mead wrote, the Ik had become "a people who have become monstrous beyond belief." Scientist Ashley Montagu wrote that the Ik are "a people who are dying because they have abandoned their own humanity."[10]

Ik families elevated wilding to a high art. Turnbull met Adupa, a young girl of perhaps 6, who was so malnourished that her stomach was grossly distended and her legs and arms spindly. Her parents had decided she had become a liability and threw her out of their hut. Because she was too weak now to go out on long scavenging ventures, as did the other children, she would wander as far as her strength would allow, pick up scraps of bone or half-eaten berries, and then come back to her parents' place, waiting to be brought back in. Days later, her parents, tiring of her crying, finally brought her in and promised to feed her. Adupa was happy and stopped crying. The parents went out and "closed the asak behind them, so tight that weak little Adupa could never have moved it if she had tried."[11] Adupa waited for them to come back with the food they had promised, but they did not return until a whole week had passed, when they knew Adupa would be dead. Adupa's parents took her rotting remains, Turnbull writes, and threw them out "as one does the riper garbage, a good distance away." There was no burial—and no tears.[12]

Both morality and personality among the Ik were dedicated to the single all-consuming passion for self-preservation. There was simply "not

room in the life of these people," Turnbull observes dryly, "for such luxu-
ries as family and sentiment and love." Nor for any morality beyond
"marangik," the new Ik concept of goodness, which means filling one's own
stomach.

THE IK IN US: O. J. SIMPSON AND THE WILDING EPIDEMIC

Long before the rape in Central Park or the Stuart murder, Ashley Montagu,
commenting on Turnbull's work, wrote that "the parallel with our own
society is deadly." In 1972, when Turnbull published his book, wilding had
not become part of the American vocabulary, nor did Americans yet face
declining living standards, let alone the kind of starvation experienced by
the Iks. Americans were obviously not killing their parents or children for
money, but they dedicated themselves to self-interested pursuits with a passion not unlike that of the Ik.

In America, a land of plenty, there was the luxury of a rhetoric of
morality and feelings of empathy and love. But was not the American
Dream a paean to individualistic enterprise, and could not such enterprise
be conceived in some of the same unsentimental metaphors used by
Turnbull about the Ik? The Ik community, he writes, "reveals itself for what
it is, a conglomeration of individuals of all ages, each going his own way in
search of food and water, like a plague of locusts spread over the land."[13]

America now faces a wilding epidemic that is eating at the country's
social foundation and could rot it. The American case is much less
advanced than the Ik's, but the disease is deeply rooted and is spreading
through the political leadership, the business community, and the general
population. Strong medicine can turn the situation around, but if we fail to
act now, the epidemic could prove irreversible.

Only a handful of Americans are "ultimate wilders" like Charles Stuart.
Such killers are noteworthy mainly because they may help wake us to the
wilding plague spreading among thousands of less extreme wilders who are
not killers. Wilding includes a vast spectrum of self-centered and self-
aggrandizing behavior that harms others. A wilding epidemic tears at the
social fabric and threatens to unravel society itself, ultimately reflecting the
erosion of the moral order and the withdrawal of feelings and commitments from others to oneself, to "number one."

The wilding virus comes in radically different strains. There is *expressive wilding*: wilding for the sheer satisfaction of indulging one's own
destructive impulses, the kind found among the Central Park kids and the
growing number of American youth who heave rocks off highway bridges
in the hope of smashing the windshields of unknown drivers passing inno-
cently below. The country's most famous perpetrator is O. J. Simpson, who

acted out the domestic violence that is one of the most common and Ik-like forms of expressive wilding. His alleged repeated abuse of his wife to sate his jealousy, maintain his control, or simply gratify his emotions of the moment evokes serious questions about the nightmarish spread of family violence among rich and poor alike. The national obsession with Simpson reflects the fear that when a country's icon beats his wife black and blue, smashes her windshield with a baseball bat, stalks her, and is finally charged with her murder, of which a jury acquitted him in a controversial verdict, we all participate in the crime, for heroes act out the passions and values of the cultures that create them.

Although mainly an example of expressive wilding, O. J. also modeled *instrumental wilding*. Not simply for fun or purely emotive gratification, this is wilding for money, career advancement, or other calculable personal gain. Simpson began as a youngster, running with gangs stealing food. Fantastically ambitious and opportunistic, O. J. later took naturally to a life of single-minded corporate salesmanship, obsessively remaking his voice, wardrobe, and demeanor according to the image lessons of the Hertz ad executives who greased his career, wheeling and dealing to sign movie deals and buy companies such as the Pioneer Chicken franchise (destroyed in the L. A. riots), and eventually succumbing to the greed-soaked financial deal-ings that led him, along with other entrepreneurial high rollers of his era, to bad loans and collapsed business deals.

Most instrumental wilding is far less dramatic or bizarre, involving garden varieties of ambition, competitiveness, careerism, and greed that advance the self at the cost of others. Expressive and instrumental wilding have in common an antisocial self-centeredness made possible by a stun-ning collapse of moral restraints and a chilling lack of empathy. I am mainly concerned in this book with instrumental wilding because it is the form most intimately connected with the American Dream and least understood in its poisonous effects on society.[14]

Although much wilding is criminal, there is a vast spectrum of perfectly legal wilding, exemplified by the careerist who indifferently betrays or steps on colleagues to advance up the ladder. There are forms of wilding, such as lying and cheating, that are officially discouraged, but others, like the fran-tic and single-minded pursuit of wealth, are cultivated by some of the coun-try's leading corporations and financial institutions. Likewise, there are important differences in the severity of wilding behaviors; killing a spouse for money is obviously far more brutal than stealing a wallet or cheating on an exam. But there are distinct types and degrees of infection in any afflic-tion, ranging from terminal cases such as Stuart to intermediate cases such as the savings and loan crooks, to those who are either petty wilders or rarely exhibit symptoms at all. The latter categories include large numbers of Americans who may struggle internally with their wilding impulses but remain healthy enough to restrain them. The variation is similar to that in heart disease; those with only partial clogging of their arteries and no symptoms are, indeed, different from those with full-blown, advanced arteriosclerosis, and those least afflicted may never develop the terminal stage of the illness. But these differences are normally of degree rather than of kind; the same underlying pathology—whether embryonic or full-blown—is at work among people with mild and severe cases.

There are, nonetheless, real differences between white lies or misdemeanors (forms of petty wilding) and serious wilding of the Central Park or Charles Stuart variety. Petty wilding occurs in all cultures, will persist as long as most people are not saints, and in limited doses does not necessarily threaten civil order. When so limited as not to constitute a grave social danger, it might better be described as "incipient wilding" and is not of concern here.

However, certain types of petty wilding are growing at an alarming rate in America, as I document in Chapter Five in my discussion of minor lying, cheating, and ordinary competitiveness with and indifference to others. Such transgressions on an epidemic scale can reach a critical mass and become as serious a threat to society as violent crime or huge investment scams on Wall Street. It is not the degree of brutality or violence but the consequences for society that ultimately matter, and I thus consider the full spectrum of wilding acts—from petty to outrageous—that together constitute a clear and present danger to America's social fabric.

THREE TYPES OF WILDING: ECONOMIC, POLITICAL, AND SOCIAL

Wilding, sociologically conceived, extends far beyond random violence by youth gangs, the current definition of the word offered by Webster's dictionary, to include three types of assault on society. *Economic wilding* is the morally uninhibited pursuit of money by individuals or businesses at the expense of others. *Political wilding* is the abuse of political office to benefit oneself or one's own social class, or the wielding of political authority to inflict morally unacceptable suffering on citizens at home or abroad. *Social wilding* ranges from personal or family acts of violence, such as child or spouse abuse, to collective forms of selfishness that weaken society, such as affluent suburbs turning their backs on bleeding central cities.

Economic wilders such as convicted savings and loan banker Charles Keating or Leona Helmsley, described as the "Queen of Mean," the hotel mogul's wife convicted of tax fraud, are a different species from the kids in Central Park. Partly because of differing opportunities and incentives, people wild in different ways and for exceedingly varied reasons and motives ranging from greed and lust to getting attention or respect. The different forms of wilding, however, are all manifestations of degraded American individualism.

Wilding is individualism run amok, and the wilding epidemic is the face of America's individualistic culture in an advanced state of disrepair. Individualistic culture promotes the freedom of the individual and in its healthy form nurtures human development and individual rights. In its degraded form, it becomes a license for unrestrained and sociopathic self-interest. Individualism—and its excesses—has a different face in the economy, in politics, and in the family. The deregulated free market created in the 1980s and 1990s established the environment for the extreme economic individualism that spawned such wilding calamities as the savings and loan crisis. Degraded individualism in politics is reflected in the explosion of government corruption, from the huge bribery and payoff scandals in the Department of Defense, Housing and Urban Development, and other federal agencies, to the Iran-Contra scandal and Whitewater. The manifestations of degraded individualism in families range from casual divorce to the emotional, physical, and sexual abuse of children.

WILDING AND NOT WILDING: VARIETIES OF INDIVIDUALISM

Wilding—a degenerate form of individualism—encompasses a huge variety of antisocial behavior. It includes so many seemingly unrelated acts that it might appear to stand for everything—or nothing. But wilding includes only a small subset of the entire range of behaviors that sociologists describe as individualistic, a term that arguably can be applied to any self-interested behavior. In a society such as the United States, dominated by individualistic values and a market system that rewards self-interest, some might argue that virtually all socially prescribed behavior has an individualistic dimension.

I propose a far more restrictive definition of wilding. Not all individualistic behavior is wilding, nor is wilding an umbrella term for any form of self-interested or "bad" behavior. As noted earlier, wilding refers to self-oriented behavior that hurts others and damages the social fabric, and this excludes many types of individualistic action. The Jewish sage, Hillel, wrote, "If I am not for others, what am I?" Yet he also said "If I am not for myself, who will be for me?" His maxims suggest that many forms of self-interest are necessary and contribute to the well-being of others.

A doctor who works hard to perfect her medical skills may advance her own career, but she also saves lives. A superbly conditioned professional athlete may enrich himself by his competitiveness or ambition, but he also entertains and gives pleasure to his fans. If I strive to be the best writer I can be—an individualistic aspiration—I am educating others while fulfilling myself. In none of these cases is individualistic behavior itself necessarily wilding. Actions that advance one's own interests and either help or do not harm others are not forms of wilding, even when motivated by competi-tiveness or acquisitiveness.

Wilding includes only individualistic behavior that advances or indulges the self by hurting others. If the doctor advances her skills and career by cheating on tests, trampling on her colleagues, or using her patients as guinea pigs, her self-interest has degraded into wilding. The ath-lete who illicitly uses steroids to win competitions is wilding by cheating against his rivals and deceiving his fans.

Whereas all wilding behavior hurts others, not all hurtful behavior is wilding. If I get angry at a friend, I may hurt him, but that does not neces-sarily make it wilding. Such anger may be justified because it was motivated by a wrong done to me, and it may ultimately serve to repair the relation even if I am mistaken. Interpersonal relations inevitably involve misunder-standing, aggression, and hurt, which degrade into expressive wilding only when the hurt is intentional and purely self-indulgent, and when the per-petrator is indifferent to the pain inflicted on the other. Motivation, empa-thy, and level of harm inflicted are key criteria in deciding whether wilding has occurred. Deliberate physical or emotional abuse is clearly wilding, whereas impulsive acts that cause less harm and lead to remorse and reme-diation are more ambiguous cases and may not constitute wilding at all.

Similarly complex considerations apply to institutional wilding enacted by corporations or governments. Instrumental wilding takes place whenever institutions pursue goals and strategies that inflict serious harm on individuals, communities, or entire societies. Some of the most impor-tant forms of economic wilding, both legal and criminal, involve routine profiteering by rapacious businesses exploiting employees, consumers, and communities. As discussed in Chapter Four, the line between corporate self-interest and economic wilding is blurring in today's global economy, but not all profits arise out of exploitation and many profitable businesses are not engaged in economic wilding. Socially responsible or employee-owned businesses that add to social well-being by creating jobs, raising the standard of living of employees, improving the environment, and enhanc-ing the quality of life of their customers may be highly profitable but are hardly wilders. Systemic connections exist between American capitalism and wilding, but not all forms of capitalism breed wilding.

Finally, not all crime, violence, or evil behavior is individualistic wild-ing as conceived here. The horrific ethnic cleansing in Bosnia and the tribal warfare in Rwanda constitute wilding by almost any definition, but such wilding is rooted in fierce and pathological tribal or communal loyalties and is hardly an expression of rampant individualism. Individualism and communitarianism can each generate their own forms of wilding; I focus on the individualistic variant in this book because it is the type endemic in the United States. This should not be viewed as a preference for the communitarian form, because wilding in many of the world's cruelest societies has its roots in the excesses of community. Wilding can be avoided only by respecting the rights of individuals *and* the needs for community, a balancing act too many societies have failed dismally to achieve.

THE TWO AMERICAS: ARE WE ALL WILDERS?

Although the epidemic now infects almost every major American institution, cooperative behavior survives, and in every community one finds idealists, altruists, and a majority of citizens seeking to live lives guided by moral principles. In 1990, seven out of every ten Americans gave money to charity and five out of ten rolled up their sleeves and volunteered or became social activists; these are among the many hopeful indications, discussed later in Chapter Eight, that America can still purge itself of this epidemic.

For an analyst of wilding, there are two Americas: the America already seriously infected, which is the main subject of this book, and the America that has not yet succumbed and remains what I call in the last chapter a civil society. The majority of ordinary Americans, it should be stressed, are part of the second America, and retain a moral compass and emotional sensibilities that inhibit severe wilding behavior. But as the epidemic continues to spread, individual interests increasingly override common purposes, and the self, rather than family or community, increasingly grabs center stage in both Americas. Not everyone will become a wilder, but nobody will be untouched by wilding culture.[15]

Wilders who catch the fever and play by the new rules profoundly infect their own vulnerable communities, families, and workplaces. One dangerous criminal on a block can make a community wild, inducing aggression, violence, and a fortress mentality among peaceable neighbors. A particularly competitive salesperson or account executive can transform an entire office into a jungle, because those who do not follow suit and sharpen their own swords may be left sundered in the dust. The new ethos rewards the wilder and penalizes those clinging to civil behavior. One defense against wilding in modern America is to embrace it, spreading wilding behavior among people less characterologically disposed to be wilders and still struggling against wilding as a way of life.

Many Americans misread the epidemiology of AIDS as a problem of deviant and disadvantaged groups. They are at risk of making the same miscalculation about the wilding epidemic, to which no sector of the society has any immunity. Its ravages may be most eye-catching among the poor and downtrodden, but the virus afflicts the respected and the comfortable just as much: It exists in the genteel suburbs as well as the inner cities. Indeed, American wilding is, to a surprising degree, an affliction of the successful, in that the rich and powerful have written the wilding rules and it is ever more difficult to climb the ladder without internalizing them.

The progress of the wilding epidemic is shaped less by the percentage of sociopaths than by the sociopathy of its elites and the rules of the success game they help to define. A wilding society is one where wilding is a route to the top, and where legitimate success becomes difficult to distinguish from the art of wilding within—or even outside of—the law.

The wilding epidemic is now seeping into America mainly from the top. Although the majority of business and political leaders remain honest, a large and influential minority are not only serving as egregious role models but are rewriting the rules of the American success game in their own interest. Michael Milken was convicted of massive financial fraud, but his more important contribution to the wilding epidemic was helping change the rules of the financial game, helping inspire the $35 trillion global market in junk-bonds, derivatives, and other speculative instruments. Similarly, Presidents Reagan, Bush, and Clinton have all helped fuel the wilding crisis, partly by virtue of the personal corruption and scandals in their administrations, but more importantly through radical new policy directions.

Our current wilding crisis is rooted politically in the "free market" revolution that began with President Reagan. As conservative analyst Kevin Phillips has noted, the Reagan revolution advanced the most ambitious class agenda of the rich in over a century, creating an innovative brew of market deregulation and individualistic ideology that, as I show in Chapter Three, helped fan the flames of wilding across the land. But the most radical and ominous changes have emerged in the mid 1990s, as both a new Republican Congressional majority led by Speaker Newt Gingrich and the "new Democrats" led by President Clinton raced against each other to dismantle the social programs that symbolize our commitment to the poor, the needy, and to each other.

WILDING AND THE AMERICAN DREAM: INDIVIDUALISM TODAY AND YESTERDAY

Many signs point to a corruption of the American Dream in our time.[16] Most Americans do not become killers to make it up the ladder or hold on to what they have, but the traditional restraints on naked self-aggrandizement seem weaker—and the insatiability greater. Donald Trump, who by 1995 had made a big comeback and ruled vast gambling and real estate empires, is only one of the multimillionaire culture heroes who define life as "The Art of the Deal," the title of Trump's best-selling autobiography. Trump feels no moral contradiction about building the most luxurious condominiums in history in a city teeming with homeless people. Trump writes triumphantly about the Trump Tower: "We positioned ourselves as the only place for a certain kind of very wealthy person to live—the hottest ticket in town. We were selling fantasy."[17]

In 1835, Alexis de Tocqueville wrote that in America "no natural boundary seems to be set to the efforts of man."[18] But inspired by the Reaganites of the 1980s and the Gingrichites of the 1990s, a new version of the Dream has now emerged, more individualistic, expansive, and morally perverted than its predecessors. America has entered a new Gilded Age, where, as John Taylor writes, the celebration and "lure of wealth has overpowered conventional restraints."[19] Laurence Shames suggests that the name of the American game has become simply *more*.[20]

Today's high rollers in Wall Street's famous investment banks are living out this new chapter of the American Dream. Youthful commodity traders fresh out of business school engage in feeding frenzies in the exchanges, pursuing quick fortunes "as if they'd invented the habit of more, when in fact they'd only inherited it the way a fetus picks up an addiction in the womb." The craving, Shames writes, is "there in the national bloodstream."[21] A dramatic model is Nicholas Leeson, the 27-year-old broker who in 1995 bankrupted the historic Baring's bank of London by losing his $27 billion gamble in the international derivatives market. Derivatives, a 1990s variant of the 1980s junk-bond craze, which we discuss in Chapter Three, are part of the global financial casino in which bankers bet on currency rates, stock prices, or pork bellies to win trillion-dollar jackpots. Many Wall Street players in the derivatives game turn to inside trading—and more serious crimes—when their risky ventures go bad. The notorious Billionaire Boys' Club—a group of youthful traders and investors—would show that respectable young men consumed by the Dream could become killers.

For less-privileged Americans the new "gilded" Dream became a recipe for wilding based on collapsed possibilities. A dream of having more had been sustainable when the pie was growing, as it had been through most of American history. But when real income begins to decline, an unprecedented development in the last decades of the twentieth century, an outsized Dream becomes illusion, inconsistent with the reality of most Americans' lives. Outsized Dream, downsized lives. To weave grandiose materialist dreams in an era of restricted opportunities is the ultimate recipe for social wilding.

A new age of limits and polarization in the mid-1990s sets the stage for an advanced wilding crisis. In an America deeply divided by class, the American Dream, and especially the new gilded Dream, can not be a common enterprise and is transformed into multiple wilding agendas, unleashing wilding among people at every station, but in different ways. Among those at the bottom, the Dream becomes pure illusion; wilding, whether dealing drugs or grabbing handbags, mushrooms as a survival option and as a fast track out of the ghetto and into the high life. Among the insecure and slipping great American middle class, wilding becomes a growth area for those endowed with classic American initiative and ingenuity and unwilling to go down with their closing factories and shrinking industries. For the professional and business classes at the top, wilding is sanctified as professional ambition and proliferates as one or another variant of dedicated and untrammelled careerism. Ensconced inside heavily fortified suburban or gentrified enclaves, these elites also pioneer new forms of social wilding in what Robert Reich calls a politics of secession, abandoning society itself as part of a panicky defense against the threat from the huge covetous majority left behind. The wilding crisis, as we see below, arises partly out of a virulent new class politics.[22]

The seeds of America's wilding plague were planted long before the current era. A century ago, Tocqueville observed that conditions in America led every "member of the community to be wrapped up in himself" and worried that "personal interest will become more than ever the principal, if not the sole spring" of American behavior. Selfish and mean-spirited people can be found in every culture and every phase of history, and wilding, as I show in the next chapter, is certainly not a new phenomenon in American life. One of the world's most individualistic societies, America has long struggled to cope with high levels of violence, greed, political corruption, and other wilding outcroppings.[23]

Over the last hundred years, American history can be read as a succession of wilding periods alternating with eras of civility. The Robber Baron era of the 1880s and 1890s, an age of spectacular economic and political wilding, was followed by the Progressive Era of the early 20th century, in which moral forces reasserted themselves. The individualistic license of the 1920s, another era of economic and political wilding epitomized by the Teapot Dome scandal, yielded to the New Deal era of the 1930s and 1940s, when America responded to the Great Depression with remarkable moral and community spirit. The moral idealism of a new generation of youth in the 1960s was followed by the explosion of political, economic, and social wilding in the current era.

American wilding is a timeless and enduring threat, linked to our national heritage and most basic values and institutions. Although we focus in this book on wilding in the 1990s, the wilding problem riddles our history, for it is embedded in the origins of free market capitalism and the individualistic culture that helped shape the American Dream and our own national character. What distinguishes the current epidemic is the subtle legitimation of wilding as it becomes part of the official religion in Washington, the severity of the wilding crisis in banking and commerce, the spread of wilding into universities and other vital cultural centers, and the subsequent penetration of wilding culture so deeply into the lives of the general population that society itself is now at risk.

ROOTS OF WILDING: DURKHEIM, MARX, AND THE SOCIOLOGICAL EYE

More than a century ago, the founders of sociology had their own intimations of a wilding crisis that could consume society. The great French thinker Émile Durkheim recognized that individualism was the rising culture of the modern age. While Durkheim believed that individualism could ultimately be a healing force, he also feared that it could poison the bonds that make social life possible. Karl Marx, who gave birth to a different school of sociology, believed that the economic individualism of capitalism might erode all forms of community and reduce human relations to a new lowest common denominator: the cash nexus.

Sociology arose as an inquiry into the dangers of modern individualism, which could potentially kill society itself. The prospect of the death of society gave birth to the question symbolized by the Ik: What makes society possible and prevents it from disintegrating into a mass of sociopathic and self-interested isolates? This core question of sociology has become the vital issue of our times.

Although sociology does not provide all the answers, it offers a compelling framework for understanding and potentially solving the wilding epidemic. Durkheim never heard of wilding or the Ik, but he focused like a laser on the coming crisis of community. Durkheim saw that the great transformation of the modern age was the breakdown of traditional social solidarity and the rise of an individual less enmeshed in community. A grave danger was egoism, arising where "the individual is isolated because the bonds uniting him to other beings are slackened or broken" and the "bond which attaches him to society is itself slack." Such an individual, who finds no "meaning in genuinely collective activity," is primed for wilding, the pursuit of gain or pleasure at the expense of others with whom there is no sense of shared destiny.[24]

The other great danger is anomie, which Durkheim defined as a condition of societal normlessness breeding crime and suicide. Anomie arises when social rules are absent or confusing and individuals are insufficiently integrated into families, neighborhoods, or churches to be regulated by their moral codes. Durkheim believed that modern, individualistic societies were especially vulnerable to this kind of failure of socialization. As community declines, it leaves the individual without a moral compass, buffeted by disturbing and increasingly limitless "passions, without a curb to regulate them." Anomie fuels instrumental wilding, making the individual more vulnerable to fantasies of limitless money and power. It also feeds expressive wilding of the O. J. Simpson variety, weakening the personal and community controls that sustain civilized values.[25]

Although Durkheim captures the kind of breakdown of community that is currently helping to breed the American wilding epidemic, he lacks the economic and political analysis that would help explain why wilding is startlingly pervasive among America's ruling elites and trickles down to the population at large. As I will argue in chapters to come, American wilding is a form of socially prescribed antisocial behavior, modeled by leaders and reinforced by the rules of our free market game. As such, it reflects less the insufficient presence of society in individuals than overconformity to a society whose norms and values are socially dangerous.

Marx wrote that the market system "drowns the most heavenly ecstasies of religious fervor, of chivalrous enthusiasm, of philistine sentimentalism, in the icy water of egotistical calculation." In capitalism, as Marx conceives it, wilding is less a failure of socialization than an expression of society's central norms. To turn a profit, even the most humane capitalist employer commodifies and exploits employees, playing by the market rules of competition and profit-maximization to buy and sell their labor power as cheaply as possible.[26]

The champions of Western capitalism—from Adam Smith to Milton Friedman—agree that self-interest is the engine of the system and individualism its official religion, but reject Marx's equation of a regime built around economic self-interest with exploitation and wilding. Marx was wrong, in fact, to assume that capitalism inevitably destroyed community and social values. In some national contexts, including Confucian Japan and social democratic Sweden, the individualizing forces of the market are cushioned by cultures and governments that limit exploitation and help sustain community.

In the United States, however, rugged individualism has merged with free market capitalism, a fertile brew for wilding. Marx's view of institutionalized wilding—and of political and business elites as carriers of the virus—helps to correct the Durkheimian hint of wilding as deviance. Durkheim, in a major oversight, never recognized that egoism and anomie can themselves be seen as norms, culturally prescribed and accepted.[27]

This is a theoretical key to understanding wilding in America. Wilding partly reflects a weakened community less able to regulate its increasingly individualistic members. In this sense, the American wilder is the undersocialized product of a declining society that is losing its authority to instill respect for social values and obligations.

But Marx's view of institutionalized wilding suggests that wilders can simultaneously be oversocialized, imbibing too deeply the core values of competition and profit-seeking in American capitalism. The idea of oversocialization, which I elaborate in the next chapter, suggests not the failure of social authority but the wholesale indoctrination of societal values that can ultimately poison both the individual and society itself. As local communities weaken, giant corporations, including the media, advertising, and communications industries, shape the appetites, morality, and behavior of Americans ever more powerfully. For the rich and powerful, the dream of unlimited wealth and glamour, combined with the Reaganite and Gingrichian revolution of corporate deregulation and corporate welfare, opens up endless fantasies and opportunities. As Durkheim himself noted, when the ceiling on ordinary expectations is removed, the conventional restraints on pursuing them will also rapidly disappear. This produces socially prescribed anomie and wilding among elites based on unlimited possibilities.

A different version of socially prescribed wilding trickles down to everyone else. For those exposed to the same inflated dream of wealth, glamour, and power, but denied the means of achieving it, illegitimate means provide the only strategy to achieve socially approved goals. Whether involving petty or serious wilding, such behavior gradually permeates the population and becomes socialized. Sociologist Robert Merton wrote that crime is a product of a disparity between goals and means. If that disparity becomes institutionalized, crime and other deviance are normalized, and officially deviant behavior becomes common practice. Wilding itself becomes a societal way of life.

New economic realities, including the fact that the coming generation is the first to face the prospect of living less well than its parents, could trigger a healthy national re-examination of our values, and the pursuit of a less materialistic and individualistic life. The polarization of wealth and opportunity could also prompt, before it is too late, a rethinking of our class divisions and economic system. But without such a rescripting of the American Dream and free market system, the new circumstances create the specter of an American nightmare reminiscent of the Ik.

NOTES

1. "Move to Kill Victim Described by Defendant in Jogger Rape," *New York Times*, November 2, 1989, p. 1.
2. "Testimony has Youths Joyous After Assault", *New York Times*, November 4, 1989, p. 1.

3. "Three Youths Jailed in Rape of Jogger," *Boston Globe,* September 12, 1990, p. 9.
4. "The Central Park Rape Sparks a War of Words," *Newsweek,* May 15, 1989, p. 40.
5. Ibid.
6. Cited in article by Renée Graham, "Fur Store, Quiet Street are Now Macabre Meccas," *Boston Globe,* January 16, 1990, p. 20.
7. Colin Turnbull, *The Mountain People* (New York: Simon and Schuster, 1987).
8. Ibid. p. 86.
9. Ibid. p. 153.
10. Ibid. Back cover.
11. Ibid. p. 132.
12. Ibid. p. 132.
13. Ibid. p. 137.
14. I am indebted to Mike Miller for suggesting the terms "instrumental" and "expressive" wilding.
15. I am indebted to Mike Miller for his suggestion of "two Americas."
16. For an excellent book on the subject see: John Taylor, *Circus of Ambition: The Culture of Wealth and Power in the Eighties* (New York: Warner Books, 1989).
17. Donald Trump, *The Art of the Deal* (New York: Warner Books, 1987).
18. Alexis De Tocqueville, *Democracy in America, Vol. II* (New York: Knopf, 1985) pp. 137–8.
19. Taylor, *Circus of Ambition,* p. 8.
20. Laurence Shames, *The Hunger for More* (New York: Times Books, 1989).
21. Ibid. p. 27.
22. Robert B. Reich, "Secession of the Successful," *New York Times Magazine,* January 20, 1991, pp. 16–17; 42–45.
23. De Tocqueville. op. cit., pp. 123–4.
24. Durkheim, cited in Steven Lukes, *Émile Durkheim: His Life and Work* (New York: Penguin, 1973) p. 207.
25. Ibid.
26. Karl Marx, cited in Robert C. Tucker, *The Marx-Engels Reader.* (New York: Norton, 1972) p. 337.
27. Lukes, op.cit., p. 218.

2

The Ultimate Wilders: Rob Marshall, the Menendez Brothers, and Susan Smith— Prisoners of the American Dream

Why should we be in such desperate haste to succeed? And in such desperate enterprises?

—Thoreau

ROBERT OAKLEY MARSHALL: "SPEED DEMON ON THE BOULEVARD OF DREAMS."[1]

After the prosecutor summed up the case against their dad, Roby and Chris, 20 and 19 respectively, were thinking the same thing. There could be no doubt in anyone's mind, not even their own, about the horrific fact that their father really had killed their mother, and that their lives were a lie. They had always been envied, admired, privileged. They had money and a perfect family. "How much in love with each other they'd all seemed. . . . The all-American family. The American Dream that came true."[2]

The sons now knew the truth: Their father, Rob, a spectacularly successful New Jersey life insurance salesman, had arranged with professional assassins in Louisiana to come up on the night of September 7, 1984, to Atlantic City, where he and his wife Maria were having dinner at Harrah's. After dinner and wine and some late gambling in the casino, Rob drove his

19

sleepy wife back toward Toms River, but pulled off the parkway at the Oyster Creek picnic area to check out what he told Maria was a problem in the tire. Going out to check the tire, he waited for the paid executioners to sneak up to the car, assassinate Maria by shooting her point-blank in the back, and swat him on the head to draw a little blood and make it look like a good robbery. (The Louisiana men wanted to inflict a shooting wound but Rob went white and almost fainted—saying "I'm not the one getting shot"—and insisted on receiving only a flesh wound.) Rob returned home looking strangely buoyant after his trauma, striking one detective as more like a man ready to go out sailing on his yacht than someone who had just lost his wife. He had reason to feel a large burden had been lifted from his shoulders; Rob Marshall now stood to recover approximately $1.5 million of insurance money he had taken out on Maria, more than enough to clear $200,000 in gambling debts he owed in Atlantic City, and to set himself up handsomely for his next steps on the ladder of the American Dream. He could pay off the mortgage, buy a new car for himself and each of his three boys, and indulge in a whirlwind romance with his sexy mistress.

Rob Marshall also had good cause to feel that the police would not come after him. Talking to Gene, his brother-in-law and a lawyer, who pointed out that it did not look especially good that Rob was deep in debt and stood to get such a huge insurance payment, Rob responded that the police could not possibly suspect him. "I'm much too high up the civic ladder. My reputation in the community, in fact, places me beyond reproach."[3]

He was right about one thing; the police themselves called Rob a "pillar" in the community. Back in the early 1970s, Rob quickly proved himself a sensational salesman, selling over $2 million in life insurance in his first year, and the next year he was again named among the top-fifty Provident Mutual Life salesmen in the country. Rob and his family moved into a big house and Rob drove around town in a flashy red Cadillac. Rob also scored big in his private life, capturing Maria, a Philadelphia Main Line doctor's daughter who was exquisitely beautiful and who always kept herself and her sons impeccably groomed.[4] Maria was Rob's proudest possession. He loved her beauty. When he was arranging to have her killed, Rob told the executioners they must not mar Maria's looks; he could not stand that idea.

Rob and Maria, Joe McGinniss writes, were like royalty in Toms River. One neighbor said they "seemed to have the ideal family and lifestyle. You know, like you'd see on TV."[5] Everyone admired how they looked; they also admired Rob's business success and the fact that the Marshalls "were always buying something new." They moved to a bigger house and joined the country club. Maria was invited to join Laurel Twigs, a prestigious charitable organization, and Rob became a mover and shaker in the Rotary Club, the United Way, and the country club.[6]

There was not much doubt about how Rob had gotten so far so fast. The man was *driven,* the most aggressive salesman Toms River had ever seen. Kevin Kelly, the prosecutor who had once bought insurance from Rob, said Rob pushed through the deal while half his hamburger was still on his plate and the engine still hot in the parking lot. "The guy could fit in three or four lunches a day, the way he hustled." His drive—and his ego— seemed as big as Donald Trump's, who happened to own the Atlantic City casinos where Rob gambled and where he staged Maria's last supper.[7]

Over the course of his nationally publicized trial, later celebrated in the TV miniseries "Blind Faith," Rob's shameless behavior confirmed the nefarious picture of a sociopathic, greed-soaked personality painted by the prosecutor. In the first few weeks after the murder, Rob could barely conceal his excitement about his new freedom, not only making quick moves to get his hands on the money, but charming at least three different women into his wife's bed before he had figured out how to dispose of her remains. He staged a phony suicide attempt, giving himself the opportunity to leave "suicide tapes" by which he could publicly display his love of his kids and Maria. However, as prosecutor Kevin Kelly showed, nobody close to Rob ever heard him weep or saw him show any real grief or sense of loss over Maria. In fact, Rob had indifferently left her ashes in a brown cardboard box in a drawer at the funeral home, while at the same time he put back on, and prominently wore at the trial, the gold wedding ring Maria had given him. Rob would embarrass his sons with public demonstrations of his love for them, wearing signs for the cameras saying "I love you," even as he was desperately urging them to perjure themselves and risk jail to save his neck.

Prosecutor Kevin Kelly summed up Rob's personality: He's "self-centered, he's greedy, he's desperate, he's materialistic, and he's a liar. . . . [h]e will use anybody, he will say anything, and he will do anything—including use his own family—to get out from under." Rob was single-mindedly out for number one; he "love[d] no one but himself."[8] Kelly was not exaggerating, but what he knew and did not say was that many of the same epithets would apply to many other Toms River residents. As one native observed, Rob was in many ways not very different from his neighbors. Rob's case, one resident wrote, was compelling precisely because there was an intimate connection between "the town's collective values and the story of Rob and Maria Marshall." Indeed, the spotlight on Rob—and the community's obsession with the murder— stemmed from the fact that it helped to bring into sharp definition what the community was really about.[9]

Toms River in the 1970s was full of people in a hurry, many of them, like the Marshalls, recent town immigrants scurrying to cash in on one of the biggest booms on the New Jersey shore. Ocean County was the second-fastest growing county in the country, causing real-estate values to soar, and triggering spectacular business opportunities. The mostly blue-collar and lower-middle-class migrants who flocked to Toms River caught the fantastic entrepreneurial fever. Everyone in Toms River was suddenly making deals—and the limits on the money to be made evaporated. Since most people were new to the community, conspicuous consumption became the quickest way to get known and command respect. "I shop, therefore I am" became the Toms River credo long before it started showing up on bumper stickers around the country in the 1980s. Lots of other Toms River folks were joining the country club and driving their Cadillacs up to Atlantic City at night, joining Rob for the big bets at the high-priced blackjack tables.

Rob was a hustler, and hustling was the name of the game in Toms River—just as it was in Atlantic City, Wall Street, and, increasingly, in Ronald Reagan's Washington. Rob, a number of commentators observed, was remarkably tuned in to the spirit of his times. The commercials about getting yours and getting it now kept ringing in his ears. And as the 1980s progressed, Rob tuned in to bigger dreams than Toms River could offer. "See, all around Rob in the eighties," one old friend said, "everybody was scoring everything: sex, dope, big-money deals. At least, he thought so."[10] If young kids fresh out of business school could make their first million on Wall Street before they were thirty, Rob was missing something he deserved. As his success grew, so did his aspirations, his sense of deprivation, and his gambling debts. Like the country as a whole, Rob was going to leverage himself into a real fortune.

Yet although the resonance between Rob and the collective values of his time was electric, most people in Toms River and Atlantic City were not murdering their spouses to cover their debts and get one more step up the ladder. Rob was different only because he personified so purely and acted out so unrestrainedly the hungers driving his neighbors. Lots of others were dreaming the same big American Dream, but Rob was completely engulfed by it; his personality was a machine perfectly dedicated to making it. Rob was abnormal because the American Dream that was becoming the new standard had penetrated every fiber of his being, purging all traces of the emotional or moral sensibilities that restrained his neighbors. Rob's aggressiveness was startling even in an age of hustlers, his narcissism was more extreme than that of most of his fellow travelers in the me generation, and in an age of moral decline, his conscience was exceptionally elastic.

Undoubtedly, Rob's abnormality had roots in his past; perhaps in the Depression, which ruined his family and turned his father into an alcoholic; perhaps in his chronic sense of being an outsider, having moved at least ten times before he was sixteen. But if Rob had not murdered his wife, he would never have come under the psychiatric microscope because his extreme traits were exactly those that people on the way up were supposed to exhibit and that would propel them to the top. For fifteen years, Rob's abnormality had helped make him the biggest success in his community.

Rob got into trouble only because his dreams finally outstripped his own formidable capacities. He probably would not have killed Maria if he had not fallen so deeply into debt, and he might not have gotten into such debt if he had not been lured by the bigger dreams and looser moral sensibilities that his friends said had gotten under his skin and now possessed him. The reckless and grandiose entrepreneurial culture of Toms River that would later sweep across America released the extremes in Rob's personality, nurturing his sense of himself as a legend in his own time, free to make his own rules and look after number one first. When he got into deep financial trouble, the culture that should have restrained him was instead unleashing his deep-seated potential for wilding.

THEM AND US: VIOLENCE AND THE OVERSOCIALIZED AMERICAN CHARACTER

Public reaction to ultimate wilders like Rob Marshall has been schizophrenic. Utter shock that anyone could indifferently wipe out a wife, husband, mother, or child like an insect for money is linked with a sliver of recognition that there is something familiar about these killers. "The first thing people want to know," Alison Bass wrote in the *Boston Globe,* is "how could anyone so carefully and coolly plan the murder of a wife, a child, anyone?"[11] But the second, usually subliminal, question is, "Could *my* husband do it?" or, even more subliminal, "Could I?"

Do ultimate wilders tell us something important about ourselves and our society—or are they just bizarre sideshows? Reassuring responses come from the many commentators who observe, as does psychiatrist Dr. Charles Ford, that although people such as Rob Marshall "on the surface look very normal," they are suffering from either mental illness or deep-seated "character disorders" such as narcissism or sociopathy that radically differentiate "them" from "us."[12] Criminologists Jack Levin and James Fox describe sociopaths such as Marshall and his remarkably similar fellow wilder, Charles Stuart, as people who "blend in well and function appropriately" but are "far from normal." Criminologists explain that sociopaths "know the right thing to do" to emulate the rest of us; they are consummate actors:

"Sociopaths lie, manipulate, and deceive. They are *good* at it. Like actors they play a role on the stage of life. . . ."[13]

When they murder, ultimate wilders clearly act differently, but the clinical accounts of their character disorders do not provide a persuasive argument for the difference between "them" and "us." The bible of psychiatry, the *Diagnostic Standard Manual*, defines narcissistic personality disorder as "[t]he tendency to exploit others to achieve one's own ends, to exaggerate achievements and talents, to feel entitled to and to crave constant attention and adulation."[14] Criminologists Fox and Levin define sociopaths as "self-centered, manipulative, possessive, envious, reckless, and unreliable. They demand special treatment and inordinate attention, often exaggerating their own importance. . . . On their way to the top, sociopaths ruthlessly step over their competitors without shame or guilt." These are common human frailties, and Fox and Levin acknowledge that they are widespread among Americans who live in a culture that often idolizes characters such as J.R. Ewing of "Dallas," the personification of virtually all sociopathic traits. In trying to predict when the difference between "them" and "us" emerges, Fox and Levin end up in another conundrum, for they acknowledge that most sociopaths rarely reach the point "at which they feel it necessary to kill. Most of them live ordinary lives." Distinguishing "them" from "us" then seems a bit like the dilemma American soldiers faced in Vietnam—trying to distinguish the guerrillas from the rest of the population.[15]

It is time for sociologists to reclaim the idea of sociopathy, a concept as useful for understanding a sick society as the sick psyche. A sociopathic society is one, like the Ik, marked by a collapse of moral order resulting from the breakdown of community and the failure of institutions responsible for inspiring moral vision and creating and enforcing robust moral codes. In such a society, the national character-type tends toward sociopathy, and idealized behavior, although veiled in a rhetoric of morality, becomes blurred with antisocial egoism. The founders of modern sociology, especially Émile Durkheim, as noted in Chapter One, worried that modernity threatened to turn the most-developed industrial cultures into sociopathic caldrons of raw egoism and anomie, and conceived of the sociological enterprise as an effort to understand how societies could find their moral compass and preserve themselves in the face of the sociopathic threat.

In sociopathic societies, the clinical effort to dissect the sociopathic personality cannot be separated from an analysis of national character and ideology. Rob Marshall may be deranged, but his derangement mirrors a national disorder. As the United States approaches the twenty-first century, the official religion of the free market increasingly sanctifies sociopathy under the guise of individual initiative, entrepreneurship, and "making it."

As the American Dream becomes a recipe for wilding, clinicians and criminologists need to deepen their sociological understanding or they will continue to misread Rob Marshall as a failure of socialization rather than a pathology of oversocialization. Rob internalized too deeply central American values of competitiveness and material success, discarding any other values that might interfere with his personal ambitions. Rob is most interesting as a prisoner of the same American Dream that compels the rest of us but does not consume us with quite the same intensity.

LYLE AND ERIK MENENDEZ: A FAMILY OF COMPETITORS

As of this writing, Erik and Lyle Menendez are awaiting a second trial on charges of murdering their parents after their first trial ended in a hung jury. I have reconstructed their case from public accounts.

On the evening of August 20, 1989, as José Menendez was watching television in the spacious den of his $4 million Beverly Hills estate, he had reason to feel pretty good about his life. José was a perfectionist who, according to his older son, Lyle, felt he could never "do something well enough." But even José, with his high standards and consuming ambition, might admit that an impoverished immigrant who by age forty-five had risen to become a millionaire in Hollywood's inner sanctum had not done too badly. He could count Hollywood celebrities Rick Springfield, Barry Manilow, Kenny Rogers, and Sylvester Stallone as his friends. Founder and president of Live Entertainment, Inc., a successful national video-cassette distributor, his was a Horatio Alger story come true. Journalist Pete Hammill wrote in *Esquire* magazine that José was a "glittering" testimony to the American Dream of the Reagan years.[16]

As he sat with his wife, Kitty, that evening eating fresh berries and cream, José would certainly have gotten deep satisfaction from the comments of his fellow executive Ralph King, who eulogized José in the *Wall Street Journal* after his death as "by far the brightest, toughest businessman I have ever worked with," or of former Hertz chairman Robert Stone, who said he "had never known anyone who worked harder, worked toward more goals." José, according to Stone, probably "would have become president of the company" had he stayed at Hertz. Coming to the United States from Cuba at age 15, José had dedicated every ounce of his being to getting ahead, vowing to "develop strip malls" if that was what it took to "succeed by age thirty." He could not have been better psychologically equipped. He was an intensely aggressive and competitive man brimming with entrepreneurial energy. Straight out of accounting school, he had hustled from Coopers and Lybrand to a Chicago shipping firm to Hertz, and then to RCA, successfully signing on performer José Feliciano. After being passed over for executive vice-president at RCA, Menendez achieved a brilliant coup by creating Live Entertainment, Inc. as the video arm of Carolco Pictures, on whose board he sat and which had gone big-time with its smash hit, *Rambo II*.[17]

Turning to his two handsome sons as they burst into the room, José could savor a different kind of pride. José had a burning desire to see his sons succeed as he had, and he had dedicated himself to that end with the same relentless passion with which he had pursued his business goals, drilling Lyle and Erik for hours on the tennis courts and constantly exhort-ing them to outperform their peers on and off the court. "There is a lot of pressure," Erik said, "to be great." Lyle, aged 22, was to graduate soon from Princeton, and José's younger son, Erik, aged 19, who had gotten into UCLA, was talking about wanting to realize his father's own ambition of becoming the first Cuban-American U.S. senator.

José was probably more puzzled than frightened when he saw that Lyle and Erik were both carrying shotguns. But he had no time to ask questions. Within seconds of barging into the den, as police reconstruct the scene, the two sons had fired eight shots point-blank at their father and five at their mother. Just to make sure, they thrust the barrel of one gun into their father's mouth and blew off the back of his head. Police would later say that the scene was so gruesome that it could not possibly have been a Mafia hit, as some had first speculated, because the Mob kills "clean." Erik later told reporters that his parents' ravaged, bloodspattered, lifeless bodies "looked like wax."[18]

Lyle and Erik claimed that they had gone out that evening to see the James Bond film *License to Kill*, but ended up seeing *Batman*. They came back late at night, they said, horrified to find the carnage at home. Neighbors reported that they heard the sons screaming and sobbing, pre-sumably after discovering the bodies. But police suspected Lyle and Erik from the very beginning, and not only because, as District Attorney Ira Reiner put it, a $14 million estate provided "an ample motive." The boys were not able to produce ticket stubs for *Batman,* and police had found a shotgun shell casing in one of Lyle's jackets. Then investigators discovered that two years earlier in high school Erik had co-written a play about a wealthy teenager who murders his parents for money, a creation that made his mother, who helped type the manuscript, proud of her son's gifts. But it was about six months later, in early March 1990, that police found the smoking pistol they were seeking when they confiscated tapes of psy-chotherapy sessions with both boys which apparently offered direct evi-dence of their involvement in the crime.

The Menendez brothers eventually confessed to the killings, acknowl-edging that they had followed through on a calculated plan to shoot their parents. But Lyle and Erik presented themselves in court not as brutal murderers but as innocent victims. They said they killed in self-defense, to protect themselves against years of emotional and sexual abuse. Erik claimed that his father had been sexually abusing him since he was 5 years old, forcing him repeatedly to have oral and anal sex.

The prosecution, however, as well as many followers of the trial, were skeptical about this "abuse excuse," noting accurately that it was one of the more fashionable and disturbing trends in legal defenses of the 1990s. It had cropped up in such infamous trials as the Bobbitt case, in which a sexually abused wife defended cutting off her husband's penis because he beat her. There were reasons to doubt the truth of the Menendez brothers' sexual abuse claims, among them the fact that the boys had never mentioned sexual abuse to their therapist, Dr. Orziel, who initially taped their confession. Erik and Lyle had given Dr. Orziel written permission when they entered therapy to share their confidences with their parents, an unlikely act for young men who would presumably be using the therapy to discuss their parents' alleged mental, physical, and sexual abuse. In addition, the defense of abuse was introduced late in the game, many months after the killings and shortly before the trial opened. Family members and others who had known the family well and were familiar with José's many mistresses and affairs, were reported to be incredulous, partly because none of them had ever heard any whisper of this other side of the macho José's sexual life.

Even if José sexually abused his sons, such abuse would neither justify the killings nor constitute proof of the real motive of the shootings. There were other ways for these smart and wealthy young men to defend themselves and escape the family's oppressive yoke, including running away and assuming new identities, seeking shelter with friends, relatives, or protective social service agencies, or going off to boarding school and college, as Lyle, in fact, did. But all of these strategies would have probably cost Lyle and Erik their inheritances, and certainly would not have given them immediate access to their parents' huge estate.

The remarkable behavior of Lyle and Erik after the killings offers the most revealing clues to why they committed them. Neither boy wasted any time. Lyle dropped out of Princeton and, after flirting with the idea of a professional tennis career (he had once ranked thirty-sixth in the U.S. juniors), decided "to build a business empire from the ground up." Taking his share of an initial $400,000 insurance payment, he bought Chuck's Spring Street Cafe, a popular student hangout near the Princeton campus specializing in fried chicken. Lyle immediately began drafting plans to open franchises in other states as part of a nationwide chain. His entrepreneurial ambitions extended far beyond restaurants. Lyle began traveling widely to help realize his dream of making a "fortune in, among other things, show business and real estate." He founded Investment Enterprises, a financing shell for channeling the millions of dollars he would inherit into quick, high-yield returns.[19]

Erik, however, was serious about professional tennis, immediately dropping out of UCLA and hiring a professional tennis coach for $50,000 a year. He moved into the exclusive Marina City Club Towers, a glamorous ocean-side setting south of Los Angeles. Erik worked as hard at his tennis career as Lyle did at his restaurant and real estate ventures, practicing for hours on the court and taking his coach along to boost his performance in tournaments. Erik, however, did not limit himself to a future in tennis. Still proud of his earlier murder script, Erik believed he had a spectacular future as a screenwriter. In his spare time, he worked on his plays and poetry. He told his roommate at Marina that he was confident he would "produce an unbelievable script."[20]

It took little imagination to view the killings, as the police did, as a grand entrepreneurial scheme, an ironic testimony to the grip of a father's own deepest values on the minds of his sons. José had wanted, more than any-thing else, Erik and Lyle to follow in his footsteps and live out the American Dream that had guided his own life. He had raised them to be aggressive competitors like himself who would seize every opportunity to get ahead and make something of themselves. "He wanted us," Erik said, "to be exactly like him." Lyle and Erik converted patricide into a carefully planned strategy for catapulting their careers into fast-forward. In a bizarre twist they proved how fully they had imbibed their father's values and opened themselves to the entrepreneurial spirit of the decade that shaped them.[21]

Lyle and Erik were themselves fully aware of the power of their ties to the father they killed. "We are prototypes of my father," Erik pronounced after the shootings. He added, "I'm not going to live my life for my father, but I think his dreams are what I want to achieve. I feel he's in me, pushing me." As for Lyle, he all but admitted that his whole life had been a prepara-tion for the day when he could jump into his father's shoes. Two days after the killings, Lyle told his friend Glen Stevens, who commented on how well Lyle seemed to be holding up, "I've been waiting so long to be in this posi-tion." Later, commenting on his ambitious business plans, Lyle said, "I just entered into my father's mode."[22]

The Menendez brothers had become prisoners of the American Dream, captives of their father's extravagant ambitions. Theirs may have been "ambition gone berserk," as a *Wall Street Journal* reporter put it, but it rep-resented less a crazy break from reality than an excessive vulnerability to the culture around them. The messages coming from their father, from Beverly Hills, from Princeton, from Wall Street, and, as we shall see, from both the

Reagan and Bush White House, were telling them the same thing: Money is good, more money is better, and they had only themselves to blame if they did not seize every opportunity to strike it rich. The seductive power of these messages on the boys is apparent in their uncontrollable orgy of spending after getting the first cut of their inheritance. Lyle bought a new Porsche, which was not especially unusual, but his spending on clothes was extravagant, even for Princeton. Upscale clothier Stuart Lindner remembers Lyle coming into his store "dressed in an expensive black cashmere jacket and wearing a Rolex watch" which Lindner priced at about $15,000. On that occasion, Lyle bought about $600 worth of clothes, including five ninety-dollar silk shirts. "We've had bigger sales," Lindner said, "but not in four minutes."[23]

The sons worshipped the same god as their father, but they gave the family religion a 1980s spin. They had grown up in the era of Donald Trump and Ivan Boesky, who made their father's career seem slow and his fortune paltry. Lyle told Venanzia Momo, owner of a Princeton pizza parlor Lyle tried to buy, that he did not want to have to struggle like his father did to succeed. "He said he wanted to do it faster and quicker," Momo said. "He said he had a better way."[24]

The seeds of Lyle's and Erik's ultimate wilding could be seen in a trail of small wildings reflecting the casual morality of the quick money culture that engulfed them. Even as an adolescent, Lyle frequently went on spending binges, once running up a huge hotel bill in Tucson that his father had to cover. He racked up so many traffic violations that his license was suspended twice, and several times he got into trouble with the police during his travels in Italy. At Princeton, he copied a fellow psychology student's lab report and was told he could leave voluntarily or be expelled. Meanwhile, Erik also had brushes with the law, ending up in juvenile court on a number of occasions. José, however, was always there to bail the boys out, perhaps a fatal source of support, for it may well have been that their success in getting out of small jams helped persuade them that they could also get away with killing.

The Menendez case "speaks to every parent," says television producer Steven White. "Matricide and patricide go back to Greek drama." But Lyle and Erik are poignant products of America in 1990. Their abnormality lies most of all in their uncritical receptivity to the "look after number one" message at the heart of contemporary American life. Lyle's and Erik's pathology was that they allowed themselves to be socialized so completely. They lacked the capacity to resist their father's dreams and the mesmerizing money obsession of the Reagan–Bush era. What José had not realized was that it was not his children's ambition he had to cultivate—the larger culture would see to that—but the tender sentiments and moral sensibilities that might have prevented their ambition from metastasizing into a cancer of wilding.

THEN AND NOW: AN AMERICAN TRAGEDY

In 1925, *An American Tragedy,* by Theodore Dreiser, was published. One of the country's great works of literature, it is about a young man, Clyde Griffiths, who plots to kill his pregnant girlfriend, Roberta, so that he can take up with a woman who is rich and well-connected. The story is based on a real murder committed in 1906 by Chester Gillette, a New Yorker who drowned his pregnant girlfriend to be free to pursue a woman in high society. The striking resemblance of Dreiser's hero to both Lyle and Erik Menendez, and to other contemporary men in a hurry such as Rob Marshall and Charles Stuart, suggests that wilding, even ultimate wilding, is not new. But if the parallels tell us something important about the deep historical roots of American wilding, there are also noteworthy contrasts that hint at how the virus has mutated for the worse.

Like Erik and Lyle, Clyde was an authentic prisoner of the American Dream (as was presumably the real Chester Gillette for, as H. L. Mencken notes, Dreiser stayed "close to the facts and came close to a literal reporting"). When Dreiser describes Clyde as "bewitched" by wealth, as a personification of desire for all the glitter and beauty that money can buy, he could have been describing Erik and Lyle. Indeed, Dreiser sees young Clyde as so vulnerable to the seductive temptations that surrounded him, so helpless in the face of the material pleasures just beyond his reach, that he asks whether the real guilt for the crime lay, not with Clyde, but with the culture that debased him. Perhaps future novelists or historians will instructively engage the same questions about the Menendez brothers, whose vulnerability to modern capitalist seduction is one of the most poignant aspects of their identity.

Dreiser selected the Gillette case, as critic Lawrence Hussman informs us, because he considered it "typical enough to warrant treatment as particularly American." Dreiser recognized that whatever psychological pathology was involved could only be understood in the context of a diagnosis of the health of American society and an inquiry into the moral ambiguity of the American Dream. *An American Tragedy* was compelling to millions of Americans in the 1920s because it held up a mirror in which they could see their collective reflection. The novel's success suggests that there was something of Clyde in many Americans of his era, which tells us how deeply the wilding virus had already insinuated itself into American life. Indeed, as early as the Robber Baron era of the late 1800s, the wilding streak in American culture had become too obvious to ignore, a matter of preoccupation for satirist Mark Twain, philosopher Henry David Thoreau, and the critic Lincoln Steffens.[25]

Yet if Dreiser's work suggests that wilding defines a continuity, not a break, in American life, it also hints at how things have changed. Unlike Rob Marshall or Erik and Lyle Menendez, Clyde could not actually go through with his diabolical scheme. After becoming obsessed with plans to kill his girlfriend, he lures her into a canoe with the intent of drowning her, but, whether out of weakness or moral compunction, he cannot do it. His problem is solved only because she accidentally falls into the water, along with Clyde himself. Clyde does not try to save her, partly out of fear that her thrashing about will drown him too, but that is quite different from deliberate murder. Perhaps in the America of 1925 it was still not credible to Dreiser or his audience that anyone could actually carry out such a crime, although the real Chester Gillette was only one of a number of such accused killers in the first quarter of the twentieth century. While such murders still shock the public, Americans today, according to pollsters, not only believe that such crimes can be committed, but, as noted earlier, worry whether their spouses, or they themselves, could succumb to the impulse.

That the constraints on wilding may have weakened over the last seventy-five years is suggested further by the centrality of the theme of guilt and moral responsibility in Dreiser's work. Clyde is a morally weak character, but he is not entirely devoid of conscience. After Roberta's death, Clyde is not able to absolve himself of responsibility as he is plagued by the question of whether he was guilty of not trying to save her. In contrast, the most extraordinary aspect of Rob Marshall and the Menendez brothers is their apparent lack of remorse. Friends of Rob, Erik and Lyle, and Charles Stuart, too, commented on how well they looked after the killings; indeed, they all seemed happier and better adjusted after their violent deeds and never appeared to suffer even twinges of conscience.

Dreiser's *An American Tragedy* is ultimately an indictment of the American Dream. The "primary message of the book," Lawrence Hussman reminds us, concerns the "destructive materialistic goals" that obsess Clyde and drive him to his murderous plot. Dreiser refused to accept that the evil could be explained away by Clyde's moral weakness or some presumed individual psychopathology; it was only the inability to question "some of the basic assumptions on which American society is based" that could lead anyone to that line of thinking. Dreiser himself concluded that Clyde had to be held morally accountable but that society was the ultimate perpetrator of the crime. He implicitly instructs his readers that such American

tragedies would recur until the country finally triumphed over its obsessions with materialism and ego and rediscovered its moral compass.

Dreiser's musings on the American Dream remain stunningly relevant
today, and the book is an eerie prophecy of current cases of wilding. But if
Dreiser saw how the American Dream of his era could beget extreme individual wilding, he could not have foreseen the historical developments that
have made the dream a recipe for a wilding epidemic. In Dreiser's day, the
"American Century" was dawning on a glorious future; the prosperity of
the 1920s was a harbinger of a new era of plenty in which all Americans
could reasonably look forward to their share of an apparently endlessly
expanding American pie. Despite the dark side of the materialistic preoccupation, which divided people as they competed for the biggest slices, the
dream also brought Americans together, for as long as the pie was growing,
everybody could win.

It took a new age of limits and decline, during which growing numbers of Americans would see their share of the pie shrinking and others
permanently removed from the table, to set the stage for a full-blown
wilding epidemic. Dreiser saw a foreshadowing of this in the Great
Depression, which turned him toward socialism. But America pulled
together in the 1930s and the wilding virus was kept largely in check, as I
discuss in Chapter Eight. It would take a very different set of economic
and political reversals, half a century later, to fuel the kind of wilding epidemic that Dreiser vaguely anticipated but never experienced.

It is apt testimony to Dreiser, as well as to the ferocious spread of the
epidemic he could only dimly envisage, to mention in conclusion the
rapidly growing crowd of modern-day Chester Gillettes. In addition to Rob
Marshall and the Menendez brothers, Charles Stuart is among the most
remarkable Gillette "look-alikes," not only because he killed his pregnant
wife, but because, like Chester, he was from a working-class background
and disposed of his wife because she had become an impediment to his
upward mobility. Stuart, of course, trumped Gillette's achievement by collecting several hundred thousand dollars in insurance money.

Getting almost as much publicity as Stuart was New Hampshire resident Pamela Smart, a young, ambitious media services director in the public school system who said she dreamed of becoming the next Barbara
Walters. Dubbed the "ice princess" because of her public demeanor, Smart
had the same drive as Rob Marshall. She was an honors student and cheer-
leader in high school and college. In 1991, Smart was convicted of seduc-
ing a teenager to help kill her husband; her motives included the desire to
pocket $140,000 in insurance money. It is unclear whether there were any
female Chester Gillettes in Dreiser's day, but that women no longer have
any immunity to the wilding virus is proven by such convicted killers as
Marie Hilary, whose successful poisoning of her husband and attempted

poisoning of her daughter for insurance money earned her national publicity and the title of "black widow" from the prosecuting attorney. At the time of Smart's conviction, another young woman in Detroit, Toni Cato Riggs, was convicted of masterminding the murder of *her* husband for insurance money. Riggs' husband had just returned from service in the Gulf war.[26]

SUSAN SMITH: INFANTICIDE AND THE HONOR STUDENT

Susan Smith, sentenced to life in prison, most hauntingly evokes Dreiser's theme in the 1990s. Smith is the young mother from Union, South Carolina, who confessed to strapping her two young sons, Michael, 3, and Alex, 14 months, into their carseats in her Mazda and driving the car onto a boat ramp leading into John D. Long Lake. She watched as the vehicle rolled into the water, carrying her two trusting infants to a grave at the bottom of the lake. The car sunk slowly, still floating as the infants cried plaintively for their mother who had run off to give her alibi to police.

Because Smith initially told police that the kids had been kidnapped by a gun-toting black man, reporters have compared her to Charles Stuart, who had concocted a similar racist story to throw off Boston police. Like Stuart, Smith triggered a national firestorm of self-examination. Americans everywhere wondered how a hard-working, church-going, honor society graduate in South Carolina's "City of Hospitality" could commit such a horrifying double murder.

Pundits and politicians offered their own explanations, including Newt Gingrich, who at the time of the killings on October 25, 1994, was leading the Republican campaign drive to take over Congress. Gingrich said the Smith murders showed "the sickness of our society" and was a "reason to vote Republican." But Gingrich, once a history professor, should have noticed the eerie resemblance of Smith to Chester Gillette and realized that both Smith and Gillette had deeply imbibed the intensely individualistic version of the American Dream which Gingrich was selling.[27]

The relevance of Dreiser's story and the American Dream to the Smith saga began with Smith's mother, Linda Sue, who in 1977 divorced her first husband, a blue-collar worker named Harry Ray Vaughan, to marry a stockbroker. Vaughan, Susan Smith's father, committed suicide a year after Linda left him to "marry up."

Susan Smith's romantic ambitions resemble her mother's and are intimately tied to the murders. Shortly before the killings, Smith had separated from her own blue-collar husband and had started to date Tom Findlay, the wealthy son of a corporate raider. Tom's father owned the textile factory where Susan worked as a secretary. Smith was struggling financially, living on $125 a week of child-support and a $325 weekly salary; she found it hard to meet her $344 monthly payments on her red-brick house. Susan dreamed of marrying Tom, who lived in a plush mansion called "the Castle." Tom, who was known to secretaries in the office as "the Catch," was feverishly pursued by many local women, and he complained to one friend not long before the killings, "Why can't I meet a nice single woman? Everyone at work wants to go out with me because of my money. But I don't want a woman with children—there are so many complications."[28]

Police regard the trigger event as the letter Tom sent Susan on·October 18, in which he broke off their relationship, explaining that he "did not want the responsibility of children." Susan got painful evidence of Tom's seriousness about leaving and enjoying a less-encumbered life when, only hours before she killed the children who had become the obstruction to her dreams, she found Tom in a bar flirting with three pretty single women.

After her confession, speculation in Union was rife that she did it for the money. In her confession, she wrote she had "never been so low" because of her financial problems, and Findlay's rejection meant not only the loss of love but of the wealthiest man in the county. Police believed that Smith's desperation "to jump from the listing boat of the working class" appeared to be "a major motive" for her crime.[29]

There are eerie similarities with the Dreiser story, down to the details of the drowning as the way to free oneself for marrying up. Like Gillette, Susan and her mother both saw marriage as their path to the American Dream. Known in high school as the most "all-American," Susan found it too painful to see her dream slip away. Wealthy Tom Findlay was the ticket, and Susan saw no way to keep him other than killing her own children.

Susan Smith and the whole rogue's list of modern-day Dreiser characters are just the tip of the iceberg; not only of the larger wilding epidemic but of the roster of ultimate wilders, male and female, rich and poor, who are now grabbing headlines. Experts conservatively estimate that hundreds of such calculated, cold-blooded family murders for money have taken place in the past decade. What is striking is not just the numbers, but the percentage of those who were described by friends, associates, and the police as all-American types, defying all suspicion because they so purely embodied the qualities and the success that Americans idealize. This leads us from the ultimate wilders themselves to the figures and forces in society that give rise to the wilding epidemic. These include, as we will see in the next two chapters, some of the most prominent politicians and business leaders in America, as well as some of America's most cherished institutions.

NOTES

1. *Los Angeles Times Book Review,* cited in Joe McGinniss, *Blind Faith* (New York: Signet, 1989).
2. Joe McGinniss, *Blind Faith,* p. 420.
3. Ibid. p. 62.
4. Ibid. p. 86.
5. Ibid. p. 89.
6. Ibid. p. 87.
7. Ibid. p. 308.
8. Ibid. p. 414.
9. Ibid. p. 297.
10. Ibid. p. 436.
11. Alison Bass, "Cold-blooded Killers Rarely Stand Out from the Crowd," *Boston Globe,* January 15, 1990, p. 34.
12. Ibid.
13. James Alan Fox and Jack Levin, "Inside the Mind of Charles Stuart," *Boston Magazine,* April 1990, pp. 66ff.
14. Alison Bass, "Cold-Blooded Killers," p. 34.
15. Fox and Levin, "Inside the Mind of Charles Stuart," pp.
16. Pete Hammill, "Murder on Mulholland," *Esquire,* June 1990, pp. 67–71.
17. Kathleen Hughes and David Jefferson, "Why Would Brothers Who Had Everything Murder Their Parents?" *Wall Street Journal,* March 20, 1990, p. A1.
18. "A Beverly Hills Paradise Lost," p. 66. *Time,* March 26, 1990, p. 24.
19. Ibid. p. 69.
20. Hughes and Jefferson, "Why Would Brothers?" p. A10.
21. "A Beverly Hills Paradise," p. 69.
22. Ibid. p. 72. Hughes and Jefferson "Why Would Brothers?" p. 1.
23. "A Beverly Hills Paradise," p. 69.
24. Hughes and Jefferson "Why Would Brothers?" p. 1.
25. Lawrence Hussman, *Dreiser and His Fiction* (Philadelphia: University of Pennsylvania, 1983).
26. Ken Englade, *Deadly Lessons* (New York: St. Martin's Press, 1991).
27. Charles M. Sennott, "Kin have Misgivings about Death Penalty," *The Boston Globe,* November 8, 1994, p.10.
28. Jerry Adler, "Innocents Lost," *Newsweek,* November 14, 1994, pp. 27ff. See also "Night That Turned Mom Into A Killer," *National Enquirer,* November 14, 1994, pp. 28ff.
29. Charles M. Sennott, "Bid to Climb Social Ladder Seen in Smith's Fall to Despair," *The Boston Globe,* November 8, 1994, pp. 1, 10.

3

A Fish Rots from the Head First: Washington and Wall Street Go Wild

Bad money drives out good.
—Henry Dunning Macleod

F ree-market societies are always in danger of succumbing to wilding. A thin line divides the capitalist quest for profit from economic wilding. The Robber Barons of the late nineteenth century who built American capitalism during the Gilded Age were spectacular wilders. Since then, we have suffered repeated cycles of wilding—the Roaring Twenties, with its huge speculative binges and political scandals, for example—that have chipped away at the nation's moral fabric.

The line between business success and wilding is being more dangerously blurred by two fundamental changes as we approach the twenty-first century. The first is the institutionalization of the radically individualistic political economy ushered in during the 1980s. The Reagan Revolution enshrined a new free-market religion which has become the dominant ideology of our times and is fanning the flames of wilding from Wall Street to Main Street.

The second change is the rise of global capitalism, the most fundamental economic shift in this century. The new global system threatens to destroy the social dikes against corporate wilding that national governments, labor organizations, and communities have struggled to build. Global capitalism is a key wilding threat of our era, but that is the subject of our next chapter.

WIN ONE FOR THE GIPPER: WILD
FOR MONEY

During the midterm Congressional elections of 1994 that led to a landslide Republican victory, the *Boston Globe* ran a banner headline with the following question: "Who's the most important politician in America? (Hint: He's not an incumbent). His name is Ronald Reagan."

The Gipper in 1994 was suffering from Alzheimer's disease. But his influence six years after his presidency, in the twilight of his life, was greater than ever before. The takeover of both houses of Congress by a militantly conservative new crop of Republican politicians led by Newt Gingrich symbolized the extraordinary staying power of the Reagan Revolution. As columnist Sandy Grady wrote, the new Republicans represented "warmed-over Reaganomics with a dash of bible-thumping Pat Robertson." Leading Republican strategist William Kristol said that the Republican Party in 1995 was "more Reaganite through its ranks than when Reagan was President." Rep. Gerald Solomon, Republican Chairman of the House Rules Committee, said flatly in 1995: "We're going to restart the Reagan Revolution. We're going to continue where he had to leave off." Bob Dole, Phil Gramm, Pete Wilson, and other Republican presidential hopefuls in 1996 all promised to finish the job that Ronald Reagan began.[1]

Reagan's signature could be seen in every line of Gingrich's Contract With America, which called for smaller government, tax cuts, term limits, a balanced-budget amendment, and the shredding of the welfare state. Even the "new Democrats," including President Clinton, followed Reagan's lead on core economic policy, embracing deficit reduction, increases in military spending, cuts in social spending, free trade, and downsized government. Reagan, like Franklin D. Roosevelt, is one of those rare presidents who pushes the nation on a new course and sets the agenda for future presidents of both parties.

Wilding is not the product of any leader—even one as important as Reagan—for wilding is systemic and long predates the 1980s. Reagan was hardly the first president to make Washington an accomplice to corporate greed; as Marx emphasized, political leaders of capitalist societies have always been subject to the influence of business. But the Reagan Revolution has definitively redefined the purposes of government, its relation with an increasingly powerful and acquisitive business world, and the American Dream itself. To understand how the government and political elites—in close collaboration with financial leaders—have helped fire up the current wilding crisis, we must revisit the core philosophy and policy of the Reagan presidency.

Reagan singled out one book that he said helped inspire his vision for America. The book was *Wealth and Poverty*, written by neoconservative writer George Gilder in 1981. Speaking on television, Reagan held up

Gilder's book and hailed its vision of a new American hero, the *entrepreneur*. Gilder had a bold and romantic script for helping America stand tall again, but it also proved to be a recipe for wilding. Born in the magical womb of Reaganomics, the new entrepreneur turned out to be an economic wilder, a deregulated personality in hot pursuit of fast fortune, who would help rewrite the American Dream.

Gilder celebrated men like Nick Kelley in Lee, Massachusetts, whose entrepreneurial juices began to stir as a sophomore in college when he got upset by the reams of wasted paper he saw on the floor of his stepfather's paper mill. Kelley figured out a new way to manufacture scratch pads from the paper his stepfather would normally throw in the Lee dump. He overcame serious technical and financial problems to create a thriving scratch-pad business. But when he realized he could not compete with an ingenious Italian family of scratch-pad producers in Somerville, Massachusetts, Nick adapted. He bought scratch pads from his competitors and began decorating them with emblems, turning some into legal pads. Then he found he could process tea bags from the paper, a creative breakthrough that led other papermaking companies to channel difficult projects to him. Eventually, he started three successful new businesses: one making women's fingernail mending tissue for such firms as Avon and Revlon; another manufacturing facial blotting tissue for such companies as Mary Kay and Bonne Belle; and the most successful, creating extremely thin, lint-free papers for wrapping silicon wafers utilized by the computer industry.[2]

Nick Kelley, like other successful entrepreneurs, had a passion for money—and made a lot of it. Gilder describes Kelley's drive to make money as a "gift" to society. Making money, according to Gilder, is the most important gift anyone can give in a market economy. Capitalism, Gilder writes, "begins with giving." Entrepreneurs like Kelley, by investing their time, creativity, and money in projects without any sure return, take risks for the well-being of others. Without their initiative and willingness to take such risks, capitalist economies would go belly-up.

The entrepreneur's contribution is as much spiritual as economic. Gilder sees the self-interest of the entrepreneur as holy, endowing it with a deep moral and religious significance. The entrepreneur's gift of investment in an uncertain market affirms the most important faith a society can have—"Faith in one's neighbors, in one's society, and in the compensatory logic of the cosmos." The entrepreneur "does not make gifts [that is, invest]," Gilder tells us, "without some sense, possibly unconscious, that one will be rewarded, whether in this world or the next. Even the biblical injunction affirms that the giver will be given unto."[3]

The entrepreneur, Gilder writes, is a great figure. Life is an "adventure" in which the entrepreneur "participates with a heightened consciousness and passion and an alertness and diligence that greatly enhance his experience of learning." Even the entrepreneur's failures are societal successes because they generate "knowledge of a deeper kind than is taught in schools or acquired in the controlled experiments of social or physical science," knowledge that "is the crucial source of creativity and initiative in any economic system."[4]

George Gilder's hero was also Ronald Reagan's. Reagan proclaimed:

> Those who say that we're living in a time when there are no heroes—they just don't where to look. . . . There are entrepreneurs with faith in themselves and faith in an idea, who create new jobs, new wealth, and new opportunities. It is time to realize that we are too great a nation to limit ourselves to small dreams.[5]

It was America's particular genius, Reagan said, to produce thousands of entrepreneurs who had big, lusty dreams for themselves and their country. "Their spirit is as big as the universe and their hearts are bigger than their spirit," Reagan proclaimed in his inaugural address. They were tough, ambitious, generous individuals whose restless dynamism was the high-octane gasoline in America's economic engine. Their dream—synonymous with Ronald Reagan's American Dream—was to make themselves and their country rich.

Yes, the entrepreneur may be driven by a large appetite for money and power. But Reagan, with his perennial optimism and his own unique reading of American history, assured the public that only good could come from unleashing the primal urge for self-aggrandizement. The magic of the market was that it directed the selfish energies of the entrepreneur into socially productive channels, yielding the bonanza of modern American capitalism. It was thus that Reagan could proclaim without any hesitation, "What I want to see above all else is that this remains a country where someone can always get rich."[6]

Reagan proceeded to engineer his own *perestroika* on the American economy, designed to liberate the entrepreneur and ensure that he or she "can always get rich." Over a compliant Congress that too readily acquiesced to his radical program (reflecting the new power of big business over Democratic Party financing), Reagan waved his magic wand in two decisive strokes, one deregulating almost the entire economy and thus freeing the entrepreneur from unwelcome government controls, another cutting taxes on the wealthy to ensure entrepreneurs that their pots of gold would not be taken away from them. Just as important, Reagan lost no time demonstrating through example his high regard for the rich. He surrounded himself with a kitchen cabinet of wealthy entrepreneurs such as beer magnate Alfred Coors. And at the outset of his administration, he threw the most opulent inauguration party in history: a four day $11 million celebration involving nine formal balls, a fireworks display of 10,000 rockets, and a parade of white ties, limousines, and minks that prompted even Arizona's conservative Senator Barry Goldwater to complain about such an "ostentatious" display "at a time when most people can't hack it." At one of the inaugural balls, Frank Sinatra, accurately sniffing the winds of the new administration, crooned to Nancy Reagan: "I'm so proud that you're First Lady Nancy / And so pleased that I'm sort of a chum / The next eight years will be fancy / As fancy as they come."[7]

The myth of entrepreneurship and the celebration of the rich is, again, nothing new in American history. Reaganism is only the latest stage in the long saga of America's economic individualism that mythologizes selfmade heroes and celebrates entrepreneurial initiative as the national religion. America's rags-to-riches legend, popularized by nineteenth-century novelist Horatio Alger, goes back to colonial days, surfacing in Ben Franklin's homespun *Poor Richard's Almanac*. Reagan's rhetoric clicked with the American people partly because it *was so* established in American tradition. The wilding forces that Reagan fired up had been germinating for decades in America's market economy and fiercely individualistic culture. Economic wilding, it should be clear, did not begin with Reaganism, nor will it end with Bush, Clinton, or his successor. The problem lies too deep for any government to invent or cure by itself.

But if Reaganism is only part of a longer story, it merits attention as an innovative chapter, because it decisively blurred the already tenuous line between American individualism and wilding. After the excesses of the Robber Barons, the Gilded Age, and the agonies of the depression, America recognized the shadowy side of the market and the moral ambiguities of the unregulated market. What made Ronald Reagan revolutionary was his capacity to see the world with the eyes of a mid-nineteenth-century cowboy or an eighteenth-century economist. Capitalism looked much to him as it had to Adam Smith when he described the famous "invisible hand" that ensured profit-seekers in the market would do good for society as well as themselves. Rhetorically championing the entrepreneur's high morality, Reagan resurrected a doctrine, created for the world in 1776, to serve as the manifesto for America going into the twenty-first century.

PAPER ENTREPRENEURS
AND CORPORATE WELFARE:
THE REAL REAGANOMICS

History would, however, play a cruel trick on America. First, Reagan's policies did not exactly square with his rhetoric, for it was not the struggling entrepreneur but the entrenched wealthy elite who reaped the bonanzas of the Reagan years. As conservative columnist Scott Burns wrote, "The facts

suggest that the eighties will be known as the decade of the fat cats, a time
when entrepreneurial pieties were used to beat the average worker into
cowed submission while America's corporate elite moved yet higher on the
hog." Kevin Phillips, perhaps the country's leading conservative analyst,
agrees: "The 1980s saw upper-bracket America pull farther ahead of the
rest of the nation. . . . No parallel upsurge of riches has been seen since the
late nineteenth century." The country's 400 wealthiest families tripled their
net worth, Phillips shows, and the trickle down effect predicted by conservative economists never seemed to occur. Income in the hands of the country's richest 1 percent increased more than 50 percent while the poorest 20
percent of the population lost ground, claiming only 1 percent of the country's pre-tax national income.[8]

The rich prospered under Reagan because the Great Communicator
never permitted his rhetorical devotion to the free market to inhibit his
underwriting of government welfare for the wealthy. Reagan's market revolution was always a selective affair, exposing most of the working population to greater market insecurities while extending corporate elites massive
government protection. Welfare statism for the rich took the forms, among
others, of increased federal loan guarantees for banks (thus taking away the
risks of speculation legalized by deregulation) and subsidies to industries
through unprecedented tax breaks and risk-free government contracts,
including billions of dollars of Pentagon contracts in the state planning system that Noam Chomsky and others aptly dub "military Keynesianism."
Indeed, Chomsky argues that the administration "had only contempt for
the 'invisible hand' and free-market doctrine, and had no faith in entrepreneurs. They wanted the state to act to eliminate risk, transfer wealth to the
rich, subsidize the functional parts of industry and agriculture and protect
them from imports." Chomsky concludes that the Reaganites were actually
"radical statists" who masked blatant use of government to support the rich
with the ideology of market conservatism.[9]

Corporate welfare was, in fact, among the most important historical
legacies of the Reagan Revolution. Lucrative give-aways to oil, gas, mining,
agriculture, and other industries, as well as gaping domestic and offshore tax
breaks and loopholes have grown larger since the Reagan years, with direct
subsidies to agriculture and industry amounting to $250 billion in 1995, and
tax breaks for excessive depreciation writeoffs and martini lunches worth $60
billion. When Reagan fundamentalist Newt Gingrich thundered he would
dismantle welfare for the poor, even moderately conservative groups, including the Democratic Leadership Council, began to wonder publically about
the obvious: Why was welfare for the rich not equally fair game for the
budget-cutter's ax? But even Clinton, as he shifted to embrace defense
increases, tax cuts, cuts in social spending, and smaller government, ended
up advancing core elements of the Reagan agenda and corporate welfare.

The Reaganite religion of self-interest and free market—one of the most powerful ideological forces feeding the culture of wilding—was thus accompanied by a cynical pragmatism in policy, with the president and his successors quite prepared to rely on either government or the market to advance their own interests. Reagan did, however, sponsor his own entrepreneurial revolution, liberating the *paper entrepreneur,* a new species born in the wild and woolly womb of a radically deregulated money economy. In previous generations, American entrepreneurs had to produce or trade in material goods that people actually could use. Reagan made it possible to make a fortune without producing anything of value. Paper entrepreneurs are lawyers, financiers, real-estate speculators, investment bankers, and others who make money through financial transactions that do not increase the economic pie (although they sometimes contribute to the rational restructuring of corporations) but, in Robert Reich's words, only "rearrange its slices." They are takeover artists who buy and sell companies, "white knights" who save companies from hostile takeovers, junk bond salesmen who peddle risky high-yield corporate bonds, "greenmailers" who make money by threatening to buy companies, and others knowledgeable in the arcane arts of modern high finance. Because they can make millions overnight for themselves and their clients through skillful "rearranging" on the commodities exchanges or the merger and acquisition markets, paper entrepreneurs have rapidly become dominant figures. Reich proclaimed unequivocally in 1988 that "the paper entrepreneurs are winning out over the product entrepreneurs."[10]

Paper entrepreneurs are the ultimate economic wilders. Their enterprises are inherently corrupt, not simply because they are dedicated to the dubious art of making quick windfalls, but because they are founded on the effort to make money without necessarily creating anything useful. President Reagan fervently believed that the unfettered market and his new entrepreneurs would simultaneously solve the nation's economic and moral crises. Instead, Reagan and his paper entrepreneurs made both problems worse. The paper entrepreneurs helped to rewrite the American Dream as the art of economic wilding, teaching thousands of admiring and envious young Americans that it was still possible to get rich if one did not permit moral sensibilities to interfere. As a case in point, consider the career of the country's leading paper entrepreneur in the Reagan years.

MICHAEL MILKEN: BILLIONAIRE KING OF JUNK

Members of the group were talking about Michael Milken. One said, "We owe it all to one man and we are extraneous." Another joined in, more grandly, "Michael is the most important individual who has lived in this century." A third added, "Someone like Michael comes along once every five hundred years."[11]

They sounded like the members of a 1960s cult, but these were savvy, millionaire participants in one of the most high-powered investment groups in America, the junk-bond department of Drexel Burnham Lambert Group, Inc., and they were talking about someone who, if not the most important figure of the last five hundred years, was indeed one of the giants of the 1980s. Richer and much more important than Donald Trump, he was Michael Milken, the founder and head of Drexel's awesome junk-bond empire, who started a revolution in Wall Street—and ultimately the whole American economy—by virtually inventing the junk-bond market. Junk bonds were discounted high-risk, high-yield bonds that had been around for years, but in Milken's hands they became the ultimate instrument of the takeover artist, the greenmailer, and the arbitrager, making possible the brand-new world of 1980s finance. Milken, who by age 40 was said to personally control a junk-bond market worth $100 billion can be called the ultimate paper entrepreneur, the entrepreneur whose creation was paper entrepreneurship itself.

Milken drew on the theory of an obscure researcher, W. Braddock Hickman, who had studied the performance of low-grade bonds from 1900 to 1943 and discovered that they outperformed more traditional high-grade bonds. In other words, junk bonds were anything but junk (Milken regretted calling "the stuff junk," and a friend later said, "Mike would kill to have everybody know it as a high-yield bond"). Milken became an evangelist for junk. One buyer remembered that when Michael was selling junk, he was not like a trader selling bonds, he was "a messiah, preaching the gospel." Milken spent the first part of his career figuring out which down-and-out companies, such as Penn Central, had low-grade bonds worth snapping up. But his inspiration came later, in marrying junk bonds to leveraged buyouts and other forms of "creative debt." Milken saw that if you wanted to buy a company and did not have the money, junk bonds were the way to go. Or, if you were a low-grade company (one assigned a poor credit rating by Standard and Poors or another certifying agency) and needed to raise money, junk was also the way to go. Junk, Milken figured out, was the paper entrepreneur's perfect plastic card, the way to buy yourself out of any predicament or into any fast deal. All the paper entrepreneur needed was the will; Milken would arrange the rest.[12]

The "high-grade bond guys considered him a leper," but by the late 1970s Milken was making millions and so were his clients. A brilliant and obsessive student of companies, nobody knew the junk market like Milken did. Pretty soon, it became impossible to deal in junk bonds without dealing with him. By the mid-1980s, when junk had become the grease for virtually every acquisition deal on Wall Street, Mike was the man who had to cut your deal. He had 70 percent of the entire junk market. One client said, "Where was Morgan? Nowhere. Who's the only one who can tell you what's going on? Mike. So you go crawling on your knees." Another described Milken as like "a god in that end of the business and a god can do anything it wants." There were the new movers and shakers, such as Carl Icahn, Henry Kravis, and Rupert Murdoch, but the man creating these new empire-builders, the man who was, as Milken's business biographer, Connie Bruck, writes, "choosing them, molding them, sitting on their boards, owning pieces of their growing companies," was Michael Milken. At Drexel, when people asked for Michael, the secretary would indicate in hushed tones the whereabouts of "the King."[13]

Milken became a legend in the business community. One of his business associates said, "I'm not much given to hero worship, but I have to tell you I never thought there would be a Michael Milken." Milken did for business what Donald Trump did for the general public: He inspired faith in a new expansive and romantic American Dream tailored for the Reagan era and beyond. One Milken colleague, who originally planned to get a doctorate in history, proclaimed he was now not studying history but *making* it:

> When I read Alvin Toffler's Future Shock, and he described
> this vortex of change that whirls around us, and it happens
> very fast in New York City, and slower in Des Moines, and
> even slower in the outback of Australia, the thing that was
> amazing to me was, when I looked at the funnel of that
> maelstrom, the vortex of that sits right in the middle of my
> desk. I am the fella who determines what the changes will
> be. If I don't finance it, it ain't gonna happen. I get to decide
> who's going to get capital, to make the future. Now, I ask
> you—what's more romantic than that?[14]

Although Milken initially terrorized "the older stuffier world of Ivily-degreed bankers and terminally tweeded fund managers," by the mid-1980s he had given businesses a new entrepreneurial identity to hang their hats on—one, however, that put wilding at the heart of American enterprise.[15]

On April 25, 1990, the King appeared in a New York City courtroom and tearfully confessed that he had committed six financial crimes that could earn him twenty-eight years in prison. Milken agreed to a plea bargain in which he would pay a $200 million fine and $400 million in a restitution fund for investors hurt by his crimes. Securities and Exchange Chairman Richard Breeden said that Milken should do time because his guilty plea "demonstrates that he stood at the center of a network of deception, fraud and deceit."[16] Indeed, Milken had been indicted in September 1988 on ninety-eight racketeering counts filed in a 184-page document alleging the most sweeping violations ever perpetrated against the securities laws. Milken, the indictment charged, had "traded on inside information, manipulated stock prices, filed false disclosure forms with the Securities and Exchange Commission (SEC) in order to disguise stock ownership, filed fraudulent offering materials, kept false books and records, and defrauded [his] own clients." Milken, the god who ruled Wall Street for a whole decade, was now shown to be a supreme economic wilder: in fact, the biggest financial criminal in history.[17]

Milken, it turned out, had for years been running the country's entire junk-bond market like a Mafia don. It was hard to tell whether his associates and clients were talking about Michael Milken or the other Michael, Mafia-head Michael Corleone, made famous by Al Pacino in the movie, *The Godfather*. A Milken intimate says, "In addition to being a talented, creative genius, Michael is among the most avaricious, ruthless, venal people on the face of the earth." Another says, "Michael is interested in power, dominance, one hundred percent market share. Nothing is good enough for Michael. He is the most unhappy person I know. He never has enough." Like Corleone, Milken stopped at nothing to get control. Even after his indictment in 1988 he succeeded in getting exclusive control of the junk-bond offerings of the biggest deals in the country, among them the RJR-Nabisco takeover. A close member of Milken's group said Mike's nickname was "the Shep," referring to the brilliant, eccentric Corsican shepherd boy in Robert Ludlum's thriller, *The Matarese Circle,* who, obsessed by the need for control, masterminded a worldwide terrorist revolution through his control of global multinational corporations.[18]

Connie Bruck concluded after extensive interviews on Wall Street that "there are parallels between traditional organized crime and the organization that the patriarchal Milken built . . . the brass-knuckles, threatening, market-manipulating Cosa Nostra of the securities world." Milken did whatever was necessary (short of physical violence) to get a client and keep a client, ending up with the world's most powerful corporations and investment banks in his stable, even though he was gouging all his powerhouse clients regularly and many knew it. One of Milken's favorite sayings was, "If we can't make money off our friends, who can we make money off of?" Milken did not favor either buyers or sellers of junk; he took both under his wing and found, as described in the SEC indictments, exquisite ways to extort money from them, whether it was taking exorbitant commissions, demanding "warrants," a type of financial sweetener for the deal-maker, or distorting the price of offerings, often by ingenious schemes involving unethical if not illegal buy-backs and trading on the extraordinary inside information available to him.[19]

Milken, virtually omnipotent, saw himself as outside both moral and legal constraints, regarding them as "mere conventions . . . for the foot soldiers of the world—the less creative, less aggressive, less visionary." Bruck writes that the King would make his own laws: "For whether it meant procuring women, or threatening would-be clients, the resounding credo at Drexel was to do whatever it took to win." At the nerve center of the American economy, Milken had created a veritable wilding machine. One Drexel associate said Mike's people "were animals, threatening companies." Another former Drexel executive was equally blunt: "It was all true, the place is a total slimebucket."[20]

Milken helped spawn a wilding culture, a kind of ethical jungle throughout the business world that went well beyond criminal activities per se. Its trademark was its lust for quick money of dizzying amounts. In 1985, Drexel paid the King a cool $40 million bonus, while his overall income for 1987 was at least as high as $550 million, inspiring none other than David Rockefeller to remark that "such an extraordinary income inevitably raises questions as to whether there isn't something unbalanced in the way our financial system is working." In 1986, Milken's group at Drexel received over $250 million in bonuses. One of his associates, who got a $9 million cut, said "This is Disneyworld for adults."[21]

Milken's company rocketed to the fastest fortune ever made on Wall Street. In 1977, Drexel's revenues were about $150 million, but by 1985, it was making $2.5 billion in revenues, and in 1986, it pulled down a record $4 billion. In 1990, Drexel filed for Chapter Eleven bankruptcy, but that did not stop every company in America from gaping at Drexel's performance and dreaming up its own strategies for the fast buck.[22]

The romance with paper entrepreneurship still mesmerizes American business, despite the fall of Drexel and Milken and the re-regulation of the most nakedly criminal practices. The events at Drexel constitute collective economic wilding against society itself, partly because it unleashed an entire culture of Milken clones. One was Ivan Boesky, perhaps Wall Street's most publicized 1980s criminal, who confessed to insider trading after making hundreds of millions of dollars on takeover deals. Boesky solemnly stated the credo of his decade when he told a Berkeley commencement gathering, "Greed is healthy. You can be greedy and still feel good about yourself." Another Milken clone, Charlie Atkins, controlled a securities market worth $21 billion at the tender age of 27, but in 1987 was convicted of creating the largest tax shelter fraud in history. Found guilty on thirty-one charges of "bogus security transactions," Atkins faked tax losses running into the billions, with clients eventually suing him to recover over $2.5 billion. And there was the Billionaire Boys' Club, a group of over-zealous yuppies smitten with the new entrepreneurial fever, who were prepared to murder for a quick fortune. Joe Hunt, club leader, was convicted on April 22, 1987, for an eerie revenge killing following a bad business deal.[23] Any hope that the criminal side of Wall Street might be fading in the 1990s has been shattered by the events catalogued later in this chapter, including the late-1991 revelation that Salomon Brothers, one of Wall Street's three largest and most prestigious trading firms admitted serious and extensive illegal trading in government securities.

Beyond such overt criminal wilding is a more insidious version in which businesses make huge pots of money without making anything useful. Corrupting in any era, its economic and moral consequences are now stagger- ing. Multiply manyfold the $6.2 billion that Henry Kravis was paying to buy Beatrice Companies, the $6 billion that Samuel Heyman was paying to take over Union Carbide, the $25 billion that Milken helped raise to pay for RJR-Nabisco, and you get a quick idea of the volume of capital—and mountain of debt—that was going, not to re-equip the American economy to compete with the Japanese and Germans, but rather to enrich America's corporate elite.

Paper entrepreneurship has become institutionalized wilding on a grand scale. "The main story," writes Michael Thomas in the *New York Review of Books,* "is the cost of these (paper) deals to society at large." Profits are some- times realized, but debt is increased, employees are often victimized, and vast resources are diverted away from more economically and socially productive uses. Robert Reich, who coined the term "paper entrepreneurship," puts the ultimate cost succinctly: "It has hastened our collective decline."[24]

BUSHWHACKED: KINDER AND GENTLER TRICKLE-UP ECONOMICS

The transitional figure between President Reagan and Speaker Gingrich, whose in-your-face version of the Reagan Revolution we discuss in Chapters Six and Seven, was George Bush. President Bush became an unexpectedly skilled salesman of the Reagan dream, giving the new wilding culture a human face. He seemed to be taking the country on a new course when he spoke of a "kinder, gentler America." In fact, during the 1988 campaign, Bush derided "this fast-buck stuff. I don't have great respect for just going out and stacking up money." In his inaugural address, Bush said: "In our hearts, we know what matters. We cannot only hope to leave our children a bigger car, a bigger bank account." Speechwriter Peggy Noonan wrote that the words Bush most prized were love, family, and children.

But if Bush dramatically shifted the tone and style of the presidency, it may have only been to defend the basic thrust of the Reagan Revolution. "Bush represented a shift from the aggressiveness of the new rich," Kevin Phillips writes, "to the defensiveness, even social conciliation of established wealth." Bush represents "old wealth"—an elite of "trust funds, third gener- ation summer cottages on Fisher's Island, and grandfathers with Dillon Read or Brown Brothers Harriman"—that seeks to govern capitalism in a decorous, restrained manner. The spectacle of "hogs feeding at the trough," David Stockman's way of characterizing the excesses of the Reagan administration, could create a public backlash, one that blue-blooded Republicans such as George Herbert Walker Bush had historically sought to avert.[25]

In 1980, Bush called Reagan's program "voodoo economics," and he was said to be personally embarrassed by the Reagan circle's shameless flaunting of wealth. But Bush was genuinely smitten with the magic of the market and the mystique of the entrepreneur. "Let individuals have as much leeway and flexibility as possible . . . as free a market as possible," Bush preached in 1988. He unleashed a series of economic policy initiatives to preserve into the twenty-first century the essentials of Reaganomics. Bush's "Read my lips. No new taxes" pose is widely credited with encouraging in the country a "may the public be damned, I'll take mine" attitude, close to the heart of the new wilding culture. Moreover, while he eventually changed course and agreed to tax revenue increases, his commitment to further liberating the entrepreneur by slashing capital gains taxes never wavered. Nor did his commitment to preserving the broader tax revolution of the Reagan years, which had eroded the progressivity of income taxes and massively redistributed income to the rich.

Meanwhile, Bush, despite his rhetoric of compassion, perpetuated a policy of benign neglect to the low- and middle-income groups that were picking up the wealthy's tax burden. His annual budgets offered slim pickings for the homeless, the poor, the uneducated, the medically uninsured, battered wives, abused children, and the millions of working families struggling harder to pay the bills and send the kids to school. Pulling the public plug on the mushrooming population of the needy and ignoring a vast menu of social problems were the most virulent forms of Reaganite public-policy wilding, a wilding that Bush embraced, lending it respectability by cloaking it in the sparkling rhetoric of "a thousand points of light."[26]

Bush's policy on deregulation, the key policy that unleashed paper entrepreneurialism and which Speaker Gingrich would take to new extremes, was also militant. He lived up to his campaign promise to "kick a little butt" by nominating Richard Breeden as chairman of the Securities and Exchange Commission, a man who espoused further deregulation of Wall Street and vehemently opposed any restraints on the corporate "urge to merge."

THE S & L SCANDAL: DEREGULATION
AND THE REAL MAGIC
OF THE MARKET

Nowhere is the thread tying Bush to Reagan more evident than in the savings and loan crisis, arguably the biggest orgy of economic wilding in history. The S&L crisis is paper entrepreneurialism run fantastically amok, bred from the pell-mell deregulation of Reaganomics. Deregulation brought out of the

woodwork two breeds of wilding entrepreneurs, the first a loosely coordinated band of Mafia-style outlaws, "mobsters, arms dealers, drug-money
launderers and the most unlikely cast of wheeler-dealers that ever prowled
the halls of financial institutions." S&L researchers Stephen Pizzo, Mary
Fricker, and Paul Muola describe this group, which took over hundreds of
banks, as a "network that was sucking millions of dollars from thrifts through
a purposeful and coordinated system of fraud." William Seidman, chairman
of the Resolution Trust Corporation, the agency set up to rescue the thrifts,
confirmed that "criminal fraud was discovered in 60 percent of the savings
institutions seized by the government in 1989." FBI director William Sessions
said in testimony before the House Banking Committee that criminal fraud
was so "pervasive" that it "is truly a national crisis."[27]

A second group of high-roller entrepreneurs who took over S&Ls
stayed within the law but made absurdly risky investments in junk bonds
and commercial real estate, as well as in high-risk car, mobile home, credit
card, and consumer loans. These investments were made possible by the
Reagan-Bush administration's deregulatory policy. The debt created by
these investments, likely to be $500 billion, was, of course, left to the
American taxpayers to pay.

During Reagan's tenure, Edwin Gray, head of the Federal Home Loan
Bank, complained that the "White House was full of ideologues, particularly
free-market types," who were rabidly stoking the S&L crisis by their mania
for deregulation. The way to solve the problem, they said, was more deregulation, which meant not only legalizing and underwriting outrageously
speculative investments and loans, but funding fewer examiners. Gray complained that he was "repeatedly turned down in his bids for more inspectors
to police, or shut down, the freewheeling thrifts created by deregulation."
The silver lining of the S&L crisis is that it has made perfectly transparent
the connection between economic policy and economic wilding.[28]

Both Presidents Bush and Clinton have been touched personally by the
S&L scandal, a symbol of its magnitude and the complicity of political elites
in the entire debacle. The public symbol of the Bush connection to the scandal is his son, Neil Bush, a director of Silverado Banking Savings and Loan,
who in 1990 was charged by the U.S. Office of Thrift Supervision with fla-
grant conflict-of-interest for approving huge loans to his business partners.
Silverado eventually collapsed in 1988 at a cost of $1 billion to the taxpayers.
The political organization Common Cause reported a more immediate connection between President Bush and the S&Ls: Bush received more than
$600,000 from S&L executives during his 1988 presidential campaign. There
is also evidence of direct connections and sweetheart deals between former
Bush aides such as Robert J. Thompson, Bush's former Congressional liaison,
and S&L entrepreneurs such as James M. Fail, who, although he controlled a
company that pleaded guilty to fraud, was permitted in December 1988 to
purchase fifteen failed S&L banks.[29]

In mid-1990, questions developed about whether President Bush had, in fact, created a second S&L crisis by dragging his feet on the prosecution of S&L criminals while helping to transfer the cost from the wilders to the public. Senator Howard Metzenbaum, investigating S&L fraud, claimed that the American people are "sick of stories about fast-living buccaneers who first escaped with their money and who are now escaping prosecution." In March 1990, *Time* magazine lambasted Bush for letting at least 1,500 of 3,500 major S&L criminal cases "gather dust," claiming that "the dire shortage of sleuths is partly caused by the Bush administration's unwillingness to lay out a measly $25 million" in a $500 billion crisis. Critics also charge that Bush engaged in a massive unloading of failed S&Ls to the very entrepreneurial crowd responsible for the crisis. William Greider minces no words in accusing the Bush administration of looking at the S&L crisis as a fire sale, an opportunity for private investors to pick over the carcasses," buying for a steal and reaping huge profits. "Big league investors and major Wall Street firms," Greider writes, "are circling around the bailout process, buying choice carcasses at concessionary prices." He maintains that this is only the beginning of a"fire sale [that] promises to be a long and costly debacle for the American taxpayers."[30]

President Clinton's connection to the S&L scandal is still being uncovered at this writing by congressional committees and Kenneth Starr, the independent prosecutor investigating Whitewater. There is no evidence so far of any criminal involvement, but the Clintons were intimate associates with James B. McDougal, head of Madison Guaranty, the nation's most famous failed S&L. McDougal, a former aide to Governor Clinton in Arkansas, was a business partner of the Clintons in Whitewater Development, a real-estate corporation subsidized by McDougal's S&L.

Clinton has been plagued by both his original dealings with a fast-money crowd in Little Rock during the early 1980s and his administration's possible involvement in efforts to suppress regulatory investigations of Whitewater. The two questions that hung over President Nixon in the Watergate scandal now plague the Clinton administration: What did the President know and when did he know it?

WALL STREET WILDING IN THE 1990s: ORANGE COUNTY AND "SPECTRONIC FINANCE"

The S&L scandal, although the most notorious symbol of economic wilding fueled by Washington, is only the tip of a huge iceberg of financial scams that are consuming Wall Street as we move toward 2000. The S&L debacle, the 1987 burst of the speculative bubble, and public disgust with

1980s-style Wall Street profiteering should have led to a thorough cleansing and reform of Wall Street, but the 1990s are witnessing a massive expansion of Wall Street greed and influence, making the 1980s look like a dress rehearsal.

In the 1990s, many of Wall Street's most famous investment houses have been implicated in overtly criminal financial wilding. In 1992, as part of its investigation into the scandal at Salomon Brothers described earlier, the SEC imposed fines on ninety-eight banks and Wall Street firms. A stunning roster of the country's most famous financial houses, including almost all of the leading Wall Street firms, admitted that they had submitted scores of phony bids in the debt markets of huge government financing organizations such as Fannie Mae and Freddie Mac. SEC investigators found long paper trails of lies and phantom financial statements, manufactured by various Wall Street banks to increase their share of the lucrative government debt-servicing business.[31]

Two years later, in late 1994, the SEC announced the first of a series of expected verdicts against leading Wall Street firms for defrauding customers in limited partnerships that invest in assets such as real estate and oil. Prudential Securities admitted in 1994 that it had criminally misled customers about the safety of its partnerships, agreeing to pay in total over $700 million in restitution, a penalty that exceeded even the $650 million paid by Drexel to settle its own mammoth financial wilding in the 1980s. Prudential's confession led the SEC in 1995 to pursue similar investigations in four of the biggest Wall Street brokerage firms, including Paine Webber.[32]

But the most important Wall Street wilding of the 1990s is not overtly criminal. New legal, greed-soaked financial strategies of Wall Street's great investment banks for making quick money at the expense of both productive businesses and ordinary citizens have become widely institutionalized. These became familiar to the public with the startling revelation in December 1994 that Orange County in California—one of the wealthiest in the country and described by the British Broadcasting Corporation as the "culmination of the American Dream"—had gone bankrupt. The cause was reckless public investments in derivatives, Wall Street's seductive and highly speculative instruments for 1990s investors.

Derivatives are central to the casino Wall Street game of the 1990s, successors to the junk-bond mentality of the 1980s. Involving a huge array of new exotic financial instruments, derivatives are paper schemes for leveraging money and quick profits which usually require risky bets on the direction of interest rates or futures commodities. Robert Citron, Orange County's Treasurer, proved a reckless gambler, borrowing billions of dollars at low short-term rates to pay for higher-yielding long-term securities. He bet that interest rates would fall, increasing the value of his long-term holdings, but the Federal Reserve's actions in 1994 pushed rates up, dri-

ving the values of long-term bonds down and eroding the county's investment fund by at least 25 percent.

If investors in derivatives have access to credit, they can keep coming
back to the table, betting over and over to make up paper losses with a big
win. Orange County, with plenty of credit and big dreams, lost over $2 bil-
lion by the time its credit had run out, behaving exactly like many of the
greedy S&L entrepreneurs who went bust. "Orange County," said Kevin
Starr, the state librarian of California, "thought it was Orange County Inc."
Starr added that "[t]his is a warning shot across the bow of those who
would like us to slowly privatize the United States. . . . How about the
embarrassment of not being able to pay the budget of the Marine Corps
because naval bond investments went sour?"[33]

Laughing all the way to the bank were the Wall Street firms who initially dreamt up and aggressively marketed the new speculative instruments, and who continued to reap enormous profits. Merrill Lynch, for
example, which is expected to be a target of lawsuits by investors who felt
defrauded, had been doing billions of dollars of business with Orange
County, pocketing a lucrative fee each time Orange County went back for
another bet at the table. Analysts agree that the greed of the Wall Street
firms, combined with the failure of regulators to control the sales of such
risky instruments, contributed to the Orange County collapse. Local governments, such as Auburn, Maine, which announced financial disaster
from investment in derivatives about a month after Orange County, private
investors, pension funds, and major corporations have all become eager
purchasers of derivatives and related speculative instruments in the mid
1990s, putting much of the economy at risk.

Financial consultant John Ellis, a Republican, writes, "[o]ne would
think that the Clinton administration and the newly elected Republican
Congress would be working frantically to rein in the Wall Street financial
community," which is shamelessly exploiting fierce "pressure to increase
yields and generate profits" throughout the country. The failure to regulate,
as well as the shamelessness of the Wall Street firms that have exacerbated
Orange County's situation by selling their bonds as collateral, is government-
fueled wilding. "There's a reason," Ellis writes, "[why] Americans have
grown increasingly disgusted with their federal government. It has spent
well beyond its means and enriched a small, elite community of Wall Street
financiers whose amorality in pursuit of profit is antithetical to the social
contract and the national interest."[34]

Kevin Phillips, one of the country's leading political analysts, places the
growing power, greed, and fortune of Wall Street in the 1990s in a larger
historical context. Financial elites, he argues, took command of such former world empires as the Netherlands and Britain at the point they began
to decline, finding ways to squeeze enormous profits out of economies that

were otherwise on the wane. Citing the speculative financial binges of the Netherlands' rentier elites during the "Tulipmania" of the mid-seventeenth century, and reckless profiteering by British financial moguls as British industry receded in the early twentieth century, Phillips argues that Wall Street is now taking the American economy down the same path.[35]

Derivatives have become the leading edge of what Phillips calls the brave new world of "spectronic finance," the use of electronic technology and new paper transactions to achieve what he calls the "financialization" of the American economy. In financialization, the resources of Wall Street and the economy as a whole are directed away from productive investment and toward enriching the tiny class of financiers and investment houses who own or manage much of America's money such as Goldman Sachs, Merrill Lynch, Salomon Brothers and other famous Wall Street banks.

Profits for Wall Street players have been stupefying. The sheer volume of trade in paper transactions in the 1990s has become forty times greater than the real dollar value of the productive economy, with the combined volume of trade of Wall Street firms such as CS First Boston, a bond-trading house, exceeding the dollar value of the American gross national product (GNP). Although Michael Milken may have gone to prison, the total profits of Wall Street firms increased from $9.8 billion in 1988 to $16.3 billion in 1992, and the biggest winners in the 1990s have been Wall Street's leading houses—flush with profits from derivatives and other speculative instruments. Merrill Lynch, Salomon Brothers, Shearson Lehman, and Morgan Stanley all reported record profits in the early 1990s. In 1993, Merrill Lynch reported profits from derivatives alone up 57 percent and Goldman Sachs' profit in 1993 increased 87 percent over the prior record year to $2.7 billion.[36]

These enormous profits are linked to a new wave of merger mania. In the 1990s, public attention to takeovers, mergers, and Wall Street high-rollers like Milken dimmed. But by the mid-1990s, the number of takeovers approached record levels. In 1994 an unprecedented 1,300 companies were involved in takeover deals worth $339 billion, rivaling or exceeding the reckless years of the late 1980s. Among the biggest deals were Disney's $19 billion acquisition of Capital Cities/ABC, Bell Atlantic's $13 billion takeover of Nynex cellular phone business, and Airtouch Communication's $13.5 billion purchase of US West's cellular division.[37] "I looked back on those glory years of the 1980s, and thought we'd never get near them again," said Steven Wolitzer, co-head of mergers at Lehman Brothers, in 1995. Commenting on the record-breaking $181.7 billion in merger activity in the first half of 1995, he added "I don't see anything that's going to stop this."[38]

Although Milken himself is out of the game, his colleagues in the mid-1990s, known as arbitragers, or "arbs," are finding it, as Richard Nye, managing partner of Baker Nye, puts it, "a very exciting time to be in business."

Arbs buy up stocks slated for takeover and seek to cash out their purchases with huge profits once the deal is finished. At Bear Stearns and Company, twenty arbs worked on seventy-five deals in 1994, more than twice that in 1992. The enthusiasm of the arbs, many of whom work in Wall Street's most famous investment houses, is easy to understand. As the volume of takeovers continues to increase, so do their profits. Some firms claim up to 30 percent return on assets managed, with billions of dollars "arbed" nationally each year.[39]

Such blue-chip companies as General Electric, which made a hostile offer for the Kemper Corporation, or I.B.M., which made an unsolicited but successful bid for Lotus, are becoming the mid-1990s corporate raiders. Seen now as sophisticated parts of corporate strategy, such deals are financed more cautiously than in the 1980s, but still aim for huge profits and market share, often at the cost of jobs and competition. In 1995, as Disney gobbled up ABC, and America's largest banks feverishly merged, a new era of monopoly looms. The new megacorporate empires make the nineteenth century monopolies of the Carnegies, Mellons, and other robber barons look like benign dwarfs. Empires such as Disney are becoming unaccountable private governments controlling our jobs, pocketbooks, and thoughts.

The surge of Wall Street greed and mergers in the 1990s has been met by less rather than more regulation. The SEC budget in the mid-1990s appears to be a casualty of Reaganite deregulatory zeal, governmental downsizing, and the new Republican power in Congress. Security law specialist Joel Seligman has argued that a near crisis exists in sectors of the financial markets due to a lack of meaningful SEC oversight, and that contemplated budgetary cuts run the risk of creating more cases like Orange County. But Texan Senator Phil Gramm, the powerful new Republican chair of the Senate Banking Committee, has said there would be new cuts in the SEC budget, expressing concern about the "intrusiveness" of the SEC and its need to be restrained from undue interference in the market. In 1995, Republican congressional leaders sponsored what some dub the Charles Keating Protection Act—a reference to the convicted S&L banker—that would render the big investment houses virtually invulnerable to litigation from aggrieved or cheated clients.[40]

FROM WALL STREET TO MAIN STREET

Wall Street was hardly the only part of the business world that took advantage of the Reagan Revolution's intoxicating brew of greed and deregulation. Kevin Phillips notes that mainstream blue-chip manufacturing corporations in the 1990s gazed with envy at the huge profits being reaped by Wall Street's great investment houses. As the money to be gained by making cars or computers diminished—at least in the short term—compared to the money to be made in pure paper transactions, Main Street began to emulate Wall Street, devoting larger shares of its business to financial services, speculation, and trading.

Greed among America's corporations, Phillips writes, spread like "measles in kindergarten." The results included the binge of 1990s mergers and leveraged buyouts discussed earlier as part of a larger shift of corporate resources and strategies toward purely financial and paper strategies for boosting the bottom line and top management incomes. Large manufacturing firms—from General Motors and Ford to American Can Company and General Electric—shifted vast resources into new financial businesses such as the Ford Credit Company and the General Electric Credit Company. They invested in derivatives, financed mergers, and developed their own global "spectronic finance."

An explosion of corporate crime in the 1990s—explicitly referred to as "white-collar wilding" by one frustrated regulator—is also consuming many of the nation's manufacturing and service industries. Corporate crime in America is hardly new, but it is growing frighteningly bigger and bolder. In the health care industry alone, experts believe that the total amount of fraud is between $50 and $80 billion a year, a total dwarfing the annual S&L tab. This fraud includes huge insurance scams such as "rolling labs," which conduct phony tests on patients recruited through telemarketing. One southern-California scam convinced many thousands of healthy people to take physical exams at health clubs, retirement homes, and shopping malls, generating unnecessary lab tests totalling over $1 billion in fraudulent insurance claims.[41]

Fraud is rife in companies that should be most sensitive to the public safety, such as giant pharmaceutical firms. In the early 1990s, many drug-companies were accused of selling medication they knew to be unsafe, concealing evidence from both patients and government regulators while piling up huge profits. Stories of guilty pleas for failure to report sickness and death brought on by medication—drugs such as Eli Lilly's Oraflex, Hoechst's Merital (an anti-depressant) and Selacryn (blood pressure medication)—became front-page stories in the nation's major newspapers. According to a report issued by the American Medical Association in 1995, Louisville-based Brown and Williamson Tobacco Corporation lied to the public about the company's own evidence of nicotine's addictiveness. The AMA's twenty-one trustees declared in an editorial in its leading weekly journal: "The evidence is unequivocal—the US public has been duped by the tobacco industry. We should all be outraged." Meanwhile, the Federal Drug Administration was suffering from the same lack of money and staff that crippled the SEC, raising questions about whether it could fulfill its mission of protecting the public.[42]

In the mid-1990s Congress, in its deregulatory zeal, considered "product liability reform" that would make it extremely difficult for consumers to sue if hurt by dangerous products, and also considered legislation that would eliminate the FDA altogether.

The dismantling of the regulatory apparatus has led to an explosion of corporate embezzlement and phony financial reporting throughout the economy that the *New York Times* dubbed the "Fraud of the 90s." A growing number of giant blue-chip public companies as well as small private firms are being convicted of falsifying corporate statements. Charles Harper, one of the SEC's most experienced fraud fighters, lamented that in the 1990s "[w]e're seeing the serious problems migrating upstream, from the brokers to the issuers"; that is, from Wall Street to Main Street.[43]

As widespread as criminal corporate wilding has become, the most important, and damaging, economic wilding is now legal and considered standard operating procedure by multinational companies in the brave new world of the global economy. That is our next subject.

NOTES

1. Richard Wolf, "GOP takes charge." the *Daily News,* Jan. 4, 1995, p. 9.
2. George Gilder, *Wealth and Poverty* (New York: Basic Books, 1981), pp. 53–54.
3. Ibid., pp. 24–25.
4. Ibid., p. 25.
5. Ronald Reagan, cited in John Taylor, *Circus of Ambition,* p. 14.
6. Ronald Reagan, cited in Lewis Lapham, *Money and Class in America* (New York: Ballantine, 1988), p. 8.
7. Frank Sinatra and Barry Goldwater, cited in Paul Slansky, *The Clothes Have No Emperor* (New York: Simon and Schuster, 1989), p. 17.
8. Scott Burns, "Disaffected Workers Seek New Hope," *Dallas News,* August 21, 1988, p. H1. Kevin Phillips, *The Politics of Rich and Poor* (New York: Random House, 1990), p. 165.
9. Noam Chomsky, personal communication, 1991.
10. Robert Reich, *The Resurgent Liberal and Other Unfashionable Prophecies* (New York: Random House, 1988), p. 8.
11. Cited in Connie Bruck, *The Predator's Ball* (New York: Penguin, 1988), p. 84. The material that follows draws heavily on Bruck's extraordinary account of Milken's career at Drexel.
12. Ibid., pp. 39, 57, 98.

13. Ibid., pp. 287, 245, 246.
14. G. Christian Anderson, cited in Bruck, *Predator's Ball*, p. 246.
15. David Nyhan, "The Land of Milken Honey," *Boston Globe*, April 26, 1990, p. 15.
16. Robert Lenzer, "A Tearful Milken Admits Guilt," *Boston Globe*, April 25, 1990, pp. 1, 25.
17. Bruck, *Predator's Ball*, p. 360.
18. Ibid., pp. 301, 314, 357–8.
19. Ibid., pp. 370, 360–1.
20. Ibid., pp. 301, 340.
21. Ibid., pp. 247–8. Phillips, *Politics of Rich and Poor*, p. 211.
22. Ibid., pp. 246–7.
23. On Atkins, see Taylor, *Circus*, pp. 22–52. Boesky's quote is cited in Slansky, *The Clothes Have No Emperor*, p. 176. Slansky also provides the data on the Billionaire Boys' Club on p. 196.
24. Robert Reich, *The Next American Frontier* (New York: Times Books, 1983), p. 141.
25. Phillips, *The Politics of Rich and Poor*, pp. xxi, 212.
26. Ibid., pp. 210ff.
27. Stephen Pizzo, Mary Fricker, and Paul Muolo, *Inside Job* (New York: McGraw-Hill, 1989), pp. 7–8. Citations from Seidman and Sessions in Thomas Hayes, "Sick Savings Units Riddled by Fraud, FBI Head Asserts," *New York Times*, April 12, 1990, p. 1.
28. "Deregulation Helped Turn S and L Problem into Crisis," *Miami Herald*, February 19, 1989. "S and L Failure: Stumbling on New Playing Field," *Boston Globe*, July 15, 1990, p. 10.
29. Stephen Kurkjian, "Bank Official Pushed Thrifts Sale," *Boston Globe*, July 10, 1990, pp. 1, 12.
30. Richard Behar, "Catch Us If You Can," *Time*, March 26, 1990, p. 60.
31. Stephen Labaton, "SEC Sets $5 Million In Penalties," *New York Times*, January 17, 1992, p. D1.
32. Kurt Eichenwald, "SEC Widens Partnership Investigation," *New York Times*, November 23, 1994, p. D1.
33. Seth Mydens, "Orange County's Prosperity Seems Dented, Not Undermined," *New York Times*, December 13, 1994, p. 1, D7.
34. John Ellis, "The Collateral Damage of Wall Street's Unchecked Power," *Boston Globe*, December 10, 1994, p. 11.
35. Kevin Phillips, *Arrogant Capital* (Boston: Little Brown and Company, 1994), Chapter 4.
36. Ibid., p. 85.
37. Zuckerman, "Shades of the Go-Go 80s, Takeovers in a Comeback," *New York Times*, November 3, 1994, p. 1.

38. Ken Kohn and Robert B. Cox, "Mergers Surge to Record $181.7 in 1st half of Year," *Boston Globe*, June 24, 1995, pp. 8, 11.
39. Laurence Zuckerman, "For Arbitragers, the Game is Afoot Once Again," *New York Times*, December 4, 1994, p. 6.
40. Diana Henriques, "Republicans May Curb SEC and Fraud Suits by Investors," *New York Times*, December 12, 1994, p. 1.
41. "Health Care Fraud," *Time*, February 22, 1992.
42. Gina Kolata, "Questions Raised on Ability of FDA to Protect Public," *New York Times*, January 26, 1992, p. 1.
43. Diana Henriques, "Falsifying Corporate Data becomes Fraud of the 90s" *New York Times*, September 21, 1992, p.1.

4

U.S. Business vs. Us: Global Capitalism and Corporate Wilding

What do you mean **we,** *kemo sabe?*
—Tonto to the Lone Ranger

On May 10, 1993, a toy factory in Thailand, near Bangkok, burned to the ground killing 188 workers, mostly teenage girls. One surviving worker who jumped out of an upper-story window told investigators that she and some of the other workers had tried to escape down the stairs, but had been commanded by supervisors to get back to work. Her sister also jumped, but died. The 188 deaths made this the worst industrial accident in history, exceeding the 146 garment workers killed in New York's Triangle Shirtwaist garment factory fire in 1911. While the Triangle fire helped to inspire an era of regulatory reform, the tragedy in Thailand stands as a symbol of a new age of unregulated global wilding.

The Thai factory was owned by Kader Industrial Toy Company, a giant, global manufacturing conglomerate that contracts with Toys "R" Us, JC Penney, Fisher-Price, and other major American companies. *New York Times* reporter Bob Herbert wrote that the company had been running a sweatshop with young girls who were "semi-slave laborers." Calling it "terror in toyland," Herbert said that workers such as these girls slave for "grotesquely low wages and in disgusting and extremely dangerous conditions."[1]

The seductions of such cheap and degraded labor have proved irresistible to multinational companies. Corporations defend the global pursuit of cheap labor using the discourse of the free market, arguing correctly that globalizing their labor markets has the theoretical potential to enhance efficiency and promote economic development both at home and abroad. Third World wages and working conditions, however, are the result not of the pure market described in economic textbooks, but rather of a politi-cally managed regime that keeps wages artificially low while subjecting workers to often brutally exploitative conditions.

CAPITALISM vs. COMMUNITY: SOCIOLOGICAL PROPHETS AND GLOBAL PROFITS

The making of a global economy is the real business of the 1990s. Huge multinational companies are spreading their wings for global flight, capi-talizing on technological and communications revolutions to produce and market their wares from the Amazon to the Pacific Basin. Wall Street is eagerly financing the new global system, more than doubling its holdings in overseas assets from $101 billion in 1988 to $210 billion in 1993. Meanwhile, America's political leaders, both Republican and Democratic, are sponsoring a torrent of free-trade treaties—from the North American Free Trade Agreement (NAFTA) and the General Agreement on Tariffs and Trade (GATT) to regional agreements in East Asia and Latin America—that lay the legal groundwork for a new economic world order.

The rush toward a global economy is the most revolutionary develop-ment of our times. It has the potential to bring many benefits, including a more robust world economy, dynamic growth in corners of the world that have known only poverty and despair, and even the development of a new world community. But as it is unfolding in the 1990s, globalization is blur-ring the already tenuous line between the quest for profit and economic wilding. Globalism in its current form threatens to pit the interests of busi-nesses against their host societies, creating a new predatory capitalism based on world-wide economic wilding.

Concepts developed a century ago by the founders of sociology are powerful tools for understanding this new wilding threat. As we saw in Chapter One, the great French sociologist Émile Durkheim argued that early industrial capitalism, by destroying traditional communities and encouraging individual ambition and mobility, endangered social solidar-ity and the survival of society itself. The burgeoning industrial era bred a culture of egoism and anomie—egoism reflecting the loss of community, and anomie the rise of socially unregulated dreams and passions. Egoism and anomie are fertile wilding states, spawning self-interest, greed, and violence that can spiral out of control and subvert society.

Globalism promises to further weaken the social ties and values that civilize both individuals and business. Unencumbered by national loyalties, corporations now roam the world searching for the cheapest labor in des-perately poor countries. As U.S. corporations move overseas, U.S. communities themselves become more vulnerable, with shuttered plants and industrial ghost towns becoming fixtures of the American landscape. Thrown into competition with workers in developing countries, millions of U.S. workers face an uncertain future, and many become "temps," unable to find steady, full-time employment. The multinational corporation is itself becoming, in the words of some observers, a virtual, or hollow, community, with transient "contractors" replacing permanent employees. This erosion of community intensifies both egoism and anomie, transforming growing numbers of employees into rootless, atomized "entrepreneurs," constantly seeking re-employment. At the same time, the multinationals and their top managers are increasingly liberated from governmental regulation, free to pursue unbounded appetites for global power and vast world-wide profits.

Although the twentieth century has proven Karl Marx's predictions about capitalism's death to be folly, globalism eerily vindicates Marx's view of the potential for capitalist wilding. The market's function of reducing all behavior to the cash nexus and naked self-interest becomes increasingly relevant in a global economy. Employees who must act as entrepreneurs find no shelter from the market, and survive only by embracing relentless self-promotion. Major American corporations, seeking bonanza profits, pursue child labor in India and prison labor in China.

Marx recognized that the great moral problematic of capitalism was the incentive of business to make money by exploiting its employees. In a global economy, this problem assumes a new scale. The core of the current wilding threat arises from the intensification of appetites whetted by the new fantastic global possibilities, and from the ingenious new multinational corporate strategies for realizing them.

THE MUSICAL CHAIRS OF GLOBAL BUSINESS: THE NEW CORPORATE WILDING

The key is a game of global musical chairs—a master strategy for maximizing profits by pitting national workforces against one another and exploiting the immense leverage of capital flight. Corporations able to hire cheap labor around the world can threaten to leave a community unless workers submit to lower pay or local governments agree to various incentives to keep companies from pulling up stakes. Such intimidation has always been one of business's trump cards, played fifty years ago by Massachusetts and New Hampshire textile mill owners, for example, who relocated from New England to the South after northern workers unionized. But musical chairs becomes a game plan for unparalleled wilding when the theater shifts from the nation-state to the world—and the mill owners can relocate to South Korea or Mexico.

Here, the analyses of Durkheim and Marx converge. Musical chairs in the national arena has been a regulated game, with national governments playing the role of arbiter and community protector of last resort. Such national regulation restricts the degree of egoism and anomie that can arise from the economic game and limits exploitation by prohibiting child labor, enforcing minimum wages, and protecting the environment. Within U.S. national capitalism, labor agreements and government programs created during and after the 1930s New Deal Era helped to ensure that higher profits for companies translated into higher wages for their workers and more resources for their host communities. This linking of corporate and community interests lent some credibility to the corporate manifesto expressed in the 1950s by the president of General Motors: "What's good for GM is good for America."

Under global capitalism today, however, there is no effective regulatory watchdog for the world community. As an unregulated game, global musical chairs opens societies all over the world to a purely egoistic and anomic world economy. The danger is that such a game veers, as we will see in the rest of this chapter, toward new rules that allow businesses to maximize profit by undermining the health of their host societies. As the global economy regresses back to the raw capitalism of an earlier era, the social protections built up over two centuries are jeopardized.

Global economic wilding is the fruit of active collaboration between multinational companies and national governments. Markets, whether national or global, are always shaped by those with power, and while it may seem strange that national governments would collaborate in their own demise, they have, nevertheless, during the last two decades, played a major role in subverting their own authority as they help write the rules of the new global game. This collaboration reflects incestuous entanglements among multinationals and political elites in both developed and developing countries who have struck deals that too often are subversive of their own societies. These deals have triggered a downward competitive spiral—a "race to the bottom" as some global observers have dubbed it—among economies around the world, pushing much of America toward Third-World wages and working conditions while intensifying the misery of already impoverished masses in poor countries.[2]

WILDING AROUND THE WORLD: THE THIRD WORLD AS GLOBAL SWEATSHOP

The fire in the Thai toy factory is only one example of economic wilding in the Third World, and the historical record suggests that the Thai sweatshop is more the rule than the exception. The lives of workers in developing countries reflect the power exercised by multinationals, the U.S. government, and repressive, often militarized Third-World regimes. While Thai workers suffer, Thai generals and business elites win generous aid and subsidies from the American government, and enjoy lucrative joint business opportunities and millions of dollars in bribes and payoffs.[3]

Nike pays contracted Indonesian peasant girls an average of 82 cents a day to manufacture running shoes that cost $5.60 to make; Nike then sells the shoes for $150. A military Indonesian government, staunchly allied with the United States and host of the Pacific Free Trade Summit attended by President Clinton in 1994, helps enforce a mandatory eleven-hour day for some of the workers, who make about $2 a day. Many of Nike's workers make the minimum wage of $1.06 for a seven-hour day, which is 14 cents less than the Indonesian Labor Ministry's estimate of the amount needed to avoid starvation.[4]

The Third-World game board, designed collaboratively by multinationals and governments, offers an endless set of moves for the nimble corporate player. The U.S. spinning industry, in its 1990 trade journal, advertised the attractions of Rosa Martinez at her sewing machine in El Salvador. Rosa can be hired for 57 cents an hour. Sears contracted with Chinese suppliers, some of whom, it was discovered in 1991, use prison labor to produce a variety of consumer products, and growing numbers of American companies are flocking to the Chinese "special enterprise zones" where the going wage rate can be an astonishing 15 cents per hour. In Manila, the capital of the Philippines, multinationals hire children as young as 4 years old to stitch or pack dresses at 5 pesos a day although the legal minimum wage is 69 pesos. In Guatemala, investigators have recently found instances of multinational assembly plants that padlock their doors until 2 A.M. to keep their workers, mostly young women, from going home; reports of sexual abuse in such plants are legion.[5]

Most developing countries have established special "export processing zones" or "free trade zones" that offer "tax holidays" to multinationals and exempt them from environmental codes and labor laws. By the mid-1990s, 175 such zones existed around the world, employing about 4 million workers, about half of these in China. Sometimes walled off behind barbed-wire fences, these zones have been described as "huge labor camp[s]," often controlled by special police forces. The most famous of these zones, and among the most important to American companies, is along the American-Mexican border, the site of the *maquiladora* plants, which now reach well into the Mexican interior.[6]

Growing out of the Border Industrialization Program in 1965, the *maquiladoras* are a classic instance of collaboration between multinationals and government. The Mexican government offered corporations favorable land deals, waived custom clearance and import duties, and agreed to low taxes and, tacitly, the right to run their businesses with a free hand, exempt from environmental and labor laws. The American government did its share by running political interference for U.S. companies and giving them technical assistance and tax breaks for going south of the border. By the end of 1990, there were 1,909 *maquiladora* plants, employing 371,780 workers mostly in assembly plant operations in industries ranging from textile to automobile to electronics. The passage of NAFTA in 1993 facilitated the huge American corporate exodus south of the border, swelling the ranks of displaced available Mexican workers in agriculture and other industries that cannot survive American competition.[7]

The *maquiladora* region is a site of devastating economic and environmental wilding, described in a recent report by researchers from the University of Massachusetts at Lowell as a gigantic collective sweatshop. Although touted as a salvation for poor Mexican workers, the *maquiladoras* have contributed to a nosedive of Mexican wages in the last decade. In 1982, the *maquiladora* hourly wage level averaged $1.38, falling to $.73 in 1985, $.69 in 1988 and $.51 in 1991. In late 1994, when the peso collapsed and the Mexican economy entered a post-NAFTA crisis of frightening dimensions, real Mexican wages declined another 30 to 40 percent. The long-term wage decline reflected not simply mushrooming numbers of displaced Mexican peasants, but political repression of independent unions and the pacification of workers by "official," or company-sponsored, unions which agreed in advance of their certification not to strike or demand higher wages.[8]

Blue-chip American companies, including Sylvania, RCA, Ford, and General Motors, have flocked across the border to reap huge wage-savings. GM alone had forty *maquiladora* plants and 40,000 Mexican workers by 1994. The wage-savings in auto assembly and parts manufacturing, a leading *maquiladora* industry, are dramatic. In the Ford high-tech assembly plant in Chihuahua, workers in 1990 made between $30 and $40 a week, among the lowest auto wages in the world. In its state-of-the-art plant in Hermosillo, Ford paid $2 an hour in the early 1990s, compared to $30 an hour in Detroit.[9]

Working conditions in the *maquiladoras* violate both Mexican and American law. Among the most serious problems is widespread sexual abuse of young female workers. Labor lawyers and social workers report that young women are often propositioned by their male supervisors and can lose their jobs if they don't sleep with them. Mexican social worker Teresa Almada reports that women are in "a lot of danger" both inside and outside of the factory gates, and that many become pregnant and are then fired.[10]

Anthropologist Maria Fernandez-Kelly, who worked in the plants in Ciudad Juarez, reported that workers' health tends to deteriorate rapidly because of the brutal work pace, unsafe machinery, and hazardous fumes, with the most frequent complaints being "eyesight deterioration, and nervous and respiratory ailments." A survey conducted by the University of Massachusetts at Lowell found widespread musculoskeletal disorders related to the pace of work and poor workplace engineering. Many studies have found serious health problems caused by toxic chemicals and other unregulated pollution. A recent study by the AFL-CIO found the water supply on the border massively polluted, threatening fish and wildlife with extinction, and the ecosystem as a whole with indiscriminate dumping of toxic waste in unsafe, often clandestine, dump sites.[11]

The prevailing subhuman conditions in the plants and the surrounding communities are a product of coordinated repression by multinational corporations and the Mexican government, which has intervened repeatedly, using the police and the army to suppress labor protest, and permitting multinational companies to evade environmental and labor laws. Wages and working conditions have declined as the multinationals have expanded, because the huge firms have worked so effectively with both the American and Mexican governments and with company-sponsored unions to erode workers' rights and community social protections. These are neither free nor fair markets, but the predictable outcome of a global game of musical chairs gone wild.

THE DOWNSIZING OF AMERICA: GLOBALIZATION AND WILDING AT HOME

By passing NAFTA, GATT, and other global free-trade agreements in the 1990s, the United States has firmly committed itself to economic globalization. Republican presidents Reagan and Bush, as well as Democratic leaders such as President Clinton, have argued that globalization will enhance American living standards by increasing jobs in export-sector industries, reducing consumer prices, increasing corporate competitiveness and profits, and promoting both understanding and efficiency around the world. But although globalization is now inevitable and has the potential to enhance well-being here and abroad, the game of global musical chairs as it is structured today will prove as selective in its payoffs at home as it has been in developing nations. Its effect, showing up already in the gradual erosion of the American Dream over the last twenty years, is to push the living standards of poor and working-class Americans down, and to create the kind of dangerous, polarized class structure prevalent in the Third World itself.

Global musical chairs as a wilding enterprise manifests itself most nakedly in the United States among workers at the bottom, where a literal

"Third-Worldization" of the economy is taking place as work in the U.S. regresses toward Third World wages and working conditions, especially for jobs held by Third World immigrants living here. Globalization increases the flow of workers across national boundaries, making immigration an explosive economic factor in the United States and other countries. The latest wave of immigrants in the United States, many from Latin America and Asia, are the nucleus of a growing Third World economy inside our borders, based on jobs which most U.S. citizens would not tolerate.

Globalization offers employers in this country new strategies for international recruitment. Outside Chicago, for example, factories have cultivated relationships with Mexican villages that are the home towns of their immigrant Mexican employees. These employees are willing recruiters in their villages, encouraging family and friends to join them in the factory when other workers quit and jobs open up. For companies, this direct line into remote Mexican towns is a godsend, a source of cheaper and more compliant workers than they can find among even the masses of desperate Chicagoans looking for work.[12]

Sweatshops in the United States are experiencing their own revival. In the second half of the 1980s, according to the Department of Labor, the number of illegal minors employed in U.S. sweatshops doubled. By 1995, about 2,000 sweatshops operated openly in New York City alone, typically garment shops employing immigrant workers for twelve hours a day at sub-minimum wage with no overtime. The dangers of U.S. sweatshops are no different from those in Thailand or Indonesia; in 1991 a horrific fire in a North Carolina poultry processing plant burned twenty-five employees to death. Management generally kept the factory doors locked, preventing the workers from escaping. The plant's owner, Emmett Roe, who personally ordered the padlocking, was sentenced in 1994 to nearly twenty years in prison after pleading guilty to involuntary manslaughter.[13]

Sweatshops and the exploitation of immigrant labor are only the exposed tip of the continuing Third-Worldization of the U.S. economy in the wake of globalization. In the United States, as in the developing nations, global musical chairs has offered corporations a way to extract from workers and communities massive givebacks and concessions, amounting in the 1990s to a wholesale rewriting of the social contract. At the heart of this change is the employment revolution that *Fortune* magazine calls the "end of the job," in which corporations turn many workers into part-timers, temps, independent contractors, and other contingent workers.

The transformation of about one-fourth of American workers, numbering about 30 million, into formally contingent workers—which *Time* calls the "temping of America"—contributes to the Third-Worldization of the American labor force. When a corporation reclassifies a worker as a temporary or part-time worker, or as an independent contractor, the firm immediately unburdens itself of obligations to pay for health care and unemployment insurance, pensions, and other benefits, while also relieving itself of any responsibility for providing long-term job security. Not all employees, however, will be turned into formal contingents, because globalization induces corporations to enhance loyalty and participation among a small, core work force in order to increase competitiveness and quality. This is one of the key contradictions of globalization, which simultaneously creates incentives for making workers disposable and for making them more closely tied to the company.[14]

Since becoming a temp or part-timer means not only the loss of fringe benefits and job security but also, on average, a wage only 60 percent that of regular employees, contingency catapults many formerly middle-class workers into a nightmare of economic uncertainty and vulnerability. For example, an accountant who was "downsized" and now finds jobs through a temp agency specializing in professionals and managers, gives a graphic view of his unanticipated poverty: "I have to cheat on my taxes because I can't make ends meet. I need brakes on my car, but I'll push it as far as I can on the old brakes. My wife needs dental work . . . because her teeth are rotting. I eat one meal a day because it curbs the appetite and helps put food on the table for the kids."

Beyond such economic problems, temps and part-timers suffer from a new crisis of community. Contingent work, a form of intensely anomic employment, exemplifies the weakening social ties that Durkheim predicted and feared. Here today and gone tomorrow, the contingent worker has been described by one scholar as "the workforce equivalent of a one night stand." Inspiring neither loyalty nor commitment, such loose connections at work tend to degrade workers socially and morally. One temp expressed a common sentiment among contingent workers: "I don't give a shit about the company. I'm here to get some money, to get everything I can. If I can take pencils from them I'll take them. I shouldn't think like that but I do. Can I steal some paper, copy software?"[15]

One temp said he felt "doubly raped, once by the company and once by the temp agency." In fact, both agencies and corporations often exploit contingent workers, sometimes criminally. The Internal Revenue Service is now closely monitoring corporate reclassification of employees as a gigantic tax scam. When companies call their workers independent contractors, they spare themselves such employer taxes as unemployment insurance, workers' compensation, and social security. These savings are illegal if the reclassification is purely a paper one and so-called independent contractors continue to work exclusively for the company, as they did in one large corporation that reclassified its mail room employees without even telling them. Believing that corporations are cheating taxpayers of millions of dollars through such ruses, the I.R.S. has made prosecution of such cases a high priority.

Temps and other contingent workers are uniquely vulnerable to other forms of corporate wilding, including sexual harassment, racial discrimination, and violations of health and safety codes and fair-labor standards. Most have no union, employee association, or other group to protect them. One Hispanic mother, who temped for over a decade, reported being "sexual harassed and discriminated against by many bosses. They know they can get away with anything because you're a temp." She said many temp agencies also discriminate: "If you're blond and blue-eyed, the temp agency will give you the best assignment." Other temps report that they are not told their wage rate, are forced to work overtime without pay, and are required to do unsafe work. Many have to wear specially colored badges. Some are denied a desk, a seat in the cafeteria, or a key to the bathroom.

The wilding dimensions of the new system of "contingent capitalism" are intimately intertwined with globalization both at home and abroad. Nike, General Motors, and other huge multinational producers use foreign workers as a huge off-shore pool of independent contractors. A slash-and-burn strategy for making profits, contingent work on a global scale redistributes corporate risks onto an unprotected and remote labor force that can be dumped with one switch of the computer to absorb the uncertainties of the global market and business cycle.[16]

Domestic contingent workers similarly sponge up corporate risk, buffering companies from business cycles and market uncertainties on the home front. Most contingent workers in the United States are minorities, females, or uneducated males—a mirror image of Third-World contingents. Globalization places domestic contingents in competition with foreign workers, so that together they function as a world-wide peripheral labor market—the global equivalent of what Marx described as "the reserve army of labor."[17]

Globalization, along with rapid technological change, also drives the downsizing that is bringing new anxieties—and a new experience of economic wilding—to the American middle class. The 1990s has become the Decade of Downsizing, with mass firings in over half of the Fortune 500 firms. Just the four leading downsizers—General Motors, IBM, Sears, and AT&T—cut over 200,000 jobs in 1993 alone. In 1993, corporations laid off a record total of 615,386 workers; in every year since 1991, the percentage of companies reporting work-force reductions has hovered at about 50 percent. Continuous downsizing has become an institutionalized strategy for increasing efficiency and global competitiveness. Respected labor economist Audrey Freedman told the *New York Times* in 1993 that downsizing "is going to be a permanent condition," and that "there are almost no long-term secure jobs" left in America.[18] The prospect of continuous downsizings blurs the division between regular and contingent employment, because even core employees have to consider themselves "temporary permanent."

Downsizing is brutal for both casualties and survivors. For many of those with long years of service to a firm, it is not only an economic catastrophe but a Durkheimian wilding blow with severe anomic consequences. Between 1991 and 1994, IBM was the biggest downsizer, announcing 85,000 cutbacks. Thousands of IBM employees had signed onto the company because of its promise of lifetime job security. Having devoted their lives to the corporate community, they had reason to feel morally betrayed when the company—which had taught them corporate loyalty as the highest value—unilaterally broke the covenant.

At Digital Equipment Corporation, another computer giant torn apart by massive downsizings, pink slips arrive on Friday afternoons, with only a couple of hours to clear off one's desk. One laid-off employee reported that as he walked back to his office to collect his belongings, long-time colleagues scooted into their cubicles without meeting his eyes. None came to say goodbye. They feared, he said, that the pink slip was contagious, a kind of corporate AIDS virus.

Survivors of downsizing report a climate of terror in many companies. A Connecticut telephone company, for example, maintained a no-layoff policy for ninety years, but in the early 1990s initiated a series of downsizings now commonplace in the communications industry. After the first wave of layoffs, the company "combined departments and then started chopping them off." Survivors, constantly at risk of losing their jobs, were continuously given new work assignments, adding stress and burnout to survivor guilt. "The panic and fear," one survivor said, was "so thick you could cut it with a knife."[19]

Underlying the downsizing panic is a new mortal threat to the American working and middle classes, which were created through a social contract delivering long-term, well-paying jobs. The contract, which partially kept at bay capitalism's egoistic and anomic tendencies, was ratified in New-Deal legislation of the 1930s and reinforced in labor agreements and social-welfare legislation through the 1960s following a century of dedicated labor and social struggles. But globalization has opened the door to a quick, corporate unburdening of the contract's good wages, expensive benefits, and long-term loyalty. As more and more corporations violate the contract, capitalism reverts to its earlier egoistic and anomic impulses, now played out by multinational robber barons on a global scale.

The collapse of the social contract is marked by the downsizing of entire core American industries and the rise of a new anomic post-industrial economy. As General Motors, Ford, and Chrysler make record profits in the mid-1990s from their Mexican production plants and their entry into the aircraft, oil, and financial services businesses, half a million American auto workers have been abandoned. They are joined in purgatory by millions of other displaced workers from textile, steel, and other industries fleeing to plants out of the country. Offered neither significant new training nor a viable safety net, many workers remain permanently unemployed or underemployed, forced into contract and temporary jobs or into low-paid service work without the protections and benefits that had been their ticket to the American Dream. This abandonment of the American working class by both government and corporate America is a spectacular variant of economic wilding, and a moral barometer of capitalism without a social contract.

The new futuristic post-industrial American economy—made up of high-tech multinational giants in communications, computers, finance, entertainment, and medical service—is, ironically, a throwback to the anomic capitalism of earlier times. High-tech corporate regions such as California's Silicon Valley have been described by both employees and researchers as dysfunctional contingent worlds, marked by ruthless competitiveness and profiteering, rootlessness, high turnover, astonishing disloyalty, and relatively invisible forms of exploitation and stratification. Supporting the highly paid computer entrepreneurs, electronic engineers, systems analysts and hot-shot programmers—described by one scholar as a class of anomic loners who flit restlessly from one company to another in pursuit of the best deal—are a global network of contingent computer assembly-line workers, from Mexico and Southeast Asia to far-flung areas of the United States. Their low wages, job insecurity, and often dangerous work with poisonous chemicals or eye-straining electronic microscopes reflect the grim realities of contingent capitalism. Although the computer professionals and the assembly workers are at the polar extremes of the new post-industrial economy, neither enjoys the benefits of the old social contract, which more effectively preserved loyalty and community in a capitalist world.[20]

POOR AND POORER, RICH AND RICHER: GLOBALIZATION AND INEQUALITY

As 1995 dawned, the New York Times ran a couple of stories about the new class structure of Manhattan. One compared the weekly expenses of an upper-east-side millionaire executive of a global communications business with that of a poor restaurant worker in mid-town. The restaurant worker spent a weekly total of $44.96, mostly on food. The executive spent

$27,338.66 the same week, including a weekend vacation for two, parking, massages, credit card expenses for toys, books, clothes, and daycare.[21]

A second article showed that the gap between rich and poor in Manhattan had grown explosively from 1980 into the mid-1990s, making it the most unequal in the country. The top fifth of Manhattan's households made an average of $174,486 compared to an average of $5,435 for the lowest fifth. The Manhattan gap is now bigger than that in Guatemala, one of the most economically polarized societies in the world.[22]

The Clinton administration's labor secretary, Robert Reich, a leading advocate of free trade, has acknowledged that globalization carries two terrible, closely related risks. One is the uncoupling of businesses from society, with business profiting handsomely from global ventures as communities around them decline. The corollary is the rise of an unbridgeable gap between corporate elites and everyone else. This threatens a new dangerous division in America between the professional and managerial classes, whose skills have currency on the global market, and the working class, which is becoming increasingly indistinguishable from the gigantic pool of unskilled, Third-World labor.[23]

Reich has recognized that such developments could reawaken class warfare, for they implicitly pit business and the rich against their own societies, the most draconian kind of economic wilding. Reich nonetheless embraces free trade because he has faith that massive government and corporate training will give the majority of American workers the skills necessary to compete globally. But the Clinton administration was unsuccessful in delivering a massive training program, and even had it succeeded, there is no guarantee that it would have led to the good jobs Reich predicted.

By 1995, Reich had to deliver the bad news: As America moved into the brave new world economy of NAFTA and GATT, which his own administration had championed, American society was internally fragmenting into a Third-World-like class division of rich and poor. A diminished and anxious middle class survived, but more fell each year into the huge new pool of the poor or working poor, numbering between 40 to 65 million Americans by the middle of the decade. The polarizing trends seen in Manhattan, while extreme, were being reproduced all over the country.

A leading chronicler of the new inequality is Harvard labor economist Richard Freeman, who reports that by 1990 the wage gap between well-paid and poor workers was higher than at any time since the Great Depression. In the 1980s alone, the wages of the top 10 percent of American workers grew relative to those of the lowest 10 percent by 20 percent for men and 25 percent for women. The wages of young men with high-school or less education plunged a remarkable 20 percent between 1979 and 1989. The poorest were getting poorer.[24]

The gap continues to get worse in the 1990s. The Department of Labor reported that between 1991 and 1994, an era of economic recovery, white-collar pay rose a modest 1.3 percent while blue-collar pay fell 7 percent. Freeman reports that wage gaps of every kind are increasing, including those between the well-educated and the unschooled, between the highly skilled and the unskilled, and between high- and low-paid workers within particular industries or age groups.[25]

Except for the wealthy, who have been enjoying bonanza gains, virtually everyone else is sinking. Labor Department data show that between 1988 and 1994 the average pay of all private sector employees fell 4 percent to $13.39 an hour. By 1995, American wages had fallen or remained flat every year since 1988, except in 1992. Census data show that the American family actually earned less income in 1993, when $35,987 was the median income (adjusted for inflation), than in 1973, when the median income was $37,156.[26]

But while most Americans have been getting poorer, the very rich are seeing fabulous increases in their wealth. During the 1980s, they appropriated a huge percentage of the rise in national income, creating what economist Paul Krugman called an "unprecedented jump in inequality to *Great Gatsby* levels." By 1992, the richest 1 percent owned a mind-bending $1.25 trillion in rental real estate, $1.12 trillion worth of stocks and bonds, $221.9 billion in trusts, and $524 billion in banks and other accounts, totalling $3.1 trillion in assets, a substantial fraction of the total privately held wealth of the country.[27]

The top one-half of 1 percent, the families worth from $5 million to the $21.5 billion of Wal-Mart's Walton family, America's richest, the $12.1 billion fortune of Microsoft's Bill Gates, and the $10 billion fortune of the duPont family, have been the real winners. This plutocracy, swollen by a quadrupling of the number of American billionaires and centimillionaires, raked in "virtually the entire gain" in the rich's share of national income in the last decade. The net worth of just the 400 richest Americans tripled from $90 billion in 1982 to $270 billion in 1989. As the middle class declines and the poor deteriorate into a vast, hopeless underclass, America's new rich coalesce into a tiny financial aristocracy with unprecedented wealth.[28]

Kevin Phillips, as noted in Chapter Three, brilliantly illuminates some of the connections between class inequality, globalization, and economic wilding. He analyzes the new American plutocracy as a mercenary "rentier class," typical of empires in their periods of decline. With the casino mentality of the idle rich, they are increasingly invested in speculative international financial markets managed through unregulated offshore banks. Instead of financing American jobs and productive capacity at home, the very rich are helping bankroll multi-trillion dollar global currency, derivatives, futures commodities, and bond trading. Some of the fabulous wealth poured into this global casino is "hot money," illegally laundered or gambled for huge, quick profits.[29]

The focus on this shameless American rentier elite, who are grossly enriching themselves at the expense of America itself, should not divert attention from multinational corporations and the institutionalized wilding of the new global order. America's decline and class polarization ultimately reflects not the whimsy of the idle rich, but a new, highly organized system of global finance and production, centered on and benefitting the largest multinational companies. As America downsizes in the 1990s, America's global corporations enjoy large profits, raking in, for example, 14 percent profits in 1993. That same year, when one in every five American children was born into poverty, average CEO compensation, excluding stock options, rose to $1.9 million.[30]

Systemic economic wilding arises from the concentration of unelected and unaccountable global power in a few hundred gigantic multinationals. Unlike the governments whose authority they have replaced, these corporations have no enforceable social ties, commitments, or responsibilities. It is hardly surprising that the accumulation of great wealth in such a system would be intimately linked with spreading poverty and social decay.

GLOBALIZATION WITHOUT WILDING: A PEEK AT THE POSSIBILITIES

As noted at the beginning of this chapter, globalization could be brought about in a different way to reap the benefits of global specialization, production, and trade without inflicting harm on millions of the world's workers and communities. Why, then, have our political leaders allowed globalization to proceed in its current form? And how might the global economy be restructured and regulated to balance the enormous power of multinational corporations and contain their greed?

The United States will retain significant influence in the new web of global institutions, from the International Monetary Fund and the World Bank to the World Trade Association, the global body replacing GATT and adjudicating world trade disputes. But the players gaining the most power in the new world economy are not the governments of the United States and other nations, but the multinationals themselves. The reason for the acquiescence of both Republican and Democratic presidents to their agenda is simple. Both political parties are dependent upon business funding to win elections and are not prepared to risk opposing huge global corporations on issues of central importance to them. Five hundred of the largest U.S. corporations have offices in Washington and employ thousands of lobbyists, as do 400 of the biggest foreign multinationals, together constituting by far the largest and most influential special interest group in Washington. Ultimately, business sets the parameters for economic policymaking in America, because members of the U.S. corporate elite themselves occupy the highest governmental economic posts and because they control the money and investment decisions essential to the survival of both the population and the government.[31]

President Clinton learned this lesson early. In his first term as Arkansas governor, he mounted a populist challenge to big industrial and utility companies. When he ran for a second term, the companies funded a campaign against him that threw him out of office. When Clinton ran successfully for a new term two years later, he had dropped his populist program and cozied up to Arkansas' paper-mill and poultry tycoons.

In his 1992 presidential campaign, Clinton again used populist rhetoric to challenge companies fleeing the country: "In a Clinton administration," he declared, "when people sell their companies and their workers and their country down the river, they'll get called on the carpet. We're going to insist that they invest in this country and create jobs for our people." Getting specific, he pledged to end tax incentives and other federal subsidies for companies shipping jobs abroad, while also insisting on tough no-nonsense measures to prevent our Third World trading partners from becoming havens for outlaw companies looking for slave wages and hands-off regulation.

After his election and the early defeat of his economic stimulus plan, Clinton looked not to populists but to Wall Street elites such as Treasury Secretary Robert Rubin to fashion his economic agenda. Clinton desperately sought corporate support to bolster his "new Democratic" image, deliberately taking on the unions and staking enormous capital on passing NAFTA and the new GATT agreement. By embracing the corporate free-trade agenda as his own, he tried, unsuccessfully, to stem the tide of the conservative movement leading to the Republican takeover of Congress in 1994. Political scientist Thomas Ferguson, a leading analyst of the role of corporate money in elections, argues that a late swing of corporate PAC money to Gingrich-sponsored candidates made the decisive difference in the GOP victory. Gingrich's national sweep also suggested the truth of the popular wisdom that in a choice between a Republican and a Democrat posing as a Republican, the public will choose the real thing every time.

Clinton and his top advisors clearly believe that globalization and free trade serve the interests of the nation. But they have not taken the initiatives necessary to build a global economy that "puts people first," the mantra of his campaign. Clinton has failed to take the fundamental steps that could make globalism work in the interests of ordinary workers and citizens around the world and protect them from the downward spiral of the current global game of musical chairs.

One necessary step is to promote global labor movements to represent the interests of the new global work force and balance the power of the multinationals. Both American workers and employees in developing nations need strong unions to prevent the horrendous exploitation of global sweatshops and contingent employment. But the Clinton administration has avoided any identification with American unions and has done nothing to support the embryonic movement for independent unions in Mexico, Indonesia, and other developing countries.

Jeremy Brecher and Tim Costello point out that American unions are starting to develop new international strategies. In 1994, workers in a Ford truck-assembly plant in St. Paul, Minnesota, voted to send funds to Ford workers in Mexico to support a union drive in the *maquiladoras*. The American workers, who recognized that wretched Mexican wages and working conditions affected their own jobs and security, wore patches on their jackets saying "Cross-Border Solidarity Organizers." The U.S. United Electrical Workers, with help from the Teamsters, has also contributed to independent labor organizing in the *maquiladoras*. The rise of new international labor confederations and new lines of communication between unions across national borders could ultimately create global unions representing workers in the same company or industry throughout the world, one of the only forces that could prevent multinationals from playing one country's workers against another's in a race to the bottom.[32]

A second positive direction would be to build up codes of international labor standards and corporate conduct that would set a humane global floor for wages and working conditions. The European Common Market has established a European Social Charter setting minimum wages, health and safety standards, and other social codes to be honored by all the European members. Although Clinton negotiated NAFTA with side agreements to protect labor and the environment, most observers saw them as pitifully weak. Citizen and labor groups are pushing for far stronger agreements and a robust social charter for *maquiladora* businesses.

Ultimately, globalization without wilding requires a global social charter that offers a rising and generous standard of protection for the world's labor force. While some corporations such as Reebok have initiated their own corporate codes of conduct, promising to avoid use of child labor or prison labor and pay prevailing wages in each country in which they operate, an effective social charter will require not only more corporate social responsibility but a new, robust, regulatory framework. Workers, citizens, and governments have to make the World Trade Organization and other regulatory bodies democratically accountable, responsive both to elected national representatives and to the concerns of ordinary workers and communities.

Multinational companies in the United States and elsewhere have used globalism to escape their social responsibilities and weaken the accountability that the workers and governments of their own nation have historically imposed on them. This will lead to a permanent regime of corporate wilding unless a new social covenant is negotiated between multinationals and workers and citizens of the world. Building a new world community through the struggle for global employee rights and democratic and accountable multinational corporations may prove the most important new social project of the coming era.

NOTES

1. Bob Herbert, "Terror In Toyland," *New York Times,* December 21, 1994, p. A27.
2. For a concise, readable interpretation of globalization as a "race to the bottom," see Jeremy Brecher and Tim Costello, *Global Village or Global Pillage* (Boston: South End Press, 1994).
3. For a general discussion of this pattern, see Noam Chomsky, *The Prosperous Few and the Restless Many* (Berkeley, CA: Odonian Press, 1993).
4. Richard Barnet and John Cavanaugh, *Global Dreams* (New York: Simon and Schuster, 1994), p. 327.
5. Ibid., p. 333.
6. Ibid., pp. 321ff. See also Annette Fuentes and Barbara Ehrenreich, *Women in the Global Factory* (Boston: South End Press, 1992), pp. 10ff.
7. Dan La Botz, *Mask of Democracy: Labor Suppression In Mexico Today* (Boston: South End Press, 1992), p. 162.
8. Ibid., p. 165.
9. Ibid., p. 185.
10. Ibid., p. 164.
11. Ibid., pp. 164–8.
12. Richard Barnet and John Cavanaugh, *Global Dreams,* op. cit., p. 303.
13. Ibid., p. 333. "Sweatshops Flourish a Century After Their Danger Was Detailed," *New York Times,* February 6, 1995, pp. A1; B4.
14. Richard S. Belous, *The Contingent Economy: The Growth of the Temporary, Part-Time and Subcontracted Workforce* (Washington D.C.: National Planning Association, 1989). For further discussion of the contradictions, see Charles Derber, "Clintradictions," *Tikkun,* Vol. 9, No. 5, September/October, 1994, pp. 15ff.

15. Quotations from contingent workers in this paragraph and below are drawn from interview transcripts of a study of temporary workers in Boston carried out by the author in 1994.

16. For a discussion of the relation between globalization and contingent work, see Bennett Harrison, *Lean and Mean: The Changing Landscape of Corporate Power in the Age of Flexibility* (New York: Basic Books, 1994), Chapter 9.

17. For a useful discussion of the relation between contingency and risk, see Debra Osnowitz, "Contingent Work As Risky Business," unpublished paper, Boston, 1995.

18. Cited in Peter Kilborn, "New Jobs Lack the Old Security in a Time of Disposable Workers," *New York Times*, March 15, 1993, p. 1.

19. Quotes of downsizing victims are drawn from the study of temporary workers discussed above.

20. See Bennett Harrison, *Lean and Mean*, op. cit., Chapters 5, 8, 9.

21. Laura Masnerus, "Money Changes Everything," *New York Times Sunday Magazine*, November 20, 1994, pp. 54–55.

22. Sam Roberts, "Gap Between Rich and Poor in New York City Grows Wider," *New York Times*, December 15, 1994, pp. 33–34.

23. Robert Reich, *The Work of Nations* (New York: Knopf, 1991).

24. Richard B. Freeman and Lawrence F. Katz, "Rising Wage Inequality: The United States vs. Other Advanced Countries," in Richard B. Freeman (Ed.), *Working Under Different Rules* (New York: Russell Sage, 1993), pp. 32–33.

25. Ibid., p. 32.

26. Peter Gosselin, "Tax Cuts Alone May Not Be the Ticket," *Boston Globe*, December 18, 1994, p. 34. See also Aaron Bernstein, "The US Is Still Cranking Out Lousy Jobs," *Business Week*, October 10, 1994, pp. 122–24.

27. Paul Krugman cited in Kevin Phillips, *Boiling Point* (New York: Random House, 1993), p. xviii. See also Kevin Phillips, *Arrogant Capital* (Boston: Little Brown and Co., 1994), p. 106, for data on wealth assets controlled by the very rich.

28. Kevin Phillips, *Arrogant Capital*, pp. 105–6.

29. Ibid., Chapter 4.

30. Jeremy Brecher and Tim Costello, *Global Village or Global Pillage*, op. cit., p. 33.

31. Richard Barnet and John Cavanaugh, *Global Dreams*, op. cit. See also Kevin Phillips, *Arrogant Capital*, op. cit., Chapter 1.

32. Jeremy Brecher and Tim Costello, *Global Village or Global Pillage*, op. cit., pp. 156ff.

5

The Dreamin' Is Easy and the Living Is Hard: A Wilding Recipe for the 1990s

This whole world is wild at heart and weird on top.
—Lula in *Wild at Heart*

There are signs everywhere that the culture of wilding is trickling down from Washington and Wall Street to Main Street. Civilized Boston woke up to the 1990s with headlines about the Charles Stuart murder. A few months later headlines told of a frail 57-year-old liquor-store manager, Jean Stranberg, executed by a 17-year-old with a sawed-off shotgun, all for a jar of Easter Seal pennies worth about twelve dollars. A couple of months earlier, on February 20, three Boston University students learned how wild Boston had become when as a joke they jumped on the hood of a stranger's car on campus, slightly damaging the vehicle. The driver pulled out an automatic weapon and shot Leslie J. Young, a 20-year-old engineering major, in the chest, then turned to Young's two friends and asked: "Does anybody want more?" When one said "No," the driver sped off and Young was taken in critical condition to an intensive care unit. The students had received a quick lesson in the cultural importance of material possessions, especially expensive ones such as cars.[1]

Perhaps more telling about the state of America in the 1990s are not such outrageous wildings, but the small wildings that ripple through our daily experiences. *Boston Globe* columnist Susan Trausch satirizes her own propensities for wilding: "An extra ten bucks dropped out of the automatic teller machine the other day and I didn't give it back." There were, after all, Trausch explains, "no guards. No middleman . . . The machine doesn't ask questions." Trausch "grabbed the bills," and stifled "the impulse to shout, 'I won!'" Later, she asks herself, "Is this why the world is a mess? People don't want to be chumps so they say, 'I'll get mine now,' and then they grab an illicit brownie from the pastry tray of life. And oh, the noise we make if we don't get what we consider ours! If, for instance, only forty dollars had come out of the slot instead of fifty dollars, my outrage would have echoed in the aisles from aerosols to zucchini." But beating the system "made me want to play again," Trausch admits. "Maybe there was a gear loose. Maybe hundreds of dollars would come out." Trausch concludes that although she'd "like to report that at least the illicit money went to charity, it didn't. I blew it on lottery tickets."[2]

Trausch's lingering moral pangs are quite unusual. One sociologist laughed after reading her story, speculating that he and most other Americans would have pocketed the illicit greenback without a second thought, with no flickering of the conscience whatsoever. According to Queens, New York, school-board member Jimmy Sullivan, a streetwise, savvy observer of American life in the 1990s, "Everybody cheats." It "isn't just some people," Sullivan emphasizes pointedly, "It's 95 percent of the people. Some cheat a little. Some cheat a lot. You work in an office, you take home supplies. People work at a construction site, they take home two-by-fours. Unfortunately, we've become a nation of petty crooks." Admitting to a reporter that his main concern as a school-board official was patronage jobs for his "people"—white political cronies in his clubhouse—Sullivan makes no apologies. Everybody is doing it, cheating to get theirs, especially now that times are getting tougher. Sullivan certainly knows what he is talking about, at least regarding the New York City school system, where three-quarters of the city's school boards have been under investigation and half are believed to be corrupt. Sullivan himself was manipulating a multimillion-dollar budget to build his own corrupt school fiefdom. Sullivan explains, "We're a nation of fucks and gangsters because that's what we glorify in Americana." It's all part of the American Dream today.[3]

Sullivan pled guilty to using coercion to support institutionalized cronyism. He had not counted on the fact that there are still honest people like his school superintendent, Coleman Genn, who switched from working with Sullivan to wearing a hidden microphone for an independent commission investigating school corruption. Genn is part of the "second America" discussed in Chapter One, the majority of Americans who have been touched but not debased by the wilding epidemic and continue to struggle honorably to maintain their integrity. Sullivan, nonetheless, has his finger on a contradiction tearing America apart in the final decade of the century. The pushers of dreams, the creators of "Americana," are feverishly selling the Reagan-Bush high-roller version of the American Dream in movies, magazines, and the ubiquitous video. While Americans are being willingly seduced, swimming in exquisitely alluring images of the pleasures only money can buy, money itself is getting harder to come by. As Americans dream big, economic shadows are lengthening and darkening. This contradiction between the glamorous life on the screen and the contrasting opportunities of real life has the potential to spread the epidemic deeply into the "second America" that, until now, has kept it at bay.

REVVING UP THE DREAM MACHINE: HOLLYWOOD GOES WILD

Tom Cruise, *People* magazine reports, has become the 1990s silver-screen idol, the star of stars in America's most enchanting dream factory. Cruise established himself early in the 1980s in a movie called *Risky Business,* which helped mold the fantasies of the Reagan era. Cruise played the modern suburban Huck Finn who finally makes good. A disappointment to his straight-arrow parents, whose dream is to get him into Princeton, Cruise enjoys going on joyrides in the family Porsche far more than studying for college board exams. But one class—on business entrepreneurship—finally does wake him up. In a Reaganesque revelation, Cruise realizes that by starting his own brothel, he can make it big and have fun too. When his parents pack off for a European vacation, he launches his business in grand entrepreneurial fashion, turning his suburban family home into a whorehouse. Cruise is transformed; the young goof-off becomes a zealously ambitious entrepreneur rivaling any Wall Street trader in his detailed attention to markets, customers, and finances. In a morality play for his times, Cruise's business is a huge success. As young women and clients traipse in, Cruise stands at the door counting the dollars, his charming, impish grin stretching from ear to ear. The skeptical Princeton admissions officer who comes to visit is so impressed that he awards Cruise the admission ticket to Princeton that his parents had dreamed of.

In a later hit film, *The Firm,* Cruise graduates law school and heads toward his first job as a tax lawyer, lured by a firm's offer of a $96,000 starting salary, all college debts paid, subsidized membership in the local country club, and a lavish home and car also financed for him by the firm. Born poor, Cruise is hungry for success and eager to play the game. His mentor at the firm, played by Gene Hackman, instructs him from the start that billing is the most important thing to worry about and that he should bill the time he spends driving in the car or going to the bathroom. His mentor also tells him that "being a tax lawyer has nothing to do with the law—it's a game. We teach the rich how to play it so they can stay rich." Cruise's firm itself stays rich by deeply involving itself with organized crime, socializing all its young recruits into a crooked professional world in which loyalty to the firm over-rides not only loyalty to the law but to all moral scruples as well.

Cruise is part of a new crop of male movie stars such as Sylvester Stallone, Bruce Willis, Wesley Snipes, Michael Douglas, John Cusack, James Spader, and John Malkovich, whose roles differ strikingly from those of the earlier generation of stars such as Dustin Hoffman, Al Pacino, and Robert DeNiro. In movies such as *Midnight Cowboy, Serpico,* and *Mean Streets,* Hoffman, Pacino, and DeNiro portrayed alienated, tormented antiheroes, struggling with and finally rejecting the values of society. In contrast, the new breed of stars are competitive "glamour boys . . . not motivated by hos-tility or angst but by the desire to succeed." They do not "question them-selves or society." They make a lot of money and have fun doing it, not letting moral compunctions interfere with their pleasures in winning big. In *Wall Street,* Michael Douglas's character speaks unabashedly for Ivan Boesky when he proclaims that "greed is good."[4]

The current stars symbolize an economic revolution in Hollywood that transformed the dreams being pumped out to wide-eyed audiences. In the 1960s and early 1970s, Warner Bros., United Artists, MGM, and 20th Century Fox were still independent studios. Politically sensitized directors often enjoyed great control, creating probing films about Vietnam, nuclear power, and other issues of the day. But by the 1980s, large multinationals had bought up virtually all the studios, installing new hard-nosed executives and business-minded producers who reined in the directors and helped rewrite the scripts. The great Hollywood Dream Machine, as Meryl Streep pointed out, was now securely programmed to the bottom line.[5]

At Paramount Pictures, producers Don Simpson and Jerry Bruckheimer personified the new Hollywood. Simpson and Bruckheimer collaborated on some of the most spectacular box-office successes of the 1980s, including *Beverly Hills Cop, Flashdance, Top Gun,* and *Beverly Hills Cop II.* Former 1960s hippies, Simpson and Bruckheimer evolved comfortably into the spirit of the 1980s and 1990s. The formula they brought to all their scripts was a fantasy of competition and triumph, the individual overcoming all odds to become a big winner. In *Flashdance,* for example, made in 1983 during the height of the Reagan recession, a young, beautiful working-class dancer beats the economic odds, dancing her way out of a desolate, industrial wasteland in a bleak Midwestern city to Cinderella stardom. "There are people," Simpson says, "who are successful and who win. They have moments of pain but they are winners. Then there are losers. Terry and I side with the winners. We aren't interested in losers. Losers are boring." Hollywood had cast its lot with Ronald Reagan.[6]

Hollywood increasingly mirrors the meaner and nastier spirit of mak-ing it in the 1990s. In *The Player,* Tim Robbins models the hypercompetitive wilding mentality of the big-time Hollywood producer who wheels and deals to get the scripts with the biggest bottom-line payoff, while happily prostituting the artistic sensibility of his writers. Robbins also seduces the girlfriend of a writer he kills in a fit of rage, attracted to the callousness of a woman who shows no remorse about sleeping with her boyfriend's executioner.

In *The Object of Beauty,* John Malkovich and Andie MacDowell model the wilding ethos of smaller-time operators, who team up to defraud an insurance company as part of their white-collar-crime career, furiously conning everyone including each other. Con artists appear everywhere in 1990s films, including *The Grifters,* a movie about a remarkable trio of mother, son, and girlfriend who are intertwined in surprisingly complex relations of mutual rip-offs. The mother, at one point, tries to seduce her son after failing to steal his money and inadvertently kills him during an effort to rob him, a scene evocative of the Ik. Meanwhile, films like *Pulp Fiction* and *Natural Born Killers,* written by Quentin Tarantino, the decade's leading writer and director, suggest that wilding for money is helping spawn a culture of extreme expressive wilding, leading to a culture on and off the silver screen saturated with manipulation, cruelty, and violence for its own sake.

In *Falling Down,* Michael Douglas models the kind of 1990s wilding that happens when the new Dream falls apart. As a laid-off engineer in Los Angeles who has lost not only his job but his wife, Douglas goes berserk when he gets stuck on the freeway on a hot afternoon. Abandoning his car, Douglas goes on a rampage with a semi-automatic weapon, blowing away Koreans, blacks, and rich country-club tycoons, and nearly killing his ex-wife and child as well. Famous also for his performances in *Disclosure, Basic Instinct, Fatal Attraction,* and a host of other films about domestic violence and the war of the sexes, no actor has better shown the poisonous link in the 1990s between instrumental wilding in the market and expressive wilding at home.

Television in the 1990s features the same obsessional intertwining of instrumental and expressive wilding in an age of big money and relative deprivation. "Melrose Place," one of the hottest TV primetime soaps, follows the exploits of a group of greedy, young professionals ensnared in careerist plots and manipulative love relationships. The characters in the series—doctors, lawyers, and advertising executives—resort to kidnappings, extortion, and even murder to get what they want.

Alongside Hollywood as a purveyor of the new mind-grabbing Dream stands the advertising industry, the master producer of "all-consuming images." The line between movies and advertising blurs, as critic Charles Champlin implicitly suggests in his description of a scene from another

Simpson and Bruckheimer film, *American Gigolo:* "Nothing, neither bosom nor buttock, is photographed more lovingly than the [Mercedes] 450SL— those taillights, winking provocatively in the velvet night, such as to drive men mad." Film directors increasingly function as advertisers, perhaps recognizing that they are playing to audiences addicted to high-priced consumption. Advertisers, in turn, exploiting the new visual technology, have become the consummate artists of the 1990s, designing the electrified commercial fantasies that define the American way of life.[7]

Television has become the advertising industry's ultimate weapon, allowing advertisers to mainline the Dream directly into the nervous system. Sociologist Stephen Pfohl describes a young girl "exposing herself to a television." He writes: "It strikes me that she is daydreaming with the machine. Her eyes are moving rapidly but her body remains still. She sits knees curled within her dress, biting her nails, clutching a doll. Wide eyes, it's electric." The young girl enters the room where Pfohl is talking with her mother. "Mommy, Mommy. They showed a KTL 191 with screaming rearview blinkers and a flashing rotary rocket launcher with a digital tracking unit. It was only $29.99 but for one time only it's $19.99. But you have to call right away. Can we Mommy? Can we? . . . All you have to do is call." The little girl has memorized the toll-free number she wants her mother to dial. Pfohl concludes that as consumers we have been "seduced into taking the media within ourselves; its screens and its terminals now functioning as our most intimate organs of sensation . . . We are the media. We are the television!"[8]

The line between regular programming and advertising on TV in the 1990s is fading. In addition to various home shopping networks, regular networks sponsor multiple hour-long extended ads, or "infomercials," for cosmetics, kitchenware, clothes, and exercise equipment that often feature celebrities such as Jane Fonda and Cher and seem less like commercials than cooking shows or fashion videos. On MTV, such paid infomercials for designer clothes by Donna Karan or Todd Oldham, modeled by the world's leading supermodels, are virtually indistinguishable from the regular programming of fashion television.

"Shop until you drop" has become the mantra of the 1990s. "Shopaholism," now the American addiction of choice, reflects the coming-of-age of conspicuous consumption, nurtured in part by advertisers selling the high-priced version of the American Dream. The supermodels set the tone, parading extravagant dresses and jackets priced at thousands of dollars. The super-rich can buy customized Hermes evening gowns for $20,000, along with alligator luggage for $75,000 a set, Russian sables starting at $40,000, silk sheets at $15,000, or a set of gold belts at $30,000 each. Upper-middle-class shoppers go to Neiman Marcus or Saks Fifth Avenue to buy Lagerfeld dresses or Chanel jackets for $1,500 and up. The middle- to upper-middle-class college crowd settles for Polo or Ann Taylor shirts for $75, Timberland boots and shoes for $150, Northface ski jackets for $300, J. Crew sports jackets for $150, and Donna Karan jeans for $75. Although not as exorbitant as the playthings of the very rich, such designer-brand consciousness helps socialize young people into the extravagant consumer consciousness of the gilded Dream.

DOWNTIME: THE AMERICAN DREAM GOES BUST

As the price of happiness ratchets up, the ability of the average American to pay is falling. The great contradiction of the 1990s may be the increasing gap between bigger American appetites and shrinking American wallets.

The Dream Machine is on a collision course with the American economy. In 1973, for the first time ever, the real wage of the American worker began falling. "The U.S. standard of living, long the envy of the rest of the world," *Business Week* proclaimed, had "hit the wall." By the time Ronald Reagan was elected, a great economic revolution was already taking shape. Wages were continuing to slip so rapidly that American workers could no longer support their families. Just to stay even, both husband and wife would have to become workers, their two incomes increasingly required to do the job that one had done before.

As Ronald Reagan began spinning his dreams of the entrepreneurial jackpot, young people woke up to the harsh possibility of downward mobility. Young men and women wondered whether, even with combined incomes, they would be able to buy a house as big as their parents'. In places such as Boston, Washington, and San Francisco, many doubted that they would be able to afford a house at all. "Is the American Dream about to end?" *Business Week* asked in the late 1980s. "For the first time since the depression," the magazine continued, "millions of Americans face the likelihood that they will not be able to live as well as their parents."[9]

Ronald Reagan and George Bush were elected on the promise that they would fix the economy, but the paper trail of the 1980s suggests that they may have done more than just renege on their promises. America in the 1980s went so deep into debt with the rest of the world—in 1988, Wall Street financier Peter J. Peterson calculated the debt at almost a half-trillion dollars—that it is losing control of its destiny. The sale of Rockefeller Center to Japanese buyers symbolized a new 1990 American reality: We are "selling off more of what this country's people own," Wellesley economist Carolyn Shaw Bell reports, simply to meet "the interest on the debt, let alone repaying any of the principal."[10] Meanwhile, American industry in the 1980s, from automobiles to machine tools to textiles, was being routed

in international competition, so thoroughly pummeled by the Japanese, the
Germans, and the Koreans that *Business Week* speculated whether "the
United States is following Britain into permanent economic decline."

By 1995, President Clinton could boast of a major economic turn-
around, with several years of robust growth, increased global competitiveness, reduced unemployment, and the creation of three million new jobs.
But as Clinton himself acknowledged, the recovery, while boosting the
profits of America's major corporations, was not creating job security or
putting more money in the ordinary American's wallet. Huge numbers of
the new jobs were temporary or part-time positions, and the majority of
both new and old jobs were low-wage. For the first time in American history, growth was leading to worse rather than better times for most
Americans, with real wages slightly falling from the Bush recession in 1990
to the Clinton recovery in 1995.

In the midst of this economic bad news, Americans continue to be
glued to the Dream Machine, creating the paradox that *Business Week* calls
the "money illusion." They keep spending as if they are "getting the kind of
real raises" that they used to get "in the 1960s." Something is profoundly out
of kilter, the magazine suggests, because in a period of "crushing new constraints, the average American appears unable to lower his [or her] sights."[11]

Of course, the contradiction cuts more or less deeply depending where
the dreamer is perched on the economic ladder. For those on top, whether
business executive or fabled yuppie, there is the problem, as the *New York
Times* reported, of "feeling poor on $600,000 a year." The *Times* describes the
misery of young Wall Street financiers and New York doctors and lawyers
feeling strapped by the costs of their million-dollar co-ops. The pain is tolerable, however, as Kevin Phillips writes, because Reaganomics unleashed an
upsurge of riches to the wealthy that "has not been seen since the late nineteenth century, the era of the Vanderbilts, Morgans, and Rockefellers." As the
economy declines, the rich can keep dreaming big dreams.[12]

Where the contradiction draws blood is at the bottom. The poor, no less
than the rich, stay tuned in to the Dream Machine in bad times as well as
good. They are always the "last hired and the first fired," so every business cycle
wreaks havoc with their dreams. Their boats did not rise with the Clinton
recovery and they got dangerously poorer, partly the result of the cutting of
the safety net under Reagan and Bush, and Clinton's willingness to follow the
leadership of Speaker Newt Gingrich and his Republican colleagues in shredding it further. By 1995, millions of the poor were left without housing, medical care, jobs, or educational opportunity; six million children—one of every
four kids under 6 years of age in America—were officially poor. Mired in
Third-World conditions of poverty while video-bombarded with First-World
dreams, rarely has a population suffered a greater gap between socially cultivated appetites and socially available opportunities.

Blood has been drawn in the great American middle as well. As they work longer and harder to get their share of the Dream, middle-class Americans are sinking. *Business Week* says that Joe Sixpack found himself badly slipping as the economy faltered in the recession of the early 1990s. "He plunged into debt, thinking 'Buy now, before the price goes up again'. With a little luck, he figured, his next raise would keep the credit-card bills and the mortgage covered." The problem was that "the real raises didn't get any better," even with the Clinton recovery. In 1995, a *New York Times* poll reported that 78 percent of Americans said their standard of living was either stagnant or getting worse, reflecting the remarkable erosion of middle-American living standards even as the economy was growing rapidly.[13]

Unable to "lower his sights," Joe kept "borrowing. He now own[ed] a house, a big, Japanese color TV and VCR, an American car, and a Korean personal computer—all bought on credit." By 1995, Joe had ten credit cards which he used to live well above his means, spending $1.03 for every $1.00 he earned. This credit financed binge gave Joe the illusion of living the American Dream, and he wasn't alone: All across America consumers were piling up unprecedented credit card debt, 25 percent more in 1994 than in 1993.

Joe Sixpack's wife is working, which helps pay the "children's orthodontist bills and family entertainment, but it falls short of what they'll need to send the kids to college." Judith Bateman, the wife of a Michigan Bell Telephone dispatcher, told *Business Week* that she and her husband run a big weekly "deficit, but until times get better, which she keeps hoping will happen, she says, 'We enter a lot of sweepstakes.'"[14]

Larry Williams, laid off from a well-paid factory supervisory position and now a security guard at Brigham and Women's Hospital in Boston, is less optimistic and sounds less benign: "Sometimes I get real touchy when I'm not working. I've been working since I was eighteen years old. The first week was like a vacation, but when you get into a month, you start getting real edgy, you know what I mean?"

"I'M GONNA GET MINE": THE NEW AMERICAN CYNIC

It is not a long journey from Larry Williams's "edgy" feeling, to anger and cynicism, and finally to wilding. Feeling that his old job is permanently gone, because manufacturing in this country is, in his view, "down the tubes," Williams is finding it harder to match his life to his dreams. His feelings are shared by millions of Americans whose dreams are threatened. Evidence is mounting that many are recruits to the culture of wilding, people in an era of decline who are increasingly prepared to do whatever it takes to make it.

Drawing on a national survey, Boston University professors Donald Kanter and Philip Mirvis report that the wilding mindset has spread across America. The prototypical American virtue of individual initiative is degrading into the cynical attitude of "I will do anything to get ahead and not be left behind." Self-interest, Kanter and Mirvis believe, has become such an overwhelming urge that it is pushing empathy and moral sensibility into the far background. They describe an American landscape in which close to half of the population takes as its basic assumption "that most people are only out for themselves and that you are better off zapping them before they do it to you."[15]

Many Americans, Kanter and Mirvis report, believe that their fellow Americans will cheat and lie to get what they want, especially when money is concerned. Sixty percent say that they expect "people will tell a lie if they can gain by it," and 62 percent say that "people claim to have ethical standards, but few stick to them when money is at stake." About half say that "an unselfish person is taken advantage of in today's world," and slightly under half believe that people "inwardly dislike putting themselves out to help other people." As among the Ik, who take positive pleasure in hurting others, none of this strikes Americans as particularly noteworthy or surprising. Forty-three percent—and more than half of young people under 24 years of age—see selfishness and fakery at the core of human nature. Millions of Americans, Kanter and Mirvis conclude, are hard-boiled cynics who, "to put it simply, believe that lying, putting on a false face, and doing whatever it takes to make a buck" are all part of the nature of things.[16]

Kanter and Mirvis have dissected wilding types at every economic level. At the top are a depressing variety of groups eager to exploit the new opportunities the Reagan-Bush era opened up for them, including "command cynics," senior managers who consider themselves "jungle fighters" and "subscribe to the Darwinian logic that they 'made it,' so everyone else must be weak, naïve, inept, or just plain dumb." They believe that "everyone has a price and can be bought." The "administrative sideliners" are another school: mid- to upper-level bureaucrats whose "view of human nature is predominantly cold" and who "have no real concern for people, save as instruments" for their own ends. Then there are "articulate players," mostly the young professionals who became the most visible symbols of greed in the 1980s. They live in the self-oriented world that Christopher Lasch describes as the "culture of narcissism," and share "a willingness to do whatever has to be done to others in order to advance." They are "porcupines whose quills are at the ready," taking pleasure in their capacity to put others down on their road to the top.[17]

At the middle and lower ends of the hierarchy are other groups, many impaled on the sharp sword of economic change and decline. Among them are the "squeezed cynics," often sons and daughters of skilled workers or lower-middle-class clericals, whose once bright aspirations "have faded along with the decline of heavy industry. The jobs they expected have been automated, eliminated, or sent overseas." Downwardly mobile, they exhibit a "dead-ender's self-interest," and their anthem is "Where's mine?" and "What's in it for me?" Then there are the "obstinate stoics," disproportionately blue-collar, who "do not trust people . . . and seem to feel more strongly than most that expecting anyone to help you makes you a damn fool." And finally there are the "hard-bitten cynics," mainly shopfloor workers and unskilled laborers who live "on the razor's edge between independent respectability and antisocial aggression." Among their life-guiding maxims: "Never give money to anyone who needs it."[18]

Kanter and Mirvis seem unsurprised by their findings. The intensely self-centered, antisocial attitudes they uncover reflect the successes of socialization rather than its failure. Making reference to the culture of the Reagan-Bush era, Kanter argues, "The tendency to behave cynically is being reinforced to an unprecedented degree by a social environment that seems to have abandoned idealism and increasingly celebrates the virtue of being 'realistic' in an impersonal, acquisitive tough-guy world." He could be talking about the Ik when he concludes that "[i]n citizen and country alike, there seems to be a loss of faith in people and in the very concept of community."[19]

DRINKING, CHEATING, AND OTHER CAMPUS SPORTS: YOUNG AND WILD 1

The young are among the more exuberant wilders in America. Progeny of the Reagan-Bush era, and the most vulnerable to the slings of economic fortune, they are an ominous harbinger of America's future.

Kanter and Mirvis report that a clear majority of youth under 24, in contrast to only 43 percent of the population as a whole, are "unvarnished cynics" who view "selfishness as fundamental to people's character." Most students do not disagree with this assessment of their generation. On the first day of the 1990 spring semester, I asked a class of about forty college students, most of them economics majors, whether the average student on campus would agree or disagree with a series of highly charged statements about selfishness and self-interest. Their answers were not reassuring. Sixty-five percent said that the average student would agree that "There is nothing more important to me than my own economic well-being," and 72 percent said that the typical student would agree that "I am not responsible for my neighbor." Seventy-five percent said their generation believed that "it's everyone for himself or herself in the American economy," and 88 percent said their fellow students would agree that "In our society everyone has to look out for number one." A stunning 96 percent thought their generation believed that "Competition is the most important virtue in a market society," and 65 percent expected a typical student to agree that "People do not let moral scruples get in the way of their own advancement." In discussion, they explained that most students were apprehensive about their economic prospects, fearing that they would not do as well as their parents. If they wanted to succeed, they said, they would have to focus all their energies on "buttering their own bread."[20]

On the positive side, significantly lower percentages of the students, ranging from 30 to 50 percent, said that they personally subscribed to the selfish sentiments enumerated above. This is an indication that a significant sector of the younger generation remains committed to moral principles. My impression as a teacher is that a large percentage of today's college students remain generous and decent, although increasingly confused and torn between "making it" and remaining faithful to their moral ideals. Unfortunately, many sacrifice their intellectual loves to make big money, such as the student with a profound passion for the study of history who decided to give it up and become a corporate lawyer so that he could live the high life.

Growing student cynicism has lead to an explosion of wilding on campuses across the country. A report by the Carnegie Foundation for the Advancement of Teaching released in 1990 found "a breakdown of civility and other disruptive forces" that are leaving campus life "in tatters." Of special concern is an epidemic of cheating, as well as a mushrooming number of racial attacks, rapes, and other hate crimes. Words, the currency of the university, are increasingly "used not as the key to understanding, but as weapons of assault."[21]

Campuses are no longer ivy-walled sanctuaries but increasingly dangerous sites of theft, sexual assault, property damage, and other crimes. The epidemic of alcoholism among students—70 percent qualify as binge drinkers at some colleges—has contributed to these rising crime rates. A study of 104 campuses conducted by the Harvard School of Public Health identified forty-four colleges in which a majority of the students were binge drinkers. On these campuses, nine out of ten students said that they had suffered assaults, thefts, or other forms of violent intrusion, often from drunk students.[22]

Much campus crime, however, is committed sober by cold, calculating student wilders. A Harvard University student pleaded guilty in 1995 to stealing $6,838 raised at Harvard for the Jimmy Fund, an annual charity event to help kids with cancer. Joann Plachy, a law student at Florida State University, was charged in 1995 with hiring a professional killer to murder a secretary who accused Plachy of having stolen a copy of an exam.[23]

Ernest L. Boyer, Carnegie's president, said that college promotional material "masks disturbing realities of student life," that mirror the "hard-edged competitive world" of the larger society.[24] Desperate for good grades, huge numbers of students routinely plagiarize papers and cheat on exams. Studies on many campuses, including Indiana University and the University of Tennessee, show that a majority of students admits to submitting papers written by others or copying large sections of friends' papers. A majority also confesses to looking at other students' answers during in-class exams. In the spring of 1991, seventy-three students in an introductory computer programming course at the prestigious Massachusetts Institute of Technology were disciplined for participating in the largest cheating scandal in the history of the school. "You could check for cheating in any class and you'd certainly find a significant portion of the people cheating," one MIT student said, adding casually, "It's one way of getting through MIT."[25]

Technology, especially computers, has made life easier for the new generation of student cheaters. Students routinely ask their friends for copies of old course papers on computer disk. It doesn't take much effort to rework a paper on a computer for a new class. One student at an elite Boston university said that nobody on campus thinks twice about the morality of such high-tech cheating.

In the 1990s, books on how to cheat are hot sellers on campus. Michael Moore, 24, has written a primer, *Cheating 101*, which has sold briskly on campuses around the country. He describes how to stuff crib sheets filled with useful facts into one's jeans or under one's baseball cap. He offers tips about how students can communicate answers on multiple choice tests by shifting their feet under the desk in a prearranged code. About cheating, Moore says that "everyone's doing it," and that he's making an "honest living." About his decision to make an "honest living" by writing a how-to-book on cheating, Moore says, "I'm just exercising my First Amendment rights."[26]

Although a significant minority of students are idealistic and intensely concerned with others, the majority appear increasingly cynical about their studies and their futures. They want to "invest as little time in their studies as possible," the Carnegie report suggests, while collecting their meal ticket and moving on to the professional gravy train. Fifty-five percent of faculty members complained that "most undergraduates . . . only do enough to get by." Carnegie president Boyer, however, noted that faculty are complicit in

the problem by pursuing "their own research at the expense of teaching."
He might have added that some faculty and administrators are providing
the worst role models, as can be seen by the growing faculty research scandal. Congressman John Dingell has uncovered science fraud in the biology
labs of MIT as well as unlawful diversion of research overhead expendi-
tures for such things as "flowers, country-club memberships, and going
away parties for departing deans" in many of the nation's most famous
universities, including Harvard, Stanford, and the California Institute of
Technology. Stanford University president Donald Kennedy resigned in
1991 after the media reported the extensive diversion of Stanford overhead
funds to pay for such extravagances as a yacht. The reputation of Nobel
laureate David Baltimore, one of the country's foremost cancer researchers
and president of Rockefeller University, has been tarnished by the National
Institute of Health's conclusion that a member of Baltimore's own labora-
tory falsified data. Campus life breaks down as students, faculty, and
administrators follow the narrow paths of their own career dictates.[27]

KIDS, MONEY, AND GENERATION X: YOUNG AND WILD 2

Today's student culture transparently reflects the intensely materialistic,
entrepreneurial ethos of the Reagan-Bush-Gingrich era. Elite institutions,
where the Carnegie report finds the most acute problems, are filled with
students driving expensive cars and wearing designer clothes. Students'
consumer appetites—and their abilities to indulge them—are enhanced by
the seductions of campus credit-card peddlers. Visa, Mastercard, Discover,
American Express and other credit-card outfits telemarket their wares to
students or set up shop in student centers, offering specially designed
preapproved lines of credit worth thousands of dollars to young students
saturated with media images of glamour and accustomed to spending
other people's money. First Financial Visa and Mastercard promise credit
lines of up to $1,000 for first-year students, $1,500 for sophomores, $2,000
for juniors, and $2,500 for seniors. American Express says "get it now" and
"use it for the rest of your life," promising to help students "get more out of
the good times . . . fly, talk long distance. Shop. Dine out. And much, much
more." Ford Citibank Card says its card can "put you on the road to a lifetime of credit . . . without a co-signer or a job." Use the Ford Credit Card
and get rebates "toward a brand new car." Citibank Classic describes its special student card as "no fee, no anxiety," promising students discounts on
music, clothing, airline tickets and other goodies that won't just relieve
stress but "relieve what gives you stress in the first place."

The Dream Machine starts its work on the young early. "It was probably inevitable," the *Boston Globe* reports, "that the baroque and pricey strollers of the eighties would be followed by a children's magazine boom in the nineties." Samir Hasni, a University of Mississippi journalism professor, estimates that "twenty-five magazines for kids have been created since 1985," most aimed "at the children of yuppies." Hasni describes their parents as the "guilty generation" who are "loading their children down with money," partly as compensation for ignoring them while pushing ahead in their careers. One magazine, formerly called *Penny Power* and now renamed *Zillions,* helps kids think about what to buy, offering reviews of such goodies as Reebok's Pump, a new $170 sneaker. Many of the magazines "are spin-offs of movies, TV, and toys," marketing accessories for Barbie dolls.[28]

Pamela Hage, director of Kids Link, a marketing agency in Atlanta, says some of her ads target children directly whereas "we have other campaigns where we use the child as a conduit to get to the parents." James McNeal, a marketing professor at Texas A&M, says children are targeted because they prefer the more expensive brand-name sneakers, clothes, and toys. The total corporate sales in such "kid-influenced spending" in 1993 was $157 billion, triple that of ten years earlier.[29]

Increasingly, children are enlisted in advertising campaigns to reach other children. One variant is Stacy Strezsak, 8, who parades down fashion runways in child beauty pageants modeling bathing suits and custom satin gowns costing $800. Some of the pageants require the contestants to deliver commercials, as when Stacy announced herself as "the newest member of the Ty-D-Bowl family . . . Let me into your home and I'll make your bowl shine like the sun."[30]

Growing up has lost its innocence. Unlike previous generations, today's students experience the great American pastime as an arena in which to cut their entrepreneurial baby teeth. In a baseball store in Arlington, Massachusetts, 9-year-old David Haroz and his buddies Rich Phillips, aged 10, and Marc Chalufour, aged 13, rifle through piles of baseball cards to find speculative bargains. Marc is betting on a "rookie sleeper—Jose Gonzales of Texas, worth 3 to 8 cents today—that Marc's dad thinks will move'up smartly in value." David's mother, Betsy Edmunds, tells a reporter, "It's like the stock market to them. Very speculative. They know the values." It's possible to make big money with cards that hit the jackpot. A collector in Chicago recently paid $115,000 for a vintage Honus Wagner. Most kids, of course, play for smaller stakes, happy to deal in the glitzy holographic card market where they can buy an Upper Deck set for $48. Some, such as Mark Perry of Chelsea, aged 25, invest for the long haul. Perry started at age 7 and stores a treasure trove of over 12,000 cards in his closets. When this generation of youth talks about knowing the score, they are not talking about which team got more runs.[31]

In the summer of 1990, the *New York Times* reported that the materialistic preoccupations of the young were turning them into the generation "that couldn't care less." The *Times* article refers to a conversation in which a young Ohio cashier, hearing a radio news report about the missing dead and wounded in a flash flood, looked up and said, "I wish they'd stop talking about it. I'm sick of hearing about it." Indifference to the pain of others, pollsters suggest, typifies the attitude of an alarming number of the young. They don't want to hear about it unless "it's knocking on my door." Young people themselves admit their self-preoccupation and indifference, talking "incessantly of stress—their preoccupation with getting jobs or grades and their concern about personal threats like AIDS or drugs."[32]

Pollster Andrew Kohut, summarizing his own 1990 national survey, describes the young as a "generation of self-centered know-nothings." Only about 25 percent put a priority on "helping make the community a better place," and many are "so self-absorbed" that they would not act to help others even in the most dire emergency. Today's youth, Kohut concludes pessimistically, are harbingers of a new "Age of Indifference."

By 1995, the youth of the 1990s were being dubbed "Generation X," a "slacker" population that had moved from indifference to nihilism. Suffering from dysfunctional families and an economy offering them "McJobs," they are hooked on TV, relate to the Brady Bunch, and have no heroes. Douglas Rushkoff says they inhabit "Wayne's World Lost in Space, both Dazed and Confused." They have "boomer envy," jealous of the wealth of the baby boomers and afraid of facing "lessness." Douglas Coupland, 29, who wrote the novel *Generation X: Tales of an Accelerated Culture,* says that "People like me—millions of us—are furious because life's getting pretty spartan for us." In fact, they are the first American generation who will live less well than their parents.[33]

ALL-AMERICAN DRUG DEALING: UNATTAINABLE GOALS AND ILLEGITIMATE MEANS

"I spend long hours, night and day, in crack houses and on drug-copping corners, observing, befriending, and interviewing street dealers, addicts, and anyone else who will pause to talk to me." Those are the words of anthropologist Philippe Bourgois, who spent five years living in an East Harlem tenement, although he was not looking to score a big drug deal; he was trying to get inside the minds of crack dealers to see what makes them tick. His conclusions are remarkable, suggesting that inner-city children bear a greater resemblance to careerist college students than anyone had imagined. Wilding at the bottom springs from the same basic recipe as wilding higher up.[34]

Bourgois describes a broken social world reminiscent of the Ik. Violence is everywhere, especially among people working or living with each other. Jackie was eight-months pregnant when her crack-dealing husband, a drug lord of substantial means, was caught and sentenced to jail. Before he left, she shot him in the stomach in front of his helpers. Instead of leaving her money before he was sent to prison, he had been squandering thousands on young women and "bragging about it."[35]

Jackie's violence so impressed the new drug lord that he hired her. About the same time, Jackie started going with Julio, another dealer, who was being stalked by the lover of his ex-girlfriend, Rose, for refusing to pay for her abortion after he got her pregnant. Julio knew how to deal with violence, for he had been hired to guard a crack den where murderous stick-ups were common. On one occasion, Julio admitted "that he had been very nervous when robbers held a gun to his temple and asked for money and crack." Julio impressed his boss when he successfully hid some of the stash in a hollowed-out statue of a saint. But he did not tell his boss the whole truth. Julio "exaggerated to his boss the amount that had been stolen; he pocketed the difference himself."[36]

Julio had started out straight, working as a messenger for a magazine. There were no career possibilities for him there, and when he needed money to support a new crack habit, he realized he needed a better job fast. Like other crack dealers Bourgois got to know, Julio had become fed up with the "low wages and bad treatment" of the jobs available to him. He had bigger dreams of a career "offering superior wages and a dignified workplace," and he found it in the underground economy. After he started dealing crack, the money and new sense of "responsibility, success, and prestige" allowed him to kick his own crack habit.[37]

Bourgois concluded from his talks with Julio and other dealers that the view that

> the poor have been badly socialized and do not share mainstream values is wrong. On the contrary, ambitious, energetic inner-city youth are attracted to the underground [drug dealing] economy precisely because they believe in the rags-to-riches American Dream. Like many in the mainstream, they are frantically trying to get their piece of the pie as fast as possible.[38]

Drug dealers such as Julio, Bourgois finds, are meticulously following the "model for upward mobility" of the Reagan-Bush era, "aggressively setting

themselves up as private entrepreneurs." Their dreams of wealth and success are precisely those of other youngsters tuned into the glitter of television and video. Rather than abandoning their dreams when the hard reality
of their economic position sets in, they adopt an ambitious strategy consistent with the opportunities open to them.

Bourgois hints that it is hard to distinguish these street entrepreneurs
from those in business schools and on Wall Street. They are equally dedicated to "making it" and equally ruthless in their business dealings. They
are prepared to take unusual risks to realize their dream of fast money. The
successful ones enjoy the same life-style, speeding "around in well-waxed
Lincoln Continentals or Mercedes-Benzes." They invite friends and
acquaintances "out to dinner in expensive restaurants almost every night."
When a dealer parks his car on the street, "a bevy of attentive men and
women . . . run to open the door for him."[39]

"Using the channels available," Bourgois writes, people such as Julio
can be seen "as rugged individualists on an unpredictable frontier where
fortune, fame, and destruction are all just around the corner."[40] Widely
presumed to be the archenemy of the American way of life, inner-city drug
wilders are instead among the purest products of the American Dream.

In 1995, William Adler published a book about ghetto children and drugs
that conveys the same sad truth. Adler focused on the four Chambers brothers, originally from rural Arkansas, who moved to Detroit and built a gigantic cocaine business with all the trappings of a Fortune 100 corporation. The
Chambers brothers were arrested and sent to jail, but not before they had created a conglomerate grossing at least $55 million tax-free a year.[41]

The Chambers story is not about inner-city youth as drug consumers,
but as capitalists. The brothers promised their young employees, recruited
both from cotton fields and the inner city, that they could get rich in a year,
but only if they would give up their girlfriends and work hard. The crack
company enforced strict discipline and work rules, offered health and benefit plans, performance bonuses, and quality improvement incentives.
When the Chambers brothers were put in jail, other young crack entrepreneurs quickly took their place. After all, for thousands of inner city youth,
crack dealing is the only path to the American Dream.[42]

NOTES

1. Jerry Thomas and Peter Canellos, "3 Shot to Death in Hub," *Boston
   Globe,* March 14, 1990, p. 1. Sean Murphy, "Driver Shoots BU Student
   After Prank," *Boston Globe,* February 20, 1990, p. 1.
2. Susan Trausch, "The Generous Greed Machine," *Boston Globe,* March
   4, 1990, p. 14.

3. Rob Polner, "A Real Education in the New York City School System," *In These Times,* April 11–17, 1990, p. 12.

4. John Taylor, *Circus of Ambition* (New York: Warner Books, 1989), p. 164.

5. Ibid., pp. 138ff.

6. Ibid., pp. 138–45.

7. Charles Champlin, *Los Angeles Times,* cited in Taylor, *Circus of Ambition,* p. 149.

8. Stephen Pfohl, "Welcome to the Parasite Cafe: Postmodernity as a Social Problem," (mimeo), Boston College, 1990, pp. 11, 27.

9. "Warning: The Standard of Living is Slipping," *Business Week,* April 20, 1987, p. 48.

10. Carolyn Shaw Bell, "Costs of the Mideast Crisis," *Boston Globe,* August 14, 1990), p. 24.

11. Ibid., p. 46.

12. Kevin Phillips, *Politics of the Rich and Poor* (New York, Random House, 1990), p. 10.

13. "Warning," *Business Week,* op. cit., pp. 46, 52. "The Face of the Recession," *Boston Globe,* August 14, 1990, pp. 24–5.

14. "Warning," *Business Week,* op. cit., pp. 46, 52.

15. Donald Kanter and Philip Mirvis, *The Cynical Americans* (San Francisco: Jossey-Bass, 1989), p. 34.

16. Ibid., pp. 9, 10, 291,

17. Ibid., pp. 27–34.

18. Ibid., pp. 35–40.

19. Kanter, cited in Charles A. Radin, "At Core, Say Analysts, U.S. Suffers Crisis of Confidence," *Boston Globe,* July 2, 1990, pp. 1, 5.

20. Kanter and Mirvis, *Cynical Americans,* pp. 10, 291.

21. Edward B. Fiske, "Fabric of Campus Life Is in Tatters, a Study Says," *New York Times,* April 30, 1990, p. A15.

22. Richard A. Knox, "Binge Drinking Linked to Campus Difficulties," *Boston Globe,* December 7, 1994, pp. 1,15.

23. Pamela Walsh, "Second Harvard Student Pleads Guilty to Stealing," *Boston Globe,* February 24, 1995, p. 8. "Florida Law Student Held in A Murder Plot," *New York Times,* February 24, 1995, p. A16.

24. Edward R. Fiske, "Fabric of Campus Life is in Tatters," op. cit., p. A15.

25. Fox Butterfield, "Scandal Over Cheating at M.I.T. Stirs Debate on Limits of Teamwork," *New York Times,* May 22, 1991, p. 12.

26. Anthony Flint, "Student Markets Primer on the Art of Cheating," *Boston Globe,* February 3, 1992, pp. 1,13.

27. William Celis III, "Blame to Share in Overcharging of U.S. for Research," *New York Times,* May 12, 1991, p. 1.

28. Elizabeth Kastor, "Magazine Boom: Mass Appeal to Yuppie Kids," *Boston Globe,* August 16, 1990, p. 85.

29. Steven A. Homes, "Shoppers! Deciding? Just Ask Your Child," *New York Times,* January 8, 1995, p. 4.

30. Nathan Cobb, "A Queen of the Pint-Size Pageants," *Boston Globe,* December 8, 1994, pp. 61,66.

31. Gordon McKibbon, "It's in the (Baseball) Cards," *Boston Globe,* April 11, 1990, pp. 1,12.

32. Michael Oreskes, "Profile of Today's Youth: They Couldn't Care Less," *New York Times,* June 28, l990, p. D21.

33. Mark Muro, "Complaints of a New Generation," *Boston Globe,* November 10, 1994, pp. 1, 12.

34. Philippe Bourgois, "Just Another Night on Crack Street," *New York Times Sunday Magazine,* November 12, 1989, pp. 53ff.

35. Ibid., p. 62.

36. Ibid., p. 64.

37. Ibid., p. 62.

38. Ibid., p. 65.

39. Ibid., p. 94.

40. Ibid., p. 94.

41. William Adler, *Land of Opportunity: One Family's Quest for the American Dream in the Age of Crack* (Boston: Atlantic Monthly Press, 1995).

42. Ibid. See also Max Frankel, "Drug War, II," *New York Times Magazine,* January 29, 1995.

6

Killing Society: The Ungluing of America

A nation never falls but by suicide.
—Ralph Waldo Emerson

T he wilding epidemic has brought American society to a critical divide. American cities and families, for several decades in a state of decline, are now beginning to unravel rapidly. If the forces behind American wilding are allowed to grow, it is possible that the fabric of American social life will decompose.

A degraded individualism, especially in the economy, lies at the root of this decline. Adam Smith, the first great economist of the modern age, articulated the idea of the "invisible hand," the mysterious market mechanism that automatically translates the selfish ambition of each person into the good of all. Always a problematic doctrine, the idea of an invisible hand has now been spun into a dream with almost surreal dimensions. In the good society, a market society, Americans now learn, the supreme virtue is to concentrate feverishly on one's own interests, for by doing so one not only maximizes one's chances of getting ahead, but also performs what George Gilder, whose book *Wealth and Poverty* is discussed in Chapter Three, calls a great "gift" to society. As with the Ik, goodness, in practice, means "filling one's own stomach"; the difference is that an Ik does not pretend that such "goodness" is good for anyone else.

An American Dream that does not spell out the moral consequences of unmitigated self-interest threatens to turn the next generation of Americans into wilding machines. In a pattern already visible today, Americans could turn, not only on each other, but on society as well, too self-absorbed to make the commitments and observe the moral constraints that hold stable communities together. There is already abundant evidence that a wilder generation of Americans is assaulting and abandoning society, allowing the guarantees of civilized behavior and the most vital social institutions to languish and die as they pursue their own selfish dreams.

The breakdown of society that I describe in this chapter—violence on the streets, family dissolution, chaos in government—is a cause as well as a consequence of the wilding crisis. The wilding culture poisons families, workplaces, and neighborhoods, which in their weakened form are fertile spawning grounds for more wilding. There is no first cause in this chicken-and-egg causal chain; the wilding virus creates social breakdown and simultaneously grows out of it.

CIVILIZATION AT THE BREAKING POINT: WILDING IN THE STREETS AND THE UNRAVELING OF SOCIETY

America's culture of wilding, at its extreme, is triggering an epidemic of bizarre and terrifying violence. The new violence constitutes a direct assault on society, undermining the social infrastructure that sustains civilized life.

In November 1989 the *New York Times* reported that ten teenage girls were arrested and "charged with jabbing women with pins in dozens of unprovoked attacks on the Upper West Side over a one-week period." The girls "thought it was fun to run down Broadway," Deputy Police Chief Ronald Fenrich said, and stick "women with pins to see their reactions." The girls expressed some remorse, Fenrich said, although mainly "they were sorry they got caught." Meanwhile, the neighborhood residents, although they had seen more vicious crimes, told reporters that they found the pinprick attacks an "intolerable invasion, both because of the cavalier manner in which the attacks were carried out, and because rumors spread early that it was possible the jabs had come from AIDS-infected needles."[1]

American cities have always been violent places, but the pinprick attacks are emblematic of a new, more menacing violence and a more profound breakdown of social life. Like the expressive wilding in Central Park, it involves taking pleasure in the inflicting of pain and complete indifference to the sensibilities of the victims. For the potential targets—anyone walking the street—the message is to remain hypervigilant and assume that every pedestrian is a potential threat.

The new phenomenon of bystander killings carries a similar message: that no place is safe and that society has become too weak to offer protection. In 1987, Darlene Tiffany Moore, a visitor to Boston, was killed by a stray bullet from nearby gang shooting while sitting on a front porch. By

1990, so many Bostonians had been hit by randomly ricocheting bullets, often inside their own homes, that 47-year-old Dorothy Ingram "sleeps on the floor, fearing stray bullets may come through her windows at night."[2]

The sheer volume of violence is also new. A resident of Ingram's neighborhood says that "the past whole year of 1990 has been killing, killing, killing; somebody got shot, somebody got stabbed. That's all I've been hearing since 1990 began." There is a new expression in Boston neighborhoods, "twenty-four-and-seven-kids," referring to children whose mothers keep them in the house twenty-four hours a day, seven days a week, because they fear for their safety.

The horrifying image of children killing children has helped define the 1990s. In October 1994 two Chicago boys, ages 10 and 11, threw a 5-year-old child, Erik Morris, to his death from a 14th floor window. The reason: Erik had refused to steal candy for them. Erik's 8-year-old brother had desperately tried to save him but was overpowered by the bigger boys.

A month earlier, Chicagoan Robert Sandifer, age 11, was killed by two boys, ages 14 and 16, who feared that Sandifer would squeal about their gang activities to police. Sandifer, shortly before his own murder, had killed a 14-year-old girl, Shavan Dean, when he fired a volley of bullets into a group of teenagers playing football. Young Sandifer was buried with his teddy bear.

On Halloween night, 1994, a 16-year-old killed Boston's youngest street-violence victim, Jermaine Goffigan, murdered on his ninth birthday. Only a few hours before his death, Goffigan's third-grade class had thrown him a surprise birthday party. Like Shavan Dean, another complete innocent, Goffigan had the misfortune to be in a crowd of kids mistakenly shot up in a mass gang shooting.

Children themselves are terrified in many neighborhoods. 14-year-old Chirll Rivers is a Boston student who says she's scared: "I don't want to die. You have to watch your back every day. Someone could mistake you for someone else and shoot you. I could be the wrong person."[3] Another kid, forced to walk home from a youth program after a van broke down, collapsed in a panic, crying "I can't walk home, I just can't walk home. Someone got killed on my street. I'll get killed too." The *Boston Globe* reported that this youth got home, running all the way, but in the next eight days, three young men did not have the same luck, killed on the same street, while a fourth was fatally shot through the window of his mother's apartment." The result of this unprecedented epidemic of violence, the *Globe* said, was that increasing numbers of city youths are arming themselves, carrying small knives and pistols tucked into their waistbands or inside their coats."[4]

Omaha Police Chief James Skinner consoled Bostonians that they have plenty of company. "Yes, you're suffering. Yes, it hurts," Skinner said, "but

Boston is not alone, it's not unique." In 1990, New York City Mayor David Dinkens had to order increased police funding after the *New York Times* reported at mid-year that nineteen cabbies had already been murdered, that four children had been killed within a single week in their apartments by stray bullets (called by the tabloids the "Slaughter of the Innocents"), and a sleeping baby had been wounded when a bullet came through the wall of his apartment. Describing it as an unacceptable surge of violence, Dinkens had to take money away from schools, city hospitals, and public transportation to finance additions to the 26,000 police officers already on the force. Felix Rohatyn, the financier known as the man who helped save New York from bankruptcy in the 1970s, feels that far more needs to be done, saying "there is no part of the city where the quality of life is acceptable." Perhaps influenced by the fact that his wife had been robbed three times in the previous few years, once by a bicyclist who ripped a gold chain off her neck on Madison Avenue and another time by a thief who stole her wallet from her handbag on Fifth Avenue, Rohatyn said "there is a qualitative difference today. . . . What you feel is the constant threat of something that's going to happen to you. It's not civilized life to consider yourself lucky when you've been mugged but haven't been killed." Rohatyn says it would not be difficult for him to relocate his business to Denver, but knows that there he would not find things much better.

Many Denverites, like Philip Connaghan, a machine-shop owner, feel they are in a "war for survival." After his shop was burglarized eight times in two years, Connaghan rigged up a shotgun booby trap (a single-barrel shotgun propped up and attached to a tripwire) that led to the death of Michael McComb, who was shot when he tried to break in to Connaghan's store. Connaghan was fined $2,500 and ordered to pay $7,000 restitution to McComb's family, but he received overwhelming support from Denver residents fed up with crime.[5]

In Philadelphia in 1995, District Attorney Lynne Abraham says that "all of our cases now are multiple gunshot executions, houses set on fire and six children burned to death. This," she says of Philadelphia, "is Bosnia."

SUBURBS, SMALL TOWNS, AND NATIONAL PARKS: NEW WILDING TERRAINS

It is not only city life that is being subverted by the new wilding. In November 1994, six teenagers from Abington Township, a quiet, middle-class suburb of Philadelphia, went on their own wilding spree when they savagely beat Eddie Polec, age 16, to death with clubs and baseball bats.

Law-enforcement officials said this might have been part of a "fun outing," although there were reports that the murder was retaliation for the alleged rape of an Abington girl.

One Abington mother, expressing the shock of the community, said, "These are suburban kids—you don't figure them to go bad. It's not their character to be a rough group of kids." An Abington father and Rabbi, Aaron Landes, said, "There was a presupposition we lived in a kind of safe cocoon because we lived in suburbia. There are many families who have struggled to buy a home in suburbia to avoid the urban ills for their children." But suburbs have become cauldrons of both street and domestic violence, including an explosion of child-abuse and neglect cases among educated and professionally successful suburban parents.[6]

Priscilla Dillon, a social worker whose caseload is in Weston, Wellesley, and other posh suburbs of Boston, says that the frequency of suburban "family cris[e]s has escalated by 50% in the last five years." The kids, she says, "act out the frustrations of the family by running away, drinking, doing drugs, confusion. The only difference is that they are not publicized as much they are in the inner city." Suburban social workers say the suburban ethos of success triggers the problem; some highly successful parents "are quite absent from their kids' emotional development" and others, who "have very, very high standards for their children," put "undue pressure" on them to replicate their parents' success.[7]

Some suburbanites are beginning to question the myth of suburbia as haven. Stephen Lutz, a 17-year-old student at Abington High, recently renamed "Murder High," aptly concluded: "Maybe we can learn violence is not a city thing. It's not a suburban thing. It's not an Abington thing. It's a society thing. It can touch you anywhere."[8]

Violence is spreading not only to suburbs but to small towns as well, where crime is growing at an alarming rate. In 1993, the small town of Ayer, Massachusetts, had a higher rate of aggravated assault than either Boston or Worcester, and in 1994 small towns in Massachusetts were experiencing the largest crime rate increases in the state. In the new climate, the traditional friendliness of small towns, ironically, is becoming a spur to crime. In Kewanee, Illinois, a tiny, close community, Roger Harlow, a 48-year-old Sunday school teacher, was arrested and charged with over eighty-five burglaries in December 1994, mostly in homes of his friends and business acquaintances. Harlow would invite friends out to lunch and arrive late after stopping to burglarize their homes. Darrell Johnson, a country club and Elks associate of Harlow, said, "I'm mad at myself, too, for leaving the house open. Not anymore."[9]

Even our national parks are becoming violent places. Paul Crawford, a national-park ranger who now wears a .357 magnum revolver on his hip alongside his billy club and handcuffs, says, "Fighting, stealing, killing, we get it all. People drop their guard when they come to the parks, and that's why the criminals follow them here." John C. Benjamin, a district ranger, agrees. "I thought I'd be out here protecting the environment," Benjamin says. "I had no idea I would be breaking up bar fights, investigating murders and making reports on assaults."[10]

National park officials in Washington have called for bulletproof vests for their rangers. "Things have gotten a lot more intense," says Robert C. Mariott. "It used to be that we'd run into a belligerent drunk occasionally. But now," says Mariott, rangers routinely "run into people who are confrontational and violent." Ranger Robert L. McGhee was shot to death in Mississippi after "making a traffic stop on a park road." Drug rings have been uncovered in several national parks, and officials say that the parks have become stalking grounds for bands of thieves hunting automobiles, camera equipment, and jewelry.[11]

People come to national parks to restore their faith in society. A Detroit truck driver says one of the reasons he likes camping is that in the park he "can leave things in the tent.... It's not like the city, where you have to lock everything up." But Jenn DeRosa, a New Jerseyite who camped across the country with her friend Steve Grillo and had her bicycle, money, and all her credit cards stolen, today prepares for camping as if she were a hardened inner-city dweller. "I feel pretty safe," DeRosa says, because she now carries a knife.[12]

THE MURDER CAPITAL OF THE WORLD: CRIME IN AMERICA

All over the country, people are plagued by an intensifying fear of violence. The Figgie Report, a national survey on fear of crime, indicates that four out of five Americans "are afraid of being assaulted, robbed, raped, or murdered." An estimated 90 percent of Americans lock their doors, and more than half "dress plainly" to avoid attracting the attention of violent criminals. Over 50 million households stock guns, including a rapidly growing arsenal of automatic assault weapons, to ward off attack.[13]

Violence has always been endemic in the United States, but national statistics suggest we are entering a new era. In 1990, violent crime in America hit a record high, including 23,348 murders, prompting Delaware Senator Joseph Biden to dub it the "bloodiest year in American history." Private security expenses—for walled or wired homes, guns, and armed guards—rose from $20 billion in 1980 to $52 billion in 1990. Thirty-four percent of the American population said they felt "truly desperate" about rising violence.[14]

In 1993, violent crime hit another peak, rising over 5.9 percent from 1992 to about 11 million reported cases—an astonishing rate of 51.5 cases per 1,000 people over the age of 12. Although FBI statistics showed a 3 percent decline in violent crime over the first half of 1994, a period of economic recovery, a special Justice Department report issued in late 1994, based on lengthy interviews with 100,000 Americans, concluded that violent crime was actually still rising. The study revealed that official FBI data severely under-represent American violence, with over half of all crimes not reported to law enforcement agencies. In 1995, compared to 1955, the rates of robberies and aggravated assaults have gone up sixfold, rapes have tripled, and the overall major-crime rate has quadrupled.[15]

The epidemic is most severe among youth. Gang violence against the young has been the fastest-growing type of killing in the nation, increasing 371 percent from 1980 to 1992. The percentage of people charged with murder who are under 18 has also been growing explosively, increasing 165 percent between 1985 and 1993, as has the percentage of victims who are teenagers and younger children. Psychologist Charles Patrick Ewing reports a burgeoning epidemic of murders by juveniles—in 1995, about 4,000 homicides. "I'm terribly pessimistic," Ewing said. He showed that the number of murders by youths doubled between 1984 and 1990 and will likely "quadruple by the end of the century." Youth suicide is also at a near all-time high: In 1995 it was more than double the rate of 1970. Paul Bracy, director of the Massachusetts Department of Health's Office of Violence, says flatly that the "youth violence we're experiencing in this country has never been to this level before." The *Journal of the American Medical Association* reports that the toll is enormous, with almost four out of every five deaths among youth between 15 and 24 years of age due to accidents, homicides, and suicides.[16]

The murder rate in 1995 will be about two-and-a-half times that of 1960. As a Senate Judiciary report noted soberly, "We are by far the most murderous industrialized nation in the world." British, Japanese, and Germans kill each other about one-tenth as often as Americans do.[17]

DOMESTIC VIOLENCE RUN AMOK: WILDING IN THE KITCHEN AND THE BEDROOM

One of the remarkable things about Ik society is the complete unraveling of the family. Consumed by the desperate quest to get food, an Ik views family obligations as "insane." Family members, the Ik believe, are either "burdens" or competitors, in either case an obstacle to filling one's own stomach. The Ik are quick to cast off old parents and children, whom they view as "useless appendages." Bila, an unexceptional Ik mother, frequently took her baby to the fields, hoping a predator would take it away. When a leopard finally made off with it, she "was delighted. She was rid of the child and no longer had to carry it about and feed it."[18]

An extreme wilding culture spells death for the family, as it does for society as a whole. The family is ultimately a set of demanding social obligations and commitments, requiring a sense of moral obligation and a robust capacity to think beyond oneself.

America's own wilding culture seems at first blush to be reinforcing the family rather than subverting it. Wilding has made the outside world a dangerous place. To protect themselves, journalist Chris Black writes, "citizens have hunkered down with their nuclear families and turned their homes into suburban bunkers against the threats" outside. Sociologist Ray Oldenburg says that as the sense of community erodes and the city streets become scary, "we have replaced the ideal community with the ideal private home." Americans try to keep off the streets, spending time with family rather than friends, watching videos at home rather than venturing out to the movies. Marketing consultant Faith Popcorn calls the trend "cocooning"—escaping into the warm bosom of one's own family and home in order to tune out the rest of the world. The family, in Christopher Lasch's phrase, beckons as the only "haven in a heartless world."[19]

Families, however, are always more a mirror of the outside world than a barrier against it, and wilding on the outside is helping to unglue the American family, turning it into an unstable and increasingly heartless haven. As Americans harden themselves to survive on the streets and compete at work, they make more conditional family commitments and may be becoming more indifferent or violent toward the people to whom they are closest. Taking violence as one indicator, veteran researchers Richard J. Gelles and Murray A. Straus report: "The cruel irony of staying home because one fears violence in the streets is that the real danger of personal attack *is in the home.* Offenders are not strangers climbing through windows, but loved ones, family members."[20]

In 1995, approximately 5,000 Americans murdered someone in their immediate family—about half of these killing a spouse and the other half a parent, child, or sibling—accounting for almost 25 percent of all murders in the country. A staggering number of Americans are physically assaulted by family members each year, including over 1.5 million elderly victims, over 2 million children, and more than 2 million wives who are severely beaten by their husbands. In America a wife is beaten, the FBI estimates, every thirty seconds, and over 40 percent of the most brutally beaten, according to researchers William Stacey and Anson Shupe, are pregnant at the time. The fantastic obsession with the O.J. Simpson case partly reflects the epidemic of expressive wilding in the form of spousal abuse that is poisoning America in the 1990s.

As for children and the elderly, the greatest threat comes not from strangers, the *Boston Globe* reports, "but overwhelmingly from their families," where new forms of abuse are on the rise. Despite all the publicity on TV and milk cartons about strangers snatching kids, the *Globe* notes, there are no more than 300 such cases a year, whereas there are now "more than 160,000 family abductions annually, and nearly 60,000 youngsters expelled from their homes and refused reentry." Typical of elderly victims, who get less public attention than battered spouses and abused or abandoned children, is a 77-year-old California woman who told police her son repeatedly "hit her on the head with beer bottles," a 71-year-old Massachusetts man who "suffered a six-inch gash in his forehead when his son struck him with a frying pan," and an 80-year-old California grandmother who was imprisoned by her grandsons. She was "isolated from all outside contact" while they cashed her Social Security checks and depleted her bank account.[21]

Representative Edward R. Roybal of California, reporting a House Aging Committee finding of a 50 percent increase in family violence against the elderly from 1980 to 1990, calls it a "crisis of epic proportions." Similarly, official statistics show astronomical increases of anywhere from 100 to 400 percent since the mid-1970s in the rate of child abuse. It is impossible to be certain that family violence is increasing, for the figures may simply reflect better reporting techniques. Nor do we know that the modern American family is more violent than families throughout history, which have often been "cradles of violence." In ancient civilizations, including the Greek and Roman, as well as among the Gauls, Celts, and Scandinavians, newborn babies were routinely drowned in rivers, abandoned as prey for birds or other predators, and buried in dung piles. One historian concludes that a large percentage of eighteenth-century European and American children, subjected to routine beatings and indentured labor, would be considered battered children today.[22]

THE UNGLUED FAMILY: DIVORCE, SINGLES, AND THE SOCIOLOGY OF THE HEART IN THE "POSTMARITAL" ERA

Whether or not it is becoming more violent, the American family is clearly becoming a less stable institution, the traditional bonds between spouses and between parents and children eroding so rapidly that some fear the nuclear

family may not survive the next century. Senator Patrick Moynihan, reviewing evidence that only 6 percent of black children and 30 percent of white
children will grow up with both parents, says we are already in a "postmari-
tal" society. "The scale of marital breakdown," writes historian Lawrence
Stone, "has no historical precedent that I know of, and seems unique. There
has been nothing like it for the last 2,000 years, and probably much longer."[23]

At least three long-term, unambiguous trends signal a dramatic ungluing of the family as we have known it: sustained high rates of divorce, a pre-
cipitous increase in the number of single-parent households, and an
extraordinary increase in the numbers of Americans living outside of any
family structure. Demographer James R. Wetzel reports that divorce rates
are now holding steady at double those "of the average for the 1950–1964
period, and about triple the average of the 1920s and 1930s." Wetzel estimates that "more than half of all marriages contracted during the 1970s
will end in divorce." Among young people marrying today between the ages
of 18 and 24, approximately 75 percent will divorce. Marriage is no longer
"for better or for worse," but on average for about seven years, after which
time a declining number of divorcees will remarry, with an even higher
probability of divorcing again for those who do. This decisive breakdown
in permanent relationships may be, as Stone suggests, the most important
revolution of modern times, a "watershed in the culture of the West."[24]

The number of single-parent households is another revolutionary
development, with about 15 million such families in 1994. This is almost
triple the number in 1950 and, remarkably, is nearly one-third of the number of "normal" families, that is, the approximately 50 million traditional
households with two parents and children. The number of mothers raising
children without a husband present has exploded from about 3.5 million
in 1950 to approximately 12 million in 1994, including a rapidly growing
number of white as well as black women. In 1995, the Census Bureau
reported that 30 percent of all families, and 63 percent of black families,
were headed by single parents. Demographer Thomas Exter projects a continued mushrooming of such "incomplete" families, with numbers estimated to soar another 16 percent by 2000.[25]

Perhaps the most dramatic signal of family unraveling is the number
of Americans living outside any family system. "Families were the order of
the day early in the twentieth century," Wetzel writes, and as late as 1940,
only about 7.5 percent of Americans lived outside of a family. Today, almost
30 percent of households are made up of single or unrelated people and
about 25 million Americans now live alone.[26]

The ungluing of the family has been visible for decades, but in the last two
decades has been accelerating at an extraordinary pace. The number of single
mothers, for example, rose 53 percent from 1950 to 1970, and then increased

an astonishing 98 percent between 1970 and 1989. The number of never-married mothers exploded tenfold during the same period, and the percentage of babies born out of wedlock mushroomed from about 5 percent of all births in 1960 to about 27 percent in 1994, constituting over 1.2 million newborns, more than one out of every four births, in that year alone.[27]

The same trends are taking place in European countries and Japan, but the rate in America is out of whack. The U.S. divorce rate is higher than any other country's: four times higher than Japan's, three times higher than England's or France's, and two times higher than Denmark's or Sweden's. The percentage of single-parent households in America is also the highest: almost four times higher than in Japan, almost three times higher than in Sweden, and two times higher than in England. Moreover, the American rate of increase in single parents far outstrips that of any other country.[28]

Family ungluing, particularly divorce, reflects some positive developments—such as the new freedom of economically independent women to leave bad marriages. But it also reflects the most radical individualistic currents of the modern era, currents far more powerful in America than anywhere else. Traditional family obligations are becoming too confining for a growing segment of Americans. Lawrence Stone argues that since 1960 American "spouses are being traded in almost as cheaply and easily as used cars," reflecting "a moral and cultural shift to untrammeled individualism." This is consistent with a long-term cultural revolution in which people withdraw some of their attachments to their communities in order to gain more freedom for themselves. As early as 1853, Horace Greeley warned of rising divorce as a by-product of an American individualism evolving into virulent egotism, "wherein the Sovereignty of the Individual—that is the right of every man to do pretty nearly as he pleases . . . is visibly gaining ground daily."[29]

As individualism intensifies, the balance of commitment can tilt so far toward the self that the family and other building blocks of society decompose. When individualism turns into rampant wilding, as among the Ik, the family is shredded, leaving atomized individuals to prey upon each other. In the Reagan-Bush-Gingrich era, as the line between individualism and wilding blurs, the American family suffers its own form of abandonment, strained to the breaking point not only by acute economic pressures but by the burden of its members' self-preoccupation. Americans converted to the reigning ideology of "looking out for number one" are proving ready to sacrifice not only outsiders but their kin on the altar of their own needs and pleasures. Divorce court judge Edward M. Ginsburg concludes that the people passing through his courtroom are so committed to putting their own happiness first that it sometimes reminds him of Rome "just before it all came undone." Ginsburg muses that the role of the family has changed from caring for children to being "eternally in love and having a good time."[30]

Abandonment is a thread common to divorce and broken households. Both reflect choices to preserve the self and enhance personal happiness at the expense of the family unit, a choice that may be rational when no children are involved, but frequently proves catastrophic when they are. L. J. Weitzman, in her study of the children of the divorced, finds that they tend to feel abandoned, often traumatically so. They, indeed, are an abandoned population, if only because divorce is typically "financially a severe blow" for children, who lose the full economic as well as emotional support of two parents. Disruptions such as sale of the family home "adds to the trauma of children," Laurence Stone notes, "who may find themselves suddenly deprived not only of their father but also of their home, their school, their friends, and their economic comforts." Summarizing research findings, *Newsweek* concludes that "divorce has left a devastated generation in its wake."[31]

The experience of stepfamilies shows that the family, once dismantled, is not easily put together again. Testimony to the new age of serial marriage is the fact that one-third of all children born in the 1980s live with a stepparent and more than 7 million kids now live in stepfamilies, often composed of conglomerates of children from several past marriages. Sociologist Frank Furstenberg says that "one of the consistent findings in research is that stepparenthood does not recreate the nuclear family. It does not put the family back together again, in Humpty-Dumpty fashion." Researcher Nicholas Zill says that, psychologically, kids in stepfamilies "most resemble kids in single-parent families—even though they may be living in two-parent households." These children often "feel they've been cast in an outsider role," says Zill, who adds that as a group stepchildren have more emotional and developmental problems and "are more likely to be victims of child abuse, especially sexual abuse." Furstenberg notes that in the stepfamily it is problematic "whether the people we count as kin can be counted on." For one thing, second marriages break up more frequently than first marriages, at an extraordinary 60 to 70 percent divorce rate. "Remarriages are very fragile," says Johns Hopkins researcher Andrew Cherlin. "These couples have gone through one bad marriage and they're determined not to go through another. Their antennae are up . . . and they're prepared to leave." Moreover, many stepparents can truly not be counted on as parents. Esther, a high-school senior in Chicago, says of her stepmother, "It's like having a permanent guest."[32]

The abandonment of children is clearest in single-parent households, whose meteoric upsurge reflects the rise of a generation of young men, themselves abandoned by society, who feel little responsibility for their progeny. The psychological neglect is compounded by economics. According to Senator Moynihan, 55 percent of children in single-parent households live in poverty, and they constitute the core of the 500,000 children who go to sleep homeless every night, the one in four children who have dropped out of high school, and the 14 million children without any health insurance. Ultimate casualties of family disintegration and of the broader wilding culture and the economic policies at its source, the worst off of these children are called by *Newsweek* "American untouchables," reflecting a journalist's reaction to the sight and smell of filthy, impoverished infants and his feelings of shame at "resisting the affections of a tiny child whose entire being seems to emanate pathology." The plight of these victimized children should not obscure the struggles of one-parent children at every income level. Many, like Andy, age 11, do not live in poverty, but live disrupted lives. When he was removed from his mother after she became abusive, Andy went to live with his aunt; but when her residence was sold and she could not bring Andy to her next home, it was left unclear where he would live next.[33]

Within the two-parent household, and at the higher income levels, the larger wilding culture may be leading to a more invisible emotional sabotage of the family and abandonment of children. *Newsweek* opened its special issue on the family with a critique of affluent professionals who prize their careers or BMWs more than their children. The fact that many upper-middle-class young people are taking longer to get college degrees, are flitting across careers, and are waiting longer before getting married and less time before getting divorced, suggests that they find it increasingly difficult to make, in sociologist David Popenoe's words, a "commitment of any kind." This may reflect aborted emotional relations with professional parents too consumed by their own career drives to invest time in their children, who get expensive stereos and cars instead of love. Although most expect to get married and have children of their own, "the prospect fills them with dread."

Summarizing research findings, Kenneth L. Woodward maintains that these children appear to constitute a generation that has "grown accustomed to keeping their options open. There are so many choices to make—in relationships, careers, and consumer goods—that they hate to limit their freedom." Many of these young people, beginning to suffer from their inability to make commitments, are flocking to codependency groups, a rapidly proliferating self-help movement focusing on the emotional devastation wreaked in dysfunctional families, a condition now said to include as many as 90 percent of American families.[34]

Dr. Benjamin Spock, America's best-known "family doctor," sees a direct connection between the undoing of the family and the values of the Reagan-Bush era. "By far the most disturbing force in America today," Spock says, "is excessive competitiveness. It keeps people obsessed with their jobs and with personal advancement," at the expense of feelings for others. Spock argues that the effects on the family are devastating, because it destroys the ethos of kindness and care upon which loving families depend. Spock has put his finger on the essential wilding drama of the current era: unmitigated self-interest inevitably means abandonment of the family and, ultimately, as among the Ik, all social commitments.[35]

FALLING BRIDGES, POTHOLES, AND PEELING SCHOOLROOM PAINT: THE ABANDONMENT OF SOCIETY

"The limo from the Honolulu airport is a lumbering, battered Buick," writes journalist Tom Ashbrook, noting his first impressions after returning from a ten-year sojourn in Asia. "The doors don't close properly. The seats are stained and torn. The suspension is dropping, cockeyed. The music is mushy. The paint is extravagantly scarred. The passengers are fat." Images of Japan still in his mind, Ashbrook is deeply concerned.[36]

In Honolulu, Ashbrook again records his impressions. "Hello Occident. Cracked highways, no service. Hotel is heavy on glitter and self-promotional hype, light on everything else. Construction quality shabby. Rusting metalwork. Cheap materials. . . . Rich next to poor. Slick by shabby. Twitchy bag ladies and a legless panhandler croaking 'Aloha.' . . . Korean cabdriver complains road repairs take ten times longer than in Seoul."[37]

"An American homecoming," Ashbrook groans, "is a journey into shades of disarray." It is downright "scary for a recent returnee." Ashbrook learns that his brother-in-law "sleeps with a large pistol in his nightstand and an alarm system that can track a burglar room by room." Turning on the radio, Ashbrook hears of "Los Angeles drivers taking potshots at one another on the freeway, American schoolchildren scoring at the bottom of the First-World heap in key subjects. Drug lords reigning over urban fiefs, Alcoholics Anonymous and its ilk as a new religion. Wall Street sapping the economy." Fresh into his hotel, Ashbrook's son flicks on a Saturday morning cartoon; "Hey fella! This is America," booms the wisecracking voice of an animated hero. "I've got the right to not work any time I want."[38]

The comparison with Asia is too disheartening for Ashbrook. "While veins of efficiency and competence feel ever-expanding in Asia, they appear to be contracting in the United States. Our cracked highways and rusting bridges seem physical reflections of falling standards, organization, simple care in the performance of jobs—of lost resolve." Ashbrook concludes that a "returning American comes home with trepidation," hoping that his or her sense of the breakdown of America "is exaggerated, fearing that it might not be, subtly prepared to accept it as fact."[39]

Ashbrook is seeing the unmistakable signs of a breakdown in both the physical and social infrastructure necessary to keep a society together. America's physical infrastructure, its grid of roads, bridges, railways, ports, airports, sewer systems, and communication nodes, is in near-terminal disrepair. This is no surprise to the folks in Covington, Tennessee, where a bridge over the Hatchie River collapsed, sending seven motorists to their death; nor to people in upstate New York, where the collapse of a bridge killed ten people. Nearly half of Massachusetts' twenty-seven bridges are officially "substandard." Two-thirds of these are so badly broken-down that they need to be replaced. Moreover, 70 percent of Massachusetts roads are rated "fair" or "poor." Almost everywhere "the nation's roads are crumbling . . . existing highways go unrepaired while new ones seldom advance beyond the blueprint stage. Forty percent of the nation's bridges have serious deficiencies. Airports, like highways, are strained beyond capacity, while potential mass transit options go unexplored. Water delivery systems are so antiquated that some cities still transport water through nineteenth-century wooden pipes." California Democratic Representative Robert T. Matsui says, "The problem is absolutely catastrophic"; perhaps an understatement given the price tag of repair estimated at over $3 trillion, which is three times the size of the annual federal budget and more than the entire national debt. Rebuilding the national infrastructure, Massachusetts Transportation Secretary Frederick P. Salvucci says, "is the greatest public works challenge since the pyramids were built."[40]

As the physical infrastructure collapses, the social infrastructure is being starved, creating an emergency in the provision of affordable housing, jobs at a liveable wage, basic health care, education, and the social services required to sustain the fabric of civilization. The crisis of affordable housing has now yielded "over three million homeless people," writes journalist Michael Albert, "who wander our backstreets eating out of garbage cans and sleeping under tattered newspapers in bedrooms shared with alley-rats." About 14 percent of Americans have fallen through gaping holes in the social safety net and are poor, partly reflecting the unpleasant reality of an economy in decline churning out a high proportion of extremely low-wage jobs: 44 percent of the new jobs created during the 1980s pay less than $7,400 a year, which is 35 percent less than the poverty-level income for a family of four. Over 36 million Americans have no health insurance. This includes one-fifth of all American children, contributing to America's life expectancy being lower and the infant mortality rate higher than in all Western European countries and some Eastern European countries as well. Meanwhile, the collapse of American public education is yielding an average American high-school student who not only has difficulty locating France, Israel, or the United States itself on a map, but scores lower across the board than students in virtually all the other advanced industrialized countries. This is well-understood by American parents who shun the public school system when they can afford to do so. An estimated nine out of ten Boston parents send their children to parochial school or any place other than a Boston public school.[41]

Parents recognize that American public schools are literally disintegrating. A 1995 report by the General Accounting Office showed that 25,000 U.S. schools housing 14 million children need extensive physical rehabilitation, including New York City schools with exposed asbestos, rotting roof beams, and broken plumbing, Montana schools where water leaks led to collapsed ceilings, and the New Orleans school where termites ate books on library shelves and then the shelves themselves. The Education Infrastructure Act, approved by Congress in 1994, allocated $100 million to help fix the problem, but the new Republican Congress sought to cut the funding; it wouldn't have made much of a dent anyway since the GAO estimates it would take $112 billion to do the job, more than a thousand times the amount originally allocated.[42]

This abject unraveling of the entire social fabric is the ultimate manifestation of the new wilding culture, an abandonment of society consciously engineered by the country's political leadership and passively endorsed by the majority of voters. The cost of maintaining and reconstructing its physical and social infrastructure is well within the reach of the world's still richest country; however, in what may be the greatest act of domestic-policy wilding in this century, recent presidents, while continuing to pour billions into the Pentagon's coffers, have refused to support the public spending that would halt and reverse the crumbling infrastructure. This refusal is rationalized under the umbrella of "free market" ideology, to wit rolling back taxes, deficits, and "big government." In contrast, Western European countries such as Belgium, France, West Germany, and the Netherlands, less wealthy than the United States, have managed to preserve much of their social infrastructure by spending a substantially higher percentage of their GNP on health care, education, and a wide range of other social programs.[43]

THE END OF GOVERNMENT?
THE THIRD WAVE AND POLITICAL
WILDING

"No new taxes" is the ultimate symbol of the new public-policy wilding, a thirty-second sound bite powerful enough to catapult two presidents into the White House. Cynically fueled by politicians, the so-called tax revolt has created the political space leaders need to defund society, and reflects the war in Americans' hearts and minds between their commitments to society and to themselves. Refusing taxes has become the respectable political vehicle for lashing out at and ultimately abandoning both government and society itself. Future historians may come to view American leaders playing the tax revolt as a sequel to the emperor playing his violin as Rome burned.

While tax cuts were at the heart of the 1980s Reagan Revolution, the tax revolt reached its full head of steam in the 1990s. Newt Gingrich and his Republican colleagues who took over Congress in 1995 put tax-cutting at the center of their Contract With America, proposing to cut $220 billion over five years. The Contract spelled out tax cuts for business investment and capital gains which, as the *New York Times* observed, would not only reward the speculative short-term investments that are sapping the economy, but would shower 30 percent of the tax savings on less than 2 percent of the richest Americans—those making $200,000 or more— and 47 percent of the savings on the richest 10 percent, thereby accelerating the "trickle-up" to the super-rich begun in the 1980s.

To pay for the tax cuts, Republicans proposed $200 billion worth of cuts in education, housing, health, welfare, and other social spending. Liberal critics noted that this meant the poor and the working class—especially poor children—would be paying for the tax cuts. Science, music, lunch programs, and sports in the public schools, health clinics, food stamps, child-care centers, legal aid, and cash income assistance to the poor could go the way of the Edsel. Gingrichites proposed to cut Medicaid, the only source of medical care for 36 million poor and elderly Americans, by as much as $125–200 billion over seven years, to be followed by huge cuts in Medicare, the lifeline of the middle class elderly. These cuts not only punch more and bigger holes in the collapsing infrastructure and safety net, but threaten to terminate the federal government's legal obligation to prevent starvation, illness, and death among dispossessed populations, the subject of our next chapter.

The Contract's tax and spending cuts were part of a systematic plan to dismantle much of the federal government itself. Gingrich described this as part of the historic Third Wave revolution, conceived by futurists Alvin and Heidi Toffler, that would sweep away central government and "devolve" power and resources to state or local governments. Despite the faddishness of the Tofflerian perspective and the dangers of "states' rights movements," which have historically helped preserve segregation and intolerance, Gingrich translated Third Wave "devolution" into a recipe for "zeroing out" a remarkable array of the most socially protective parts of the government. Among the hundreds of agencies targeted for extinction or zero public funding were the Department of Education, the National Public Broadcasting Service, the Department of Housing and Urban Development, the National Endowment for the Humanities, the National Endowment for the Arts, much of the Environmental Protection Agency, and the Federal Drug Administration.

The attacks on the EPA and the FDA make clear that the tax-cutting revolution of the mid-1990s was a wedge designed not to reform but destroy government. The new Contract with America would effectively end the capacity of the EPA to regulate by mandating prohibitively complex or expensive forms of cost-benefit analysis and compensation to property owners, essentially gutting prospects for the Superfund, meaningful enforcement of the Clean Air and Safe Drinking Water Acts, and threatening many of the other environmental, health, and workplace regulations put in place since the New Deal. EPA chief Carol Browner said, "This is about shutting us down, there can be no mistake." As for the FDA, Gingrich has called it "the leading job killer in America" and dubbed FDA Commissioner David Kessler, appointed by President Bush, a "thug." Renowned *New York Times* columnist Anthony Lewis, reviewing the FDA's role in saving Americans from the Thalidomide tragedy, which led to the birth of over 10,000 deformed babies in Europe, recognized the wilding side of the tax-cutting and spending revolution, saying that although there is a need for regulatory reform, "there are some things that a civilized society needs government to do. One of them is to protect its citizens from untested drugs that may do terrible harm."[44] Another is to protect Americans from contaminated meat; as President Clinton said in 1995, the proposed deregulation would make it difficult to "stop contaminated meat from being sold." Clinton was referring to the recent case of Eric Mueller, a 13-year-old Chicago boy who died after he ate a hamburger with toxic levels of *E. coli* bacteria.

While Speaker Gingrich was leading the assault on the national government, more than thirty states were planning to cut taxes and radically downsize their own governments, led by rising Republican stars such as New Jersey Governor Christine Whitman, New York Governor George Pataki, and Massachusetts Governor William Weld. Whitman gave the GOP response to President Clinton's 1995 State of the Union address to showcase her own 30 percent cut in the state income tax, which critics charged would gut many of New Jersey's crumbling public schools, shut down hospitals and mental-health clinics, undermine the solvency of New Jersey's pension system, and lay off thousands of public employees. Pataki, also elected on the basis of radical tax-cutting fever, is cutting billions in state funds for New York's rotting schools and its increasingly punitive welfare and Medicaid programs. Promising to change "Taxachusetts" into a business paradise, Weld slashed capital gains and business taxes while proposing to cut within months thousands of welfare mothers and their children off the rolls forever. While Whitman, Pataki, and Weld parrot the praises of Tofflerian devolution, they seem unaware of the irony that their programs are undermining the very state and local services that could conceivably replace the federal ones sledge-hammered to death by the Gingrichites.

Although in his 1995 State of the Union address President Clinton repeated his rhetorical commitment to a "New Covenant" for social reconstruction, in practice he rushed to join the Tofflerian and tax revolutions, entering into competition with Republicans to see who could cut taxes and government faster. Not only did he propose his own multibillion dollar tax cuts, targeted largely to the educated middle class rather than the rich or poor, but he also sponsored, in the name of "reinventing government," an unprecedented Democratic war on government itself. Among the agencies that the Clinton administration proposed to eliminate, privatize, or radically shrink were the Federal Aviation Administration, the Department of Transportation, the Interstate Commerce Commission, the Department of Energy, the Department of Housing, the General Services Administration, and the Office of Personnel Management. One hundred and thirty programs, including many for education, scientific research, environmental protection, and welfare would be terminated. As one Washington observer noted: "You expect to see Republicans, when they are in power, do this—it's what they've been pushing for years. But to see Democrats doing it, and to see the competition between the White House and the Congress as they race to privatize—it's amazing."[45]

Making government the enemy has dangerous consequences. The right-wing terrorists who blew up the Alfred P. Murrah Federal Building in Oklahoma City on April 19, 1995, were influenced by a quarter century of relentless attacks on government by politicians such as Ronald Reagan, Newt Gingrich, and Pat Robertson, talk-show radio personalities such as Rush Limbaugh, and the militant anti-government ideologues who lead the "patriot militias" of the 1990s. Oklahoma bombing suspect Timothy J. McVeigh is not an isolated psychopath but a devoted disciple of extreme right-wing militia movements which have caught fire from Montana to Massachusetts. Such militias teach not only hatred of Jews, Blacks, and immigrants, but a perverted individualism that sees drivers licenses, public schools, and social security cards as extreme infringements on personal freedom. They preach that government is the ultimate enemy of the people and should be demolished through bombings or other acts of sabotage of government installations. McVeigh and thousands of other militia militants are the bastard stepchildren of the conservative free-market fundamentalism that captured much of the nation in the 1980s and mid-1990s, and horrific wilding such as the Oklahoma City bombing will continue until the nation repudiates the extreme antigovernment ideology that is the hallmark of the Gingrich era. Tax cutting can serve the public interest only if it preserves the social infrastructure and protects the poor and middle class, who in the current tax revolution are paying more to support new business depreciation, capital gains, and offshore tax credits for the rich. As for government downsizing, the *New York Times,* noting that only 1 percent of the federal budget goes to welfare for the poor, proposes that human lives and much more money can be saved by slashing corporate welfare, including the billions of dollars now subsidizing agribusiness, oil, and mining industries and the billions more lost in outrageous business tax loopholes.

Jill Lancelot and Ralph De Gennaro suggest a "green scissors" approach to both tax cutting and government pruning which would eliminate tax credits for companies and government programs that are ruining the environment at public expense. For starters, they suggest ending costly give-away programs to the big mining corporations, such as the 1995 deal in which the Chevron and Manville corporations sought to pay $10,000 for national forest land in Montana estimated to be worth $4 billion in platinum deposits. To add insult to injury, such publicly subsidized mining deals lead to massive pollution which ends up costing taxpayers an estimated $30 billion more to clean up.[46]

The assault on government is an intimate, perhaps suicidal, wilding dance between leaders and voters. Politicians and business conservatives are orchestrating the dance, according to Bob Kuttner "channeling the raucous popular energy of the tax revolt into an orderly drive for systematic limitations on the welfare state and reductions in taxes on the well-to-do." The rich are using legitimate grievances by overtaxed home owners and working people to reduce their own obligation to society. This proved to be such a fortuitous political recipe for the affluent that it has become the bible of the Republican Party; however, what has proved to be a guaranteed ticket to elected office may prove disastrous to society as a whole, for it is doubtful that a society can survive when those governing it become accessories to its breakdown.[47]

Ordinary voters are, at minimum, being willingly seduced to dance. John Powers argues that "cafeteria-style government is on the rise in Massachusetts as more taxpayers believe that they need pay only for what they order. Yes for plowing, no for schools. Hold the bridge repairs." Powers believes that Massachusetts voters may be breaking faith with their constitution, defined as "[a] social compact, by which the whole people covenants with each Citizen and each Citizen with the whole people." In the tax revolt each voter is for himself or herself. Elderly and childless couples vote against raising taxes for schools. The young seek to ration health care for the elderly. And the well-to-do are prepared to cut back social services for the poor because in their eyes such programs are wasteful and create dependency. "Whatever happened," Powers asks, "to the common good?"[48]

Suzanne Gordon, an Arlington, Massachusetts, writer watching her neighbors acquiesce in the closing of one junior high school, two branch libraries, and the cutback of 30 percent of the city's work force, sees the emergence of the "No Cares Cohort"—a "vast group of professionals between the ages of about twenty-five and forty. A lot of them don't have children till they're older, so they don't have to worry about taking care of them. They're young and healthy, so the disastrous decline in our health care system doesn't affect them. If they're married or living with someone, they're probably co-workaholics. . . . They are as removed from the social contract as those minority kids the system has truly abandoned." Gordon concludes that "our town is crumbling" because these residents are content to "sit idly by," with many "sucked into a swirl of antigovernment, antihuman frenzy. . . . The spirit of generosity seems to have been executed in Massachusetts, if not in the nation as a whole."[49]

Yet substantial majorities of taxpayers continue to tell pollsters they support earmarked spending for public universities, universal health care, and other specifically targeted social services, even as they vote against general tax increases, suggesting caution in proposing that voters have turned wholesale into mean-spirited Scrooges. Many voters say that they want to continue to help those truly in need but see government programs as a gigantic hoax and a waste, subsidizing bureaucrats rather than the poor. The public response is as much an attempt to deliver a swift kick to an overfed public bureaucracy as it is an abandonment of the needy.

My own interviews with about thirty Massachusetts voters suggest that suburbanites, affluent and geographically insulated from city life, most closely fit the "mean-spirited" image. Many seem prepared to see the cities abandoned if their own comfortable lives could be preserved. The wilding ethos of the suburbs and the more affluent urban neighborhoods expresses itself less as a frenzied, "antihuman" rage than as an increasingly thick wall that makes the suffering of others emotionally tolerable. Most of the voters I interviewed believe that the larger society may be in danger of falling apart, but find, nonetheless, a remarkable capacity to enjoy their own lives. That a growing segment of the population is hell-bent on having a good time even as they recognize that the ship may be sinking is one of the most telling marks of the new wilding culture.[50]

NOTES

1. Craig Wolf, "Ten Teen-Age Girls Held in Upper Broadway Pinprick Attacks," *New York Times,* November 4, 1989, p. 27.
2. "Fears Rise of a City Consumed by Violence," *Boston Globe,* March 15, 1990, p. 12.
3. Ibid.
4. Ibid. Sally Jacobs, "As Streets Turn Deadly, Youths Revise Their Survival Code," *Boston Globe,* February 24, 1990, p. 1.
5. "Gang Violence Afflicts Cities Nationwide," *Boston Globe,* March 26, 1990, p. 10. Sam Roberts, "No, This City Is Not the One He Helped Save," *New York Times,* April 12, 1990, p. B1. "Booby Trap Death Brings Fine," *New York Times,* August 22, 1990, p.8.

6. Michale Janofsky, "A Youth's Fatal Beating Sends Ripples Through Philadelphia," *New York Times,* December 5, 1994, p. A16.

7. Linda Matchan, "Suburban Strife," *Boston Globe,* October 28, 1991, pp. 1, 6.

8. Charisse Jones, "An Act of Youthful Savagery Stuns a Suburb," *New York Times,* November 19, 1994, p. 1.

9. "Friendliness May Have Been Ruse for Burglaries in Small Town," *New York Times,* December 25, 1994, p. 21.

10. Dirk Johnson, "In U.S. Parks, Some Seek Retreat, But Find Crime," *New York Times,* August 21, 1990, pp. 1, A20.

11. Ibid.

12. Ibid.

13. Richard J. Gelles and Murray A. Straus, *Intimate Violence* (New York: Simon and Schuster, 1988), p. 18.

14. Paul H. Robinson, "Moral Credibility and Crime," *Atlantic Monthly,* March 1995, pp. 72–78.

15. Ibid., p. 72.

16. Peter S. Canellos, "Killings by Young Believed on Rise," *Boston Globe,* August 13, 1990, pp. 1, 18. "Boston Tries to Stem Tide of Violence Among Young People," *Boston Globe,* February 25, 1990, p. 31.

17. "Record U.S. Murder Rate Seen," *Boston Globe,* August 1, 1990, p. 1.

18. Turnbull, *Mountain People* (New York: Simon and Schuster, 1987), pp. 133–4, 136.

19. Chris Black, "The High Cost of a Gimme-Gimme Culture," *Boston Globe,* August 26, 1990, pp. A15–16.

20. Gelles and Straus, *Intimate Violence,* p. 18.

21. "Poll: 1 in 4 Jailed Killers Was Friend, Kin of Victim," *Boston Globe,* July 30, 1990, p. 5. William Stacey and Anson Shupe, *The Family Secret* (Boston: Beacon Press, 1983), pp. 2–3, 31, 66. Ethan Bronner, "For Youths, Family More a Threat than Strangers," *Boston Globe,* May 3, 1990, p. 1. Robert A. Rosenblatt, "Abuse of the Elderly, Most Often in Family, is Soaring, Panel Says," *Boston Globe,* May 1, 1990, p. 10.

22. Lloyd de Mause, (Ed.), *The History of Childhood* (New York: Psychohistory Press, 1974).

23. Patrick Moynihan, "Toward a Post-Industrial Social Policy," *The Public Interest,* Fall, 1989. Lawrence Stone, "The Road to Polygamy," *New York Review of Books,* March 2, 1989, p. 14.

24. James R. Wetzel, "American Families: 75 Years of Change," *Monthly Labor Review,* March 1990, pp. 4–5, 9. Desiree French, "Second Marriages," *Boston Globe,* September 19, 1989, pp. 61–62. Stone, "The Road to Polygamy," pp. 12–15.

25. Wetzel, p. 9. Thomas Exter, "Look Ma, No Spouse," *American Demographics,* March 1990, p. 83. See also Constance Sorrentino, "The

Changing Family in International Perspective," *Monthly Labor Review,* March 1990, p. 50.

26. Wetzel, "American Families," p. 11.

27. Ibid. Associated Press, "Over a Quarter of Babies Were Born to Unwed Mothers in '88, Study Finds," *Boston Globe,* June 14, 1991, p. 6.

28. Sorrentino, "The Changing Family," op. cit., pp. 46–47.

29. Stone, "Road to Polygamy," p. 15.

30. Edward Ginsburg, cited in Barbara Carton, "Divorce: What the Judge Sees," *Boston Globe,* May 22, 1991, pp. 79, 81.

31. L. J. Weitzman, *The Divorce Revolution* (Glencoe, IL: Free Press, 1985). Stone, "Road to Polygamy," p. 14. Jerrold Footlick, "What Happened to the Family?" *Newsweek* Special Issue on the Family, 1989, p. 16.

32. Barbara Kantrowitz and Pat Wingert, "Step by Step," *Newsweek* Special Issue, pp. 24, 27, 34.

33. Jonathan Kozol, "The New Untouchables," *Newsweek* Special Issue, p. 52.

34. Kenneth L. Woodward, "Young Beyond Their Years," *Newsweek* Special Issue, p. 57.

35. Dr. Benjamin Spock, "It's All Up to Us," *Newsweek* Special Issue, p. 106.

36. Tom Ashbrook, "A View From the East," *Boston Globe Sunday Magazine,* February 19, 1989, p. 16.

37. Ibid., p. 71.

38. Ibid., pp. 71–72.

39. Ibid., p. 76.

40. Philip Mitchell, "Saving State Roads," *Boston Globe,* March 1990, p. 11. "Aging Roads, Bridges, Get Scant Notice," *Boston Globe,* April 11, 1990, p. 20.

41. Michael Albert, "At the Breaking Point?" *Z Magazine,* May 1990, p. 17. Susan DeMarco and Jim Hightower, "You've Got To Spread It Around," *Mother Jones,* May 1988, p. 36. Irene Sege, "Poverty, Disease, Poor Education Imperil Nation's Youth, Panel Says," *Boston Globe,* April 27, 1990, p. 6.

42. William Honan, "14 Million Pupils in Unsuitable or Unsafe Schools, Report says," *New York Times,* February 1, 1995, p. A21.

43. "Consensus Fuels Ascent of Europe," *Boston Globe,* May 13, 1990, p. 19.

44. Anthony Lewis, "Reform or Wreck," *New York Times,* January 27, 1995, p. A27.

45. Michael Kelly, "Rip It Up," *New Yorker,* January 23, 1995, pp. 32–39.

46. Jill Lancelot and Ralph de Genero, "Green Scissors Snip $33 Billion," *New York Times,* January 31, 1995, p. A21.

47. Robert Kuttner, *Revolt of the Haves* (New York: Simon and Schuster, 1980), p. 10.

48. John Powers, "Whatever Happened to the Common Good?" *Boston Globe Sunday Magazine,* April 1, 1990, pp. 16–17, 38–42.

49. Suzanne Gordon, "Our Town Crumbles as Residents Idly Sit By," *Boston Globe,* February 24, 1990, pp. A1, A22.

50. These interviews were skillfully carried out by Boston College graduate students David Croteau and Mary Murphy.

7

Welfare, Prisons, and Orphanages: Social Wilding and the Politics of Triage

The poor in this country are the biggest piglets at the mother pig and her nipples. The poor ... give nothing back. Nothing.

—Rush Limbaugh

On April 29, 1992, after four police officers were found innocent of assaulting Rodney King, an African American man they had arrested and brutally beaten, armed conflict erupted in Los Angeles. Blacks, Hispanics, and whites—almost all poor and from the inner city—set fires inside City Hall and in front of police headquarters. Wielding knives, axes, and guns, rioters swept down main commercial avenues, torching and looting hundreds of shops, cars, and homes. It would take 8,000 L.A. police officers, 2,000 California National Guard troops, hundreds of California highway patrol officers, and, finally, 5,000 heavily armed federal troops, who occupied Los Angeles for weeks, to put out the fires and restore order. Before the riots were over, fifty-two people had died, 2,000 were wounded, over 12,000 were arrested, and property worth over $1 billion was burned or stolen by looters.[1]

For many Americans, this was the wilding nightmare writ large. On that Wednesday evening at 6:30 P.M., millions saw live on television the horrific beating of Reginald Denny, a white truck driver trapped in the worst area of the riots. Several black men, apparently spurred on by the presence of a news helicopter overhead, dragged Denny out of his truck, bashed him with a fire extinguisher, shot him at close range, and took his wallet. They beat him further with beer bottles and karate-kicked him in the head before leaving him blood-soaked and unconscious on the ground. Denny required four hours of brain surgery at a nearby hospital, evoking the memory of the Central Park jogger who also ended up on a brain surgeon's table.[2]

These scenes of violence convinced millions of Americans that civilization had completely broken down in the inner cities. But as in the Central Park case, many failed to see the whole picture. Fearful fascination with prime-time wilding by poor people once again distracted viewers from more important lessons about the veiled political wilding by our government, economic wilding by our great corporations, and social wilding to which all of us outside the inner cities are acquiescing.

WILDING IN L.A.: INNER-CITY TRIAGE

The riots were triggered by a form of official wilding as blatant as the wilding on the streets that followed. The horrifying tape of the Rodney King beating, replayed on television sets across the country, showed police officers hammering King sixty-one times in eighty-seven seconds with a metal baton, and continuing to kick and hit him pitilessly as he lay face down and motionless on the ground. Struck initially by two police Taser darts carrying 50,000 volts of electricity each, King suffered a broken leg and several broken bones in his face.[3]

Eerily foreshadowing the savage assault on Denny, King's beating constituted expressive wilding by police who were very much "out of control," as one of the four police officers charged later testified. This was only the first act of the grim judicial-wilding drama that sparked the riots. The second came on the sunny steps of the Simi Valley courthouse, where a nearly all-white jury made public its "not guilty" verdict, exonerating the police in the King case.

In all but the most conservative quarters, the Simi Valley decision raised suspicion of institutional wilding in the judiciary system. "How could they?" was the question that *Newsweek* headlined, reflecting the incredulity of viewers across the country who had seen the taped beating. A national survey by *Time* reported that 92 percent of blacks and 62 percent of whites would have voted guilty if on the jury, and 82 percent of blacks and 94 percent of whites thought the verdict would have been different if the police and the man they had beaten had all been white. 84 percent of blacks and 44 percent of whites also said that the criminal justice system routinely favors whites over blacks.[4]

Kid Frost, an L.A. rapper, told *Rolling Stone* that "Rodney King was just the icing on the cake, the straw that broke the camel's back." Although the King case was the trigger, the riots were ultimately an inevitable response to a far more important and long-term systemic wilding: For several decades, South-Central Los Angeles and hundreds of other inner-city neighbor-hoods have been socially "triaged," uncoupled from the lifelines of the larger society and consigned to social death.

Triage is a term originally used in military medicine for the decision to abandon terminally ill or horribly injured patients in order to save others less time-consuming or costly to treat. It has been employed in a different sense by sociologists to mean the sacrifice of the socially weakest sector of society. One reviewer of the literature defines social triage as "a sorting on social grounds" which diverts the goods or services from those found to be most wanting. In urban planning, another area that has adopted the term, *triage* means a decision to stop assisting—with money, housing, or other services—the worst neighborhoods, assuming that they will cost too much to save. Triage allows policy-makers and the public "not to become involved, to be insulated from the horrors of a situation." The ultimate social abandonment, social triage is an extreme form of social wilding, cutting the umbilical cord of the weakest and most vulnerable communities.[5]

MOVING JOBS OUT OF TOWN: CORPORATE FLIGHT AND ECONOMIC TRIAGE

The economic face of triage appears in the grim statistics on disappearing inner-city jobs. Sociologist John Kasarda has shown that between 1970 and 1984 almost 450,000 industrial jobs employing low-skill inner-city workers vanished from New York City, about 175,000 from Philadelphia, 89,000 from St. Louis, 73,000 from Baltimore, and 44,000 from Boston. Cutting economic lifelines this way produced soaring unemployment rates among young, urban black males: about 50 percent out of work in the country as a whole and an astounding 68 percent in the Northeast.

In South-Central Los Angeles, more than 75,000 jobs vanished between 1975 and 1985. In the three years leading up to the riots, Los Angeles lost more than 100,000 additional manufacturing jobs, helping reduce South-Central to what one L.A. official called an "economic Mojave Desert." Between 1990 and 1992, South-Central unemployment had, by some estimates, more than doubled, reaching almost 50 percent. One rioter shouted, "It's not black versus white. It's rich versus poor. And we're poor." L.A. sociologist Joel Kotkin declared simply, "It was a class riot."[6]

The inner city, once a mecca for Southern blacks who migrated north to work in the factories, got no substitutes for the manufacturing industries fleeing town. The economically triaged population was therefore left in a radically different situation than the traditional poor. In earlier times, the lower classes were a reserve army of labor, hired last, fired first, and always useful for keeping the price of labor cheap. Today, big business has the entire Third World as its reserve labor army, and no longer needs the domestic poor. The inner city houses a new triaged class permanently frozen out of the labor market.

Economic triage reflects old capitalist logic in a new global economy. American business now makes money by disinvesting in America—or at least in America's central cities. New York City's manufacturing jobs have shrunk from 1.1 million in 1951 to 300,000 in 1995; between 1990 and 1995, three of four jobs lost in California came from Los Angeles County. There are faster and cheaper profits to be made overseas, and cheaper land or lower taxes to be found in the suburbs. Government policies have abetted triage, giving corporations tax incentives for closing shop here and investing abroad. As Clinton charged during the 1992 campaign, the government was using workers' tax money to finance export of their jobs.

As manufacturing and the national economy soured, businesses became even less willing to risk investing in the inner cities, instead stepping up corporate wilding policies that sink them faster. Commercial and residential "redlining" in cities increased, notably in Los Angeles, which boasts 20 percent of all American banks classified as substantially non-compliant with the Community Reinvestment Act. Rather than use deposits to fund local projects, Los Angeles banks were shunting investments away from poor areas, effectively drawing a red line around some communities. After the Watts riot in 1965, viable small businesses in South-Central were "asphyxiated by discriminatory bank 'redlining' practices."[7]

A more novel development is the deliberate corporate strategy to flee to the peripheries of metropolitan areas—which in far-flung Los Angeles means more than fifty miles from the inner city. Businesses are relocating, as Christopher B. Leinberger has shown, partly "to escape the crime and the minority work force in the center city. . . . In Chicago, Sears is moving its merchandising division to Hoffman Estates—which is unreachable by public transportation." Some leading Chicago realtors have privately remarked that Sears is making the move to unload its predominantly inner-city black labor force, which has no means of commuting thirty-seven miles to the new site.[8]

CONTAINING THE ENEMY AT HOME:
THE NEW CLASS WAR

Economic triage is reinforced by nightmarish forms of geographical and physical triage. The poor are ever more isolated in urban ghettos such as

South-Central. Mirroring South African black "homelands," inner cities are increasingly walled off from the rest of society, while suburbs are fortifying themselves to prevent the triaged population from breaking in. One chronicler of Los Angeles writes of "spatial apartheid," suggesting comparison with South Africa's former policy of rigid racial separation.

Poor blacks and other minorities have always lived in ghettos, but never has the country enforced such extreme physical concentration of poor people. Calling this segregation "the melting pot in reverse," social researchers William Goldsmith and Edward Blakely show that almost three out of every four poor inner-city blacks now live in "high poverty tracts" populated mainly by other poor blacks or, as in the case of South-Central L.A., poor Hispanics. William Julius Wilson emphasizes that the inner-city neighborhoods are "very different from their economic and ecological makeup of several decades ago," when they mixed middle-class and poor people. This momentous change has led to the cutting off "of contact or sustained interaction with individuals and institutions representing mainstream society."[9]

Such uncoupling is increasingly being enforced with military measures capable of maintaining the new order. The riots produced the biggest jump in gun sales and home security systems ever seen, but triage was producing an eerie and inevitable militarization of urban life in Los Angeles much earlier, with the number of jobs in the private security industry tripling to 75,000 in Los Angeles County between 1980 and 1990. Triage creates a civil war between castoffs and defenders, turning American urban terrain into a bizarre patchwork of prison ghettos and fortressed suburban enclaves. Urban planning boils down to a brazen species of social wilding: military containment of the triaged groups.[10]

Well before the riots, L.A. leaders had contemplated "final solutions" for the inner-city poor and homeless, including "deporting them to a poor farm on the edge of the desert or confining them in camps in the mountains." The policy actually implemented has been containment of the homeless within the smallest space possible: the gruesome ten blocks of Los Angeles' skid row. In addition to deploying police around the edge of the ghetto to restrict movement, containment strategies include designing benches in most of the city to be impossible to sleep on and removing public toilets, which are scarcer in Los Angeles than in any other large U.S. city. A deadly cat-and-mouse game goes on every night between indigents trying to escape skid row and police determined to quarantine them there.[11]

Containment requires massive police surveillance and repression. Before the riots, the L.A.P.D. mounted a daily nineteen-hour helicopter vigil over inner-city turf—more intense, as Mike Davis points out, than British surveillance of Belfast during the I.R.A.'s armed insurgency. Meanwhile, city officials were literally turning inner-city areas such as

Downtown East Los Angeles into jails by holding over 25,000 prisoners in detention centers, the highest concentration of inmates in the country. The inmate population in the nation blurs with that on the street; about half of inner-city black males between ages 18 and 35 are either in jail, on probation, under arrest, or are ex-cons.[12]

Suburban populations, increasingly terrified of triaged populations, build their own walls. Los Angeles suburbs have become fortresses "complete with encompassing walls, restricted entry points with guard posts, overlapping private and public police services, and even privatized roadways." Developers around Los Angeles report that the demand for gated communities outstrips any other kind by three to one. Some communities are using neighborhood "passport control" systems to exclude outsiders, while also closing down public parks and parking spaces on weekends.[13]

Militarization of the suburbs is a logical extension of suburbanization as a social movement. As discussed in Chapter Six, the flight to the suburbs has long been a veiled secessionary movement—the attempt to put as much geographical, administrative, and fiscal distance as possible between the white middle classes and impoverished urban minorities. Its political face, nowhere more aggressively displayed than in the L.A. metropolitan area, has ranged from separate incorporation—allowing suburbs to escape the schools and budgetary burdens of the central city while zoning out low-income renters and other undesirables—to the national politics of Reaganomics, the tax revolt, and the war on the welfare state. Inner-city triage consummates suburbanization as social wilding, marking the collapse of American civil society and the triumph of the politics of abandonment.

THE GINGRICH REVOLUTION: THE NEW POLITICS OF TRIAGE

Three years after the L.A. riots, in early 1995, Speaker of the House Newt Gingrich became America's most publicized politician, getting almost as much newsprint as O. J. Simpson. Pictured on the cover of *Time* magazine as "Uncle Scrooge," Gingrich stood for a new era of mean-spirited conservatism devoted to making triage the centerpiece of American politics. At this writing, it is unclear whether Gingrich or his Contract With America will endure very long, but the spirit of triage that they represent seems destined to deeply shape American politics and perpetate L.A.-style riots well into the next millennium.

Gingrich himself has proclaimed that he intended nothing less than to dismantle Franklin Delano Roosevelt's New Deal and Lyndon Johnson's

Great Society, which he called fifty years of "disaster." Gingrich blew the lid off traditional Washington polite speech, introducing raw talk about welfare, prisons, and orphanages. Although the Statue of Liberty has as its inscription, "Give me your tired, your poor," Gingrich asserted that that was written "before welfare." Generations of the welfare state, he proclaimed, were producing a population of "dependents" and undermining American civilization. Many could not be saved and would have to be kept in prisons, and the children would have to be committed to orphanages.

Gingrich was clear about the roots of the problem. "Countercultural McGovernicks," the left-wing followers of 1972 Democratic Presidential nominee George McGovern, had helped spawn the Great Society of the 1960s and 1970s, which in the name of compassion created an "entitlement revolution." New Deal and Great Society social legislation had guaranteed all American citizens, whether they worked or not, food, shelter, and other basic necessities. Gingrich's counterrevolution, in the name of personal responsibility, would destroy the entitlements of the dependent populations. Henceforth, Americans could survive only by taking responsibility for themselves; the shiftless and irresponsible would lose their life support system and sink or swim on their own, a solution deeply resonant with the individualism of the American Dream and with the mood of hard-pressed Americans seething with rage about welfare, crime, and riots.

The Gingrich revolution gained force because it translated abstract philosophical individualism into a radical and concrete legislative agenda, the Contract With America. As noted in the last chapter, the Contract proposed to dismantle much of the federal government, but it was not government downsizing per se but the change in its "covenant" with the people that turned the Contract into a manifesto of triage. The Contract came closest to the explicit language of triage in denying welfare benefits to single poor mothers, but this was folded into a broader new social contract that terminated the federal government's obligation to provide for the "life, liberty, and happiness" of all its citizens.

The Contract sought to do this by permanently abolishing legislative entitlements. The most discussed and maligned entitlement programs were food stamps, school lunches, Medicaid, and Aid to Families With Dependent Children (AFDC), the core safety nets for the poor. But Social Security and Medicare, which serve the broader population, are also entitlements. The Contract's call for "fiscal responsibility" and "personal responsibility" put all such programs potentially on the chopping block, because the Gingrichites construed every manner of entitlement (except those—such as oil-depletion write-offs or the home ownership interest deduction—that are disguised entitlements for the comfortable) as fiscally reckless, sources of the "culture of dependency."

Instead of entitlements protecting all in need, the Contract proposed programs with restrictive caps. Whatever the social need, Congress would legislate a fixed amount to be spent by each state according to its own discretion. If more people needed subsidized food or health care than the cap permitted, a selection process would be required to determine who received aid. This is explicit political triage in which government, rather than ensuring the survival of the entire population, designates certain sectors of the population as undeserving of support.

Although Gingrich did not say so explicitly, his Contract was taking dead aim at the dispossessed inner-city populations like those who rioted in Los Angeles. Gingrich's anti-entitlement revolution was, in part, a backlash movement, scapegoating and abandoning groups for whom the majority of Americans, themselves economically squeezed, could muster little sympathy or generosity. Conservative Republican Jack Kemp, sensing the exclusionary direction of his own party, pulled himself out of the Republican race for the presidency in 1996, saying, "I believe in inclusion, not exclusion. I believe that the party will never be whole again until blacks feel comfortable in our party." Registering his dissent with the Gingrichites, Kemp added that his party "is coming dangerously close to being portrayed as though all we want is little government and big prisons." [14]

The triage sensibility has seeped deeply into the political culture of both parties. In 1995, when a *New York Times* reporter asked Avis LaVelle, an assistant secretary in Clinton's Department of Health and Human Services, whether she could defend welfare and Medicaid as entitlements, she responded, "No, I can't. . . . It's just not smart for us to take an advocacy position one way or another. The ground is shifting under our feet." [15]

The new politics of triage emerged in the mid-1990s as the cutting edge of domestic policy. It is most obvious in the welfare reform debate, but it is also, as I show below, deeply affecting immigration and other policy areas, creating larger and more diverse triaged populations, both within and outside America's inner cities.

"WELFARE QUEENS" AND THE UNDESERVING POOR: TARGETS OF TRIAGE 1

Although the landmark welfare legislation in the House of Representatives that I discuss below was modified by the Senate and did not get enacted into law as written, it represents the knife-edge of triage that is likely to dominate the political scene for years to come. Such triage proposals will

assuredly be reintroduced until triage is discredited or succeeds in dispos-
ing of the growing "surplus" populations.

The Contract With America proclaimed it was time to cut off life support for anyone who didn't go to work. Speaker Gingrich proposed that the
core welfare programs—Aid to Families With Dependent Children
(AFDC), school breakfast and lunch programs, the Women's Infant and
Children supplemental nutrition program (WIC), and food stamps—be
abolished as entitlements. Federal welfare guarantees in place since the
Great Depression would be eliminated, and each state would be free to dis-
pense or withhold welfare as it saw fit.

On March 24, 1995, the House of Representatives passed a harsh version of the Contract's welfare reform proposal. It abolished federal programs such as AFDC and repealed entitlement laws such as the Food Stamp
Act of 1977, the Child Nutrition Act of 1966, the National School Lunch Act
of 1946, and the Emergency Food Assistance Act of 1983, replacing them
with block grants to the states. The legislation removed any individual entitlement to welfare, cut off unmarried mothers under the age of 18 from cash
benefits, stripped non-working recipients of benefits after two years, and
eliminated benefits to all recipients after five years. It also banned disability
payments to drug addicts, alcoholics, and some disabled children, while radically cutting the Low Income Home Energy Assistance Program, which
helps pay winter heating bills for the poor, disabled, and elderly. Although
the legislation retained food stamps as a federal entitlement, largely because
Republicans from agricultural states feared loss of income to their farmer-
constituents, it reduced food-stamp funding by $20 billion, or 14 percent,
and kicked off impoverished, childless adults from food stamp support.

The legislation proposed to save in total $69 billion over five years and
was billed as "tough love." Such "love" is actually a form of misogyny, targeting intensely vulnerable young women and children, many of whom
were not only the victims of irresponsible young men who had impreg-
nated and abandoned them, but also of the general social backlash against
women that the Gingrichites opportunistically exploit. The Congressional
Budget Office reported that in five years the House legislation would cut off
more than half of the 5 million mainly female-headed families currently on
welfare. Clinton's Secretary of Health and Human Services, Donna Shalala,
asserted that 5.3 million children nationally would be stripped of benefits,
a number confirmed by a Republican spokesperson.

Governor Howard Dean of Vermont said that "when Americans elected
the new majority" in 1994, "they voted to do things in a new way, but I don't
think they voted to starve children." Gingrich responded, however, that the
most vulnerable could be taken from their mothers and put in orphanages
subsidized by the savings from welfare cuts. He recommended that critics

such as Hillary Clinton—who called it "unbelievable and absurd" to put "children into orphanages because their mothers couldn't find jobs"— watch *Boys' Town,* a 1938 Spencer Tracy film celebrating the rehabilitation of a boy in a group home. Secretary Shalala, however, pointed out that Gingrich's plan would return only $293 million in welfare savings to the states, which would fund only 8,029 spaces in orphanages for the millions of kids who might need them.[16]

Gingrichite representative Jim McCrery of Louisiana admitted that many welfare mothers who could not become self-sufficient after five years might have to give their "children up for adoption, place them in a group setting or foster care." He said this would be "a price worth paying" to solve the welfare mess and help future generations. The Republican plan raised the specter of thousands of new "boarder babies," such as those taken from mothers on crack during the 1980s. At places like Manhattan's cavernous Children's Center, the babies received "custodial care," said social worker Lois Hines. They "were being fed, kept dry," but they did "not have that love and caring."

Under the House plan, the states would become the effective executors of triage, forced to find strategies for selecting recipients who would be cut off and exposed to starvation or homelessness. State welfare monies would be mercilessly squeezed by the immediate five-year cut of $69 billion, and by future federal cuts due to deficit pressures, recessions which would wreak havoc on overburdened state budgets, and competition between states to "lowball" welfare out of fear that states with more generous bene-fits would attract more of the poor. Governor Mel Carnahan of Missouri, chairman of the Democratic Governors' Association, said that in the next recession, state revenues would decline and "we will have to cut people off the welfare rolls in their time of need." Governor Dean of Vermont was more blunt, saying the new plan would "starve children and kick old peo-ple out of their houses." Even extreme conservatives such as Pennsylvania Republican Senator Rick Santorum acknowledged, "You're going to have millions of women and children with absolutely no support out there."[17]

Radical Gingrichites such as Governor John Engler of Michigan, who eliminated the welfare program for presumed able-bodied recipients in his state, zealously embrace this new states' rights regime, saying that the fed-eral government should "concentrate on foreign affairs" and butt out of most domestic policy altogether, leaving the states free to do their own thing. Without federal regulations, states could be innovative in designing their own triage strategies, such as putting their own time limits on welfare, refusing to add any payments, food stamps, or school lunches to support a new child born to a welfare mother, or denying any payments at all to sin-gle mothers under a particular age, such as 18 or 21, the cutoffs usually pro-posed by Gingrichites.

Even before passage of the House legislation, governors were experimenting with triage. Governors Engler in Michigan, Tommy Thompson in Wisconsin, Pete Wilson in California, George Pataki in New York, and William Weld in Massachusetts had all deeply slashed their welfare budgets, typically targeting teenage welfare mothers and, in Pataki's case, the blind and elderly disabled as well. The governors pioneered strategies to cut off entirely those who didn't get a job quickly; Weld gained national attention for a proposal that gave thousands of Massachusetts recipients only days to find a job or lose all public support.

The block-grant program gives states and local governments new and powerful incentives to cut welfare spending as a way to induce poor people to leave their regions. When Michigan ended its general relief program to childless adults in 1991, about one-third of the 80,000 recipients left the state, presumably for more prosperous or generous states where they could find a job or receive welfare. The idea of using welfare reform as a strategy for kicking poor people out was introduced in a *New York Times Magazine* article in 1973 by Roger Starr, then city housing director in New York City, who argued that officials should organize "planned shrinkage" of its poor population because the city could not support all of them. Many believe that Starr's article influenced welfare planners in the Gingrich era and can help explain the apparently senseless welfare reform strategy of New York City Mayor Rudolph Giuliani, who, in the midst of a major budget crisis in 1995, requested Governor Pataki to cut back even further his aid to the city, including hundreds of millions of welfare and medical dollars for the Big Apple's poorest inhabitants.

Malcolm Gladwell, the New York bureau chief of the *Washington Post*, suggests that Giuliani was consciously planning to force the poor out. Among his sources is political scientist Ester Fuchs of Columbia University, who said, "When you talk to people at City Hall, their voices drop very low and that's what you hear. Maybe the poor will leave." New York currently gives welfare families of three $286 per month for rent, but a two-bedroom apartment in the city rents for $850 and 280,000 were on the waiting list for public housing even before Pataki's welfare cuts. Among Pataki's proposed cuts, which Giuliani endorsed and asked the governor to extend even further, were emergency rent subsidies for welfare families facing eviction. Because state law requires the city to house homeless families, and it costs $32,000 a year on average to do so, Giuliani's proposals make no sense even in financial terms unless he is assuming that welfare families facing eviction will actually leave the city. This would once and for all unburden the city of its overwhelming welfare costs and fulfill the triage vision enunciated many years earlier by conservative William Buckley when he ran for mayor of New York: "What is the point in encouraging them to stay, when they might go elsewhere, where employment opportunities are greater, the cost of living less, living conditions better? . . . What is the argument that holds that New York is better off now than it would be with several thousand fewer people living here . . . ?"[18]

SAVING THE POOR? WELFARE, WORK, AND TRIAGE

Gingrich's defense of triage politics rests on the notion that it will save the "deserving poor" who are willing to work, and would destroy the incentives that encouraged generations of "welfare queens" to freeload off of hard-working citizens. The conservative worldview to which Gingrich and his colleagues adhere holds that the leading cause of poverty is poverty programs; they thus frame welfare abolition as a movement not to abandon the poor but to rescue them. For example, during the floor debate on the House welfare bill, Republican Representative Dan Mica of Florida said that "unnatural feeding and artificial care creates dependency." Celebrating after the passage of the House legislation, Mica made reference to the zoo sign, "Don't Feed the Alligators," noting that alligators can feed themselves and their children when left to fend for themselves. In the same debate, GOP Representative Barbara Cubin of Wyoming took the microphone to compare the "induced" dependency of welfare mothers with that of caged wolves: "What has happened with the wolves, just like what happens with human beings, when you take away their incentive, when you take away their freedom, when you take away their dignity, they have to be provided for." Now, she said, it was time to liberate them to survive on their own.

This point of view has enjoyed mainstream political consensus, with President Clinton and most other Democratic leaders accepting Gingrich's argument that welfare entitlements undermine personal responsibility. Underlying this point of view, however, is the questionable assumption that the poor could find jobs that paid living wages. Critics such as sociologist William Julius Wilson note that high national unemployment rates, the flight of corporations from the inner cities, and the decline of unskilled jobs make it impossible for many of even the most motivated welfare mothers or fathers, living in ghetto poverty zones with unemployment rates hovering as high as 50 percent, to find any jobs at all. Philadelphia Mayor Edward Rendell said that there are no jobs for single mothers in his city who want to work, indicating that in 1995 welfare reform had terminated benefits for 5,500 Philadelphians although only 355 jobs were created in all of Pennsylvania.[19]

But even assuming jobs were available, Northwestern University sociologist Christopher Jencks shows that most would not pay enough to allow single mothers to support their children. Reviewing studies carried out in

Chicago, Boston, San Antonio, and Charleston, Jencks shows that the majority of welfare mothers are barely surviving, despite unreported income that lifts them above the official poverty line. More revealingly, interviews of single working mothers in the same cities showed that they are in the same borderline economic peril, largely because of the high costs of doctor bills and child care.[20]

Jencks concludes that the average single working mother in 1995 would need $1,500 a month to get by without help from the government, requiring a much higher wage than the going rate of $5 to $6 dollars an hour that poor working women can expect. If subsidized child care or national health care were available, the gap between their wages and the cost of basic necessities would be narrower, but the Gingrichites oppose health and child care as entitlements; in 1995, House Republicans proposed cutting the already sparse federal aid to child care $2.5 billion over five years. Jencks suggests that unless the government were to ban single parents from having kids, the drive to end welfare is doomed—unless Americans are prepared to see many families, including those with single parents who work, go hungry or homeless. Put differently, welfare reform as currently envisioned is inevitably a triage strategy, not only for welfare mothers, but for a vast pool of poor working parents whose jobs will not pay enough to feed their children.

Radical changes in the welfare system—or even its abolition—is not necessarily triage or wilding. Welfare has failed to end poverty, reintegrate the poor into society, or make the lives of the underclass tolerable. A government-sponsored program to guarantee full employment with a higher minimum wage, combined with national health care and subsidized child care, would permit a humane elimination of much of our archaic welfare system, allowing welfare recipients to move into the labor force and support their families.

Full employment would require, however, that government and business join forces to develop and retain jobs, especially in areas devastated by triage policies. Many other innovations are also possible and promising. Among these are pilot programs in Canada and New York City that convert welfare payments into money and training for new small businesses owned and operated by welfare mothers. Even orphanages, restructured as community homes where both mother and children are brought together to live, receive emotional support, and learn parenting and employment skills are an imaginative possibility—assuming they are adequately funded and democratically administered by the residents.

The Contract With America's welfare proposals are a form of political wilding not because they dismantle the current entitlement structure but because they fail to ensure viable alternatives. Both Gingrichites and Clintonites are unwilling to finance the job creation, skill training, health care, and child care necessary to abolish welfare as we know it. Reflecting the Washington mood, Republican Representative Jim Nussle of Iowa mocked ideas about guaranteeing child care for welfare mothers transitioning to work: "Pretty soon we'll have the department of the alarm clocks to wake them up in the morning and the department of bedtime stories to tuck them in at night. It's not the government's responsibility." Speaker Gingrich, dismissing the idea that poor children have an entitlement to school lunches, said it was too costly and that "it doesn't say anywhere in the Declaration of Independence . . . that anyone is entitled to anything except the right to pursue happiness." But if the Congress and the president were prepared to attack and dismantle the corporate welfare structure described in earlier chapters, embodied in outlandish subsidies to business and tax loopholes to the rich, money could be freed up without ballooning the deficit, thereby permitting a radical shrinking of the welfare system supporting both the rich and poor—without allowing anyone to starve.

UNWELCOME IMMIGRANTS: TARGETS OF TRIAGE 2

In late 1994, California passed Proposition 187 by a 59 percent majority, a possibly unconstitutional measure which would ban state services such as health care, education, food stamps, and welfare for illegal immigrants. The Prop 187 initiative, led by Republican presidential hopeful Governor Pete Wilson, and the larger anti-immigrant movement it symbolizes, is perhaps the clearest model of triage politics, for it explicitly delineates a sector of the population as unworthy and strips it of resources necessary for survival. In addition to withdrawal of government support, many private California charities and donors have also made explicit that none of their funds were to be used to help illegal aliens.

The consequences were immediately apparent in California after Prop 187 passed. Fearful illegal immigrant parents stopped sending their children to schools, clinics, and hospitals for treatment. An 11-year-old boy died because his undocumented parents were afraid that bringing him to the emergency room would lead to deportation. Critics warned of public health disasters and riots in California counties with high percentages of illegal aliens, while noting the hypocrisy of Prop 187 sponsors who hired illegal immigrants as gardeners or nannies. Wilson himself had only a few years earlier fought hard to allow California growers to bring in cheap, undocumented workers from Mexico, which led, by some estimates, to over 3 million new illegal aliens in the country.

Prop 187's victory helped spawn similar initiatives in other states with large illegal alien populations including Florida, Texas, New York, Arizona and Illinois. Republican leader Henry Hyde of Illinois, chairman of the

House Judiciary Committee, promised that he would introduce a national variant of Prop 187 in Congress in 1995. Some saw Prop 187 foreshadowing a grim nativist politics of the late 1990s, much as California's Prop 13, the original tax revolt initiative, anticipated the antitax revolution of the 1980s.

Stronger efforts to seal the borders may reduce the inflow of illegal aliens, but they are unlikely to satisfy the cruel political impetus that underlies the new anti-immigrant politics. Republican leaders such as Wilson have found in Prop 187 a powerful political wedge for diverting middle-class rage about dwindling paychecks toward "undesirables"—scapegoat populations who can be portrayed as unfairly competing for jobs and draining public budgets. Despite protests by "compassionate conservatives" such as Jack Kemp, who opposed Prop 187 as a callous betrayal of the American spirit of inclusiveness, the national Republican Party sees anti-immigration politics as a ticket to the White House in 1996 and beyond.

Triage politics has spilled over from illegal aliens to legal immigrants. The Contract With America proposed to save $22 billion by kicking legal immigrants off of Medicaid and Supplemental Security Income and barring them from sixty other health, education, housing, and other programs, including school lunches, foster care, and emergency home heating assistance. States would be free to follow suit; a few hard-hearted states that cut off legal immigrants would likely trigger a stampede in other states, who fear that more generous provisions could attract excessive immigrant inflows. For a nation of immigrants to so harshly repudiate legal immigrants shows both the fever pitch of triage politics and its utility to leaders desperately seeking to manipulate the acute economic frustrations of ordinary Americans in the 1990s.

APARTHEID IN AMERICA? HARD TRIAGE AND THE NEW UNDERCLASS

The L.A. riots suggest that multiple forms of triage could produce an American Apartheid, similar in some ways to the former racial system in South Africa, which created separate physical homelands for blacks and a militarily enforced racial caste system that divided the population into unbridgeable worlds of rich and poor. By the early 1990s, sociologists were seeing evidence of a new American underclass, physically, economically, and socially separated from the rest of the population. Consisting primarily of blacks and other minorities packed into urban ghettos around the country, this new underclass was becoming a separate nation within a nation, cast off by the rest of society and controlled by police and prisons.[21]

Apartheid, American style, is a culmination of economically systemic and politically purposeful triage strategies, coming to fruition in the 1990s. In the 1980s, the rise of the global economy and the flight of American factories to developing nations fused with the politics of Reaganism to lay the foundations for the triage of inner-city minorities. A "soft triage" was emerging; driven by global competition and greed, corporations downsized and relocated to the suburbs and overseas. In the 1990s, greater economic globalism, technological change, and deindustrialization, combined with the new explicit exclusionary politics of the Gingrich era, have contributed to a "hard triage." The abandonment and physical containment of the new underclasses is planned and ideologically justified.

Hard triage is grounded in economics. As globalization progressed and more corporations fled to developing nations through the 1980s into the 1990s, the U.S. poor lost their usefulness as a reserve labor force, becoming permanently expendable. The increasing capacity of the poor in developing nations to take over the role of the reserve labor force for American multinationals, together with the growth of labor-saving technology that eliminated huge numbers of unskilled jobs, froze more and more of America's poor out of the labor force for life.

As economic triage hardened, so did politics. Under Reagan's soft triage, the still-functional underclass would be supported, albeit marginally, through welfare; Reagan himself always insisted that he would sustain a safety net for the truly needy. In the Gingrich era, this softness has given way to hard political triage, embodied in the abandonment of the poor explicitly rationalized and spelled out in the Contract With America.

THE BELL CURVE: SOCIOBIOLOGY, INTELLECTUALS, AND THE CULTURE OF TRIAGE

This new purposefulness was accompanied by a rising culture of hard triage offering formal intellectual and moral legitimations of abandonment. One of the leaders was Charles Murray, who first came to national attention during the Reagan years. In his 1984 book, *Losing Ground*, Murray proposed as a "thought experiment" the idea of abolishing welfare and letting recipients sink or swim on their own, an idea viewed at the time as too socially inhumane. Murray had offered the moral defense of triage resurrected by Gingrichites ten years later: destroying the safety net was the only way to end the culture of dependency and nurture personal responsibility among the poor.[22]

In 1995, when his welfare proposals had shifted from social-science fiction to actual government policy, Murray wrote a more expansive moral tract, *The Bell Curve,* based on a genetic interpretation of the failures of the poor. Co-authored with prominent Harvard psychologist Richard Hernstein, who died in 1994, Murray's book argued that biologically rooted racial differences in intelligence explained the emergence of the new underclass and the increasing economic division between rich and poor. Murray suggested that the gap would inevitably grow, because the high birth rate of the genetically unendowed underclass, combined with the new cognitive demands of a high-tech economy, would turn a mushrooming number of poor Americans into a useless surplus population.[23]

Murray made triage of the poor a matter of biological destiny and moral necessity. Efforts to integrate them into the economy through training or social programs, he argued, were genetically doomed. The genetic differences, Murray claimed, offered a foundation in nature for an emerging Apartheid-like caste system that would physically, politically, and economically separate the underclass from the larger society.

The moralizing of triage has a long history. When German leaders in World War I decided to let thousands of handicapped and emotionally disturbed patients die in hospitals from starvation, German doctors and psychiatrists argued that the deaths were compassionate to the victims and good for the health of the nation. By World War II, when Nazi physicians began gassing their patients, health officials and intellectuals sought to persuade the public that physically and mentally handicapped people were subhuman and unworthy of help. This twentieth century euthanasia movement in Germany, a prelude to the Holocaust directed against the Jews, was itself a legacy of earlier intellectual movements that had used biological or biblical arguments to legitimate triage.

From its earliest days, capitalism has created surplus populations, among them the English peasants thrown off the land during the seventeenth and eighteenth century enclosure movements. Like today's inner-city poor, these "extra" people stood in the way of progress and needed to be removed. Intellectuals and their cultural movements have historically helped rationalize the segregation or elimination of such surplus populations.

In the nineteenth century, for example, when British politicians debated how to dispose of the London poor, intellectual disciples of Thomas Malthus and Charles Darwin suggested that the dangers of overpopulation could only be resolved by a competition for survival in which the genetically talented would rise and the unfit sink. Malthus himself opposed any public funds to help the London poor during the Poor Law debates in the 1830s, citing his theory of a divinely based natural selection of populations. Later in the nineteenth century, noted physician and philosopher Francis Galton helped promote the medical eugenics movement, which advocated that doctors kill their terminal patients or other biologically and socially unfit people.

Herbert Spencer, a leading American social Darwinist in the late nineteenth century, explicitly opposed welfare on Malthusian and Darwinian grounds. "The whole effort of nature," Spencer wrote, "is to get rid of such [the poor] to clear the world of them, and make room for better. . . . It is best that they should die." William Graham Sumner, a colleague of Spencer and fellow champion of free-enterprise capitalism, offered biological explanations not only of the poor's failure but the rich's success: "The millionaires are a product of natural selection, acting on a whole body of men to pick out those who can meet the requirements of certain work to be done." Such sentiments eerily foreshadow the contemporary arguments of today's neo-conservative intellectuals, who have created a new mainstream punitive discourse of responsibility and explain poverty as shiftlessness grounded in genetic defect.[24]

The American public's receptivity to Murray and other creators of triage culture reflects both new economic stresses and the virtually unbridgeable gaps that already separate them from the new underclasses. The economic squeeze on the middle class saps their generosity and inclines them toward Scrooge-like sentiments toward the poor. A *Time* magazine poll at the end of 1994, a month after the election of the Gingrichites, showed over 60 percent of Americans agreeing that people had to worry more about themselves and "less about helping others." Other polls showed Americans were donating less time and money to charity because they were so "insecure about their [own] financial well being."[25]

National empathy is also dwindling because of the growing economic gulf between the very poor and everyone else. Economic triage has so marginalized the new underclasses that they seem more a part of the Third World than of the United States. Middle- and upper-class Americans have lost their sense of common destiny with the new poor and, according to both Christopher Lasch and Robert Reich, are happily reducing their own sense of obligation.

Fear, however, is the core cultural sensibility signaling the rise of hard triage and of the kind of social wilding that could lead to an American Apartheid. Hard triage draws a line in the sand between worthy members of society and those to be cut off. Triage inevitably creates desperation, rage, and violence among the abandoned populations and intense fear among everyone else.

After the L.A. riots, many Californians already living in gated suburbs lined up at gun shops. Almost crazed with fear, they wanted to beef up their home security systems and arm themselves on the street. By 1995, national fear of crime was so inflamed that both political parties competed to see which could spend more money on police and be tougher on criminal offenders from the underclasses. Polls repeatedly showed crime to be near or at the top of public concern, with a growing thirst for retribution. A growing number of states passed legislation permitting citizens to carry concealed handguns, evoking images of Dodge City and vigilantes taking the law in their own hands.

Hard triage leads inevitably toward a militarized social order in which undesirable populations are physically segregated and confined. Urban geographers Goldsmith and Blakely concluded from their analysis of census tracts that the American urban underclass, even under the soft triage of the 1980s, was already more geographically concentrated in isolated or barricaded ghettos than any prior generation of American poor, and that "American society is like water just above the freezing point, dangerously close to disassociating into separate parts."[26]

As the Cold War faded in the 1990s, Americans turned to fight and control the new enemy at home. In 1995, for the first time, more than one million Americans were in prison, the greatest number incarcerated in any society other than Russia, which was suffering its own wilding crisis, marked by economic collapse and the rule of its new Mafia. As prisons became the hottest growth industry in America, with more than $12 billion in 1995 allocated to build new jails, Republicans fought to put assault weapons back into the gun stores and President Clinton approved extending the death penalty for multiple new offenses.

Hard triage ends in civil war. The blasts of gunfire on the streets of urban America may mark the first stage of that inevitably bloody conflict, but, as we will see in the next chapter, there is still time to turn things around.

NOTES

1. "The Siege of LA," *Newsweek,* May 11, 1992, p. 30.
2. David Ellis, "LA Lawless," *Time,* May 11, 1992, p. 26.
3. Bob Cohn and David A. Kaplan, "How the Defense Dissected the Tape," *Newsweek,* May 11, 1992, p. 36.
4. *Time,* May 11, 1992, pp. 26–32.
5. Gideon Sjoberg, Ted Vaughan, and Norma Williams, "Bureaucracy as a Moral Issue," *Journal of Applied Behavioral Science,* 1984, vol. 20, no. 4, pp. 441–53. Stuart Hinds, "On the Relations of Medical Triage to World Famine: An Historical Survey," *Soundings,* 1976, vol. 59, no. 1, pp. 29–51. For a discussion of triage in urban planning, see Donald E. Strickland and Dennis R. Judd, "Capital Investment in Neighborhoods Which Inform National Urban Policy in the United States," *Population Research and Policy Review,* 1982, vol. 1, no. 1, pp. 59–78.
6. Ronald Grover, "Can Anything Rise from the Ashes?" *Business Week,* May 18, 1992, pp. 42–43. Troy Siegal, "The Riots: Just as Much About Class as About Race," *Business Week,* May 18, 1992, p. 47. "The Siege of LA," *Newsweek,* May 11, 1992, p. 30.
7. Mike Davis, *City of Quartz* (New York: Vintage, 1992), p. 242.
8. Christopher B. Leinberger, "Business Flees to the Urban Fringe," *The Nation,* July 6, 1992, pp. 10–12.

9. William W. Goldsmith and Edward J. Blakely, *Separate Societies* (Philadelphia: Temple University Press, 1992), pp. 2, 46ff. William J. Wilson, *The Truly Disadvantaged* (Chicago: University of Chicago Press, 1987), pp. 60–61.
10. Davis, *City of Quartz,* pp. 244–250.
11. Ibid., pp. 232ff.
12. Ibid., pp. 250ff.
13. Ibid., pp. 244–45.
14. Alan Eisner, "Kemp says he won't seek presidency in '96," *Boston Globe,* January 31, 1995, p. 31.
15. "President Clinton's Welfare Waffle," *New York Times,* January 9, 1995, p. A14.
16. Elizabeth Shogren and Marlene Cimons, "White House takes aim at GOP on welfare," *Boston Globe,* December 30, 1994, p. 3.
17. Bob Hohler, "Democratic governors issue threat on welfare," *Boston Globe,* January 10, 1995, p. 10.
18. Malcolm Gladwell, "A Plot to Shrink New York City?" *Washington Post Weekly,* March 27–April 2, 1995, p. 23.
19. John W. Mashek, "How Big are Cities in the GOP 'Contract'?" *Boston Globe,* February 26, 1995, p. 6.
20. Christopher Jencks and Kathryn Edin, "Do Poor Women Have a Right to Bear Children?" *American Prospect,* Winter, 1995, pp. 44–52.
21. William W. Goldsmith and Edward J. Blakely, *Separate Societies,* op.cit.
22. Charles Murray, *Losing Ground* (New York: Basic Books, 1983).
23. Richard Hernstein and Charles Murray, *The Bell Curve* (New York: The Free Press, 1994).
24. Cited in Richard Rubenstein, *The Age of Triage* (Boston: Beacon Press, 1983), pp. 220ff.
25. "Down on the Downtrodden," *Time,* December 19, 1994, pp. 30ff. Also "Less Money and Time for Charity," *New York Times,* October 20, 1994, p. A22.
26. William W. Goldsmith and Edward J. Blakely, op.cit., p. 2.

8

Beyond Wilding:
Resurrecting Civil Society

> *An injury to one is the concern of all.*
> —Knights of Labor Motto

Wilding has taken a devastating toll on America, but it has not permanently incapacitated it. Societies, like individuals, have powerful natural resistances and remarkable capacities to regenerate themselves. While Ik society was destroyed, America, always a resilient society, has far greater economic and cultural resources to revitalize itself. To succeed, however, it will have to focus all its efforts on the task, which involves shoring up the ideal of a "civil society" at its very foundations.

Civil society is the underlying antidote to the wilding virus, involving a culture of love, morality, and trust that leads people to care for one another and for the larger community. A civil society's institutions nurture civic responsibility by providing incentives for people to act not just in their own interest but for the common good. Governments can provide a supportive framework, but a robust civil society cannot be legislated. Civil society must arise from the cooperation and moral sensibilities of ordinary people who understand that their own fulfillment requires thriving communities and an intact society.

Reflections on civil society date back to Aristotle, but have been revisited in modern times following the cataclysmic changes in Eastern Europe and the Soviet Union. The dictatorial governments ruling for decades in the name of Communism systematically undermined civil society, crushing all independent groups or communities that resisted their rule. As the people, already suffering from preexisting ethnic and nationalist conflicts, became increasingly atomized, unable to trust either their governments or their fellow citizens, a wilding culture emerged. It remained largely invisible, held in check by the all-powerful authorities. But after 1989, with the collapse of the Berlin Wall and the government it symbolized, the wilding forces, suppressed for so many years, were now free to surface. An epidemic erupted in the form of revived antisemitism, with other ethnic and ultranationalist poisons spreading through the region, including the horrific "ethnic cleansing" in Bosnia. After the initial revolutionary euphoria had worn off, civic indifference, apathy, and a lack of trust and cooperation developed among citizens. Calls for the resurrection of civil society have reverberated from Budapest and Prague to Moscow, with some leaders, such as the Czech Republic's president Vaclav Havel, recognizing that the biggest challenge, ironically, after decades of rule under the rhetoric of collectivism, is the rebuilding of community.

The wilding crises in Eastern Europe and the United States are different from one another; one was bred by coercive collectivism and the other by untrammeled free-market individualism. Sociologist Alan Wolfe writes that both an overreaching government and an overblown market can, in different ways, colonize civil society and destroy it—the market, by glorifying selfishness, and the state, by substituting paternalism or coercion for conscience. Civil society blooms only where markets and governments are kept in reasonable check, and families, communities, and voluntary associations, the institutional seedbeds of love, morality, and trust, are free to prosper. The bonds of conscience and caring, as well as mechanisms of social accountability to be discussed below, help to ensure that private interests do not override the common good.[1]

Although there is no magic formula and no perfect model, civil society, in the United States as well as Eastern Europe, is the strongest and most suitable medicine for the wilding epidemic. Americans now urgently must recognize, as do virtually all Eastern Europeans, that they must dedicate themselves unwaveringly to reconstructing their society. America desperately needs its own *perestroika*. There are staggering obstacles, including the self-serving denials by many American leaders that a real domestic crisis exists. But if Americans can see through such happy-hour rhetoric, there are many reasons to believe that they can succeed.

THE CASE FOR HOPE

Over one hundred years ago, Alexis de Tocqueville worried that America was vulnerable to an individualism that "saps the virtues of public life," and "in the long run" might "attack and destroy" society itself. Tocqueville described it as an individualism "which disposes each member of the community to sever himself from the mass of his fellows," and to "feel no longer bound by a common interest." Americans must always be on guard, Tocqueville advises, against the deterioration of their individualistic culture into "a passionate and exaggerated love of self, which leads a man to connect everything with himself, and to prefer himself to everything else in the world."[2]

Tocqueville did not disapprove of the healthy self-interest that energized Americans, but he saw the thin line separating American individualism from wilding. Without strongly developed moral codes, the restless pursuit of self-interest inherent in a market economy could at any time degrade into an egoistic menace that might destroy society. But Tocqueville, a sober observer, was also extraordinarily optimistic about the American experiment. Counteracting the wilding virus was another side of America, the strength of its civil society. One manifestation was the personal generosity and helpfulness that he observed in all his American travels. "Although private interest directs the greater part of human actions in the United States," Tocqueville wrote, "it does not regulate them all. I must say that I have often seen Americans make great and real sacrifices to the public welfare; and I have remarked a hundred instances in which they hardly ever failed to lend faithful support to each other." Because an American is neither master nor slave to his fellow creature, "his heart readily leans to the side of kindness."[3]

Tocqueville recognized that the kinder and gentler side of American life was grounded in the political rights and free institutions which "remind every citizen, and in a thousand ways, that he lives in society." Tocqueville marveled at the Americans' propensity to "constantly form associations" of a thousand kinds in which they "voluntarily learn to help each other." Americans were constantly connecting and spontaneously creating the bonds of friendship, trust, and cooperation that lie at the heart of civil society.[4]

In the 150 years since Tocqueville's visit, the wilding epidemic has spread throughout America, but it has not totally destroyed the civil society that made such an impression on him. Much evidence suggests that Americans retain some of the openness, generosity, and moral idealism that, in Tocqueville's view, differentiated them from Europeans. Likewise, the free institutions and "propensity to associate" have not vanished. It is the sturdiness of this base, its survival in the face of the wilding onslaught, that offers grounds for optimism and a direction for the future.

Although wilding stories make sensational copy and fill the newspapers, there are also plenty of stories testifying to the survival of the side of the American heart "that readily leans toward kindness." On May 15, 1991, next to a story about the drug-related murder of an entire family, the *New York Times* reported that a woman fell six stories to her death while trying to rescue a friend's child. To reach the child, trapped near the top of a West

Side hotel, she had secured a sturdy television cable around her waist, tied the other end to a pipe, and tried to lower herself from the roof. The cable broke and she fell sixty feet. The woman, Jackie Knight, age 31, was a former foster child and had a child of her own.[5]

Each year in Boston, where stray bullets now terrorize entire neighborhoods, a remarkable number of people, 40,000 in 1994, join the Walk for Hunger. The marchers hike for twenty miles, often in inclement weather, to raise money for Project Bread, a group that helps provide meals for the homeless and hungry. Each participant takes time to approach sponsors, who agree to donate a certain amount of money for each mile that the walker completes. As one curbside viewer said, "You've got the elderly walking, you've got kids walking, you've got families walking. To me, it's the most beautiful sight to see all the people walking." Such walks are only one of a cornucopia of charitable endeavors that take regularly place in cities and towns across the United States.

At the very time that taxpayers are revolting and turning off the public spigot, volunteers are stepping in to help stop the bleeding that their own votes have precipitated. In many towns across the country, playground construction is done mainly by volunteers, in the spirit of traditional community barn-raising. In Plymouth, Massachusetts, the town library stays open only because of the generosity of over fifty volunteers; in nearby Raynham, the school libraries are run entirely by volunteers. Community booster groups rally to raise money to keep public buildings painted, keep school sports programs going, and plant trees and maintain the city parks.[6]

Even in the heart of Wall Street there are signs of the other America. Several multimillionaire commodities traders created the Robin Hood Foundation, an offbeat center that scours New York City "looking for neighborhood foundations that rescue the homeless, care for children with AIDS, fight drug abuse, or rebuild families." The organization raised over $2 million in 1990, and seeks to link community activists to business sponsors or technical experts who can be helpful. One of the founders says, "I couldn't sleep if I did not have a part in this sort of thing," and another says, "I love this city with a passion. I'm a walking poster for New York. I don't want to see the city go under."[7]

Such anecdotes are backed up by hard statistics documenting the generous side of America. About seven out of every ten households contribute to charity, donating an average of almost 2 percent of household income, a figure almost four times greater than that in Canada and England (a comparison that should take into account the national health plans and large social welfare programs that taxpayers in the latter countries support, thereby reducing the need for charity). About 45 percent of Americans over the age of 18 sacrifice their own time to volunteer, averaging about four hours a week, and totalling almost 20 billion hours of volunteer time nationwide.[8]

How can the wilding epidemic spread at the same time that moral commitments and compassionate behavior persist at these levels? As I argued in Chapter One, America in the 1990s is host simultaneously to a wilding culture and a civil culture, with sectors of the elites increasingly immersed in wilding and a vast number of ordinary Americans uneasily straddling the two cultures. Most Americans' lives are a struggle to reconcile wilding impulses with a nagging conscience that refuses to die. Many succumb to wilding pressures at the office but discover their humanity with family or friends. Conversely, some become wilders in their personal lives but express their conscience in admirable careers dedicated to constructive professional or business enterprise, public service, or social change.

The stubborn persistence of civil society and moral commitment provides a fertile seedbed for social reconstruction. The way to stop the wilding epidemic is to bolster all the empathic and moral sensibilities that Americans already display. Although these need to be fortified and mobilized with new visions, the project is more akin to catalyzing the surviving immune system of a weakened patient than seeking to transplant a new immune system to the patient whose own defenses have been destroyed.

But solving the problem will take serious cultural and institutional change. As I have argued, wilding grows out of an American individualism that is deeply rooted. America's leadership and major institutions increasingly fuel Americans' wilding side and provide serious disincentives to their less egoistic inclinations. We need the culture, economics, and politics of a civil society, where the rules of the success game encourage attention to morality and the common good. More precisely, we must rewrite the rules of the game such that those who neglect the collective interest will not prosper, and those who take it into account will realize their just rewards.

RETHINKING THE AMERICAN DREAM: A NEW COMMUNITARIANISM?

The American Dream has not always been a cultural template for wilding. As we consider rewriting the dream for a better future, we have the consolation that we can look to our history for guidance. Through most of America's past, the purely materialistic and individualistic side of the dream has been balanced by a moral and community-oriented side, preventing the dream from transmuting into a wilding recipe. Moreover, the dream has been inclusive, defining a set of common purposes to which all Americans could aspire. These historical features of the dream need to be recaptured in order to fortify civil society and purge the wilding epidemic.

The individualistic dream dominating today has its roots in the mythology of the self-made man and, as James Combs argues, "stems from the ideology of capitalism and the myth of unlimited abundance." As noted in Chapter Three, the nineteenth-century novelist Horatio Alger immortalized the materialist dream in his rags-to-riches fables. In its current form, it celebrates American heroes like basketball superstar Michael Jordan, who rose to fabulous success through his extraordinary individual talent and hard work.[9]

The materialistic dimensions of the dream have become so dominant that most Americans have forgotten that there was once another side to the dream. America has traditionally defined itself in terms of a set of high moral ideals, including democracy, equality, and tolerance. Values growing out of the religious and political foundations of the country, including the Puritan zeal for community and the American Revolution's idealization of civil democracy, helped to shape another dream, one that mythologized family, community, and civic responsibility. Through most of American history, the materialistic dream prevailed, but the dream that elevated community values warned that success should not be achieved at any price. America idealized its rural and small-town communities where, to a greater or lesser degree, as Combs notes, "religion, family, and democratic good feelings tempered the quest for power and money." Small-town community is still part of American mythology, helping explain why President Clinton has proudly publicized his roots in the tiny town of Hope, Arkansas.[10]

The two dreams define a creative tension in American history. In the 1930s, the Great Depression mobilized Americans to rally together and fashion a collective lifeline to ride out the economic storm. President Franklin Delano Roosevelt reinvigorated the dream of moral community, using the government to affirm that in a time of desperate need, Americans would take care of each other. Three decades later, in the 1960s, a whole generation of youth plunged into social activism and communal experiments, seeking a morally attractive alternative to the materialist dream of their 1950s childhoods.

The failure of the aspirations of the 1960s led, in the 1970s and 1980s, to perhaps the most extensive subordination of the moral dream in American history. Of the presidents since the 1960s, only Presidents Carter and Clinton, both inept and unsuccessful, sought to revive the moral quest. But to purge the wilding epidemic, Americans in the 1990s will have to rediscover and refashion a version of the moral dream in order to temper the current fever of individualistic materialism and resurrect civil society.

The moral vision will have to be creative because of the new threats that unchecked materialism now poses. It will have to encompass an ecological morality, for we now know that the untrammeled materialist dream is incompatible with planetary survival, becoming a form of wilding directed against nature itself. The greenhouse effect, the catastrophic heating up of the earth through promiscuous use of fossil fuels, is only the most frightening of the legacies of such environmental wilding. If Americans cannot learn to live within the limits dictated by the environment, they will be engaged not only in crimes against nature, but in a form of wilding against future generations who will bear the ultimate consequences.

Americans find it hard to accept any limits on materialism, for the dominant dream has equated freedom and fulfillment with the right to get as rich or famous as luck, talent, or hard work permits. To suggest that Michael Milken should not have been allowed to make or keep the $550 million he made in 1987 strikes us as un-American. But a civil society must respect not only ecological limits but also those dictated by the traditional American morality of fair play and egalitarianism. Uncapping all limits in the recent orgy of greed and deregulation has polarized the country, creating, as Kevin Phillips has argued, an unprecedented and morally unbearable division between rich and poor.[11]

Civil society is a society of inclusion, and the new dream will have to script new trade-offs between individual freedom and the survival of the community. This ultimately requires reviving a moral dream of community; not the utopian vision of communes that failed in the 1960s, but something simultaneously more modest and more ambitious: the reawakening of the American sense of community that can mobilize the country to unify and preserve itself in an era of unprecedented division.

Today, when the wilding epidemic has placed the survival of society itself in jeopardy, the new dream has to focus Americans on the common task of saving their society. Ironically, as suggested above, Americans have been led by their present leaders into thinking about saving every society but their own. President John Adams said in the eighteenth century that America should try to help other nations but "should go not abroad seeking monsters to destroy." Such common sense is reinforced when there are real dragons at home to slay. James Reston, senior *New York Times* political commentator, writes that rather than dreaming of a "new world order," we should be urgently dedicating ourselves to "a new American order" at home.[12]

As the world shrinks, Americans may be influenced by examples of civil society abroad, especially those of new global winners such as Japan. Japan has sensational financial and political scandals of its own, and new urban violence, such as the gas attacks in Tokyo subway stations, yet has managed to preserve its social infrastructure and is far less plagued by wilding. There is relatively little crime in the streets of Tokyo or Osaka and the Japanese family is intact; indeed, the entire society maintains the sensibility of one extended family. Although Americans are hardly likely to embrace the Japanese model, the Japanese economic miracle may jolt Americans into the recognition that tilting the balance back toward community is not only a recipe for success, but is essential for our survival.

Although the Japanese are passionate baseball fans and avid consumers of Steve's Ice Cream and Big Macs, they are anything but converts to the American Dream. Michio Morishima, seeking to answer the question "Why has Japan succeeded?" observes that beneath the glittering Western facade, Japanese culture remains profoundly shaped by Confucianism. A deeply nonindividualistic philosophy, Confucianism holds up the love of the group rather than the success of the individual as the highest virtue. Only "when the natural human affection found within the family [is] extended absolutely freely beyond the confines of the family, both to nonfamily members and to complete strangers," Confucius believed, could human nature reach "perfection and the social order [be] appropriately maintained." Japanese corporations remain as much Confucian as capitalist, thriving on the loyalty of employees who view the company as their second family. The entire Japanese economy is a Confucian marketplace that Adam Smith might not recognize, because everyone acts to benefit not so much themselves as their companies and communities and to solidify their connections to them.[13]

Americans do not have to embrace Confucianism to recognize that the country needs to strike a better balance between the individual and the group, both to survive as a civil society and to prosper in the world economy. Such a profound cultural shift, however, will happen slowly and arise as much from a reinterpretation of America's own experience as from any influences abroad. America's love affair with sports is only one of many areas where Americans already understand, without fully appreciating the implication of their own knowledge, that success is a team effort. The case of Michael Jordan is instructive. Polls in 1991 showed that Jordan, after he led the Chicago Bulls to the National Basketball Association world title, was one of the five best-known and most admired figures in America. The public assimilated Jordan into the heroic tradition of the individualistic dream, a man who literally soared to fame and fortune through his own efforts. But the fans knew that the real lesson of Jordan and the Bulls was that winning comes only when the individual, no matter how extraordinary, subordinates his or her own game to the team effort.

Jordan was the Michael Milken of professional basketball, piling up points as fast as Milken accumulated junk bonds. He led the league in scoring for five years running, awing fans and players alike with the most graceful and dazzling moves ever seen on a basketball court. But it was a one-man show and his teammates seemed unable to muster the spirit to win.

By 1990, Jordan and his team had worked out a new social contract. Jordan would still be the prime mover, but he would concentrate more on opening up opportunities for his teammates. He would drive to the center or one side, and when double-teamed or triple-teamed, he would whip the ball back to one of his open teammates. Jordan became as good a passer as a scorer and fully integrated his team into the offense. When the Bulls won the championship in 1991, the key to that victory was not Jordan's pyrotechnics, still dazzling as ever, but the new team chemistry. In the final championship series, there was one game where the Bulls seemed to slip back into their old ways, with Jordan carrying the entire offense. Jordan never allowed that to recur, however, taking hardly any shots in the first quarter of the game that followed to ensure that his teammates got into the game early. Jordan's sacrifice brought his team victory and greater glory than he could have ever achieved on his own.

Jordan fully understood that the victory was the team's, not his own. Every year after the championship series, the individual selected as Most Valuable Player is touted in a Disney commercial. Jordan refused to do the commercial unless the recognition, including the money, was extended to the whole team. In what should be a symbol for America in the 1990s, the camera showed not a lone, triumphant Michael Jordan, but a Jordan embracing his teammates, celebrating the Bulls as a winning family.

Jordan's generosity does not extend, however, to other "teammates," including the thousands of Third-World Nike shoe-factory workers who are collectively paid less than the $20 million that Jordan got in one year to advertise the product. Nonetheless, America needs to rewrite its social contract in the spirit Jordan displayed with his Chicago team. The culture of civil society is one of cooperation, invoking equal respect for the rights of individuals and the needs of the collective. Americans already intuitively recognize that the community has its own legitimate aims, responding positively a generation ago to John F. Kennedy's call to "ask not what your country can do for you, but what you can do for your country." As civil society disintegrates, Americans need to ponder seriously such rhetoric and translate it into a new way of life. This will require a rewriting of the American Dream and an initially painful acceptance of limits on individual self-aggrandizement. But as the Jordan case suggests, such restraints on the self will ultimately serve the collectivity and each self within it.

Rescripting the American Dream will demand a recharging of American cultural institutions responsible for moral development, especially schools, churches, and families. Unfortunately, wilding culture has already taken a deadly toll on these institutions, and the public debate about reviving them has been dominated by well-heeled groups who seek mainly to buttress free market morality. Yet, as sociologist Amitai Etzioni argues, these are the key institutions that can "serve to countervail excessive individualism" if they can rediscover a moral compass to counteract the market ethos of their host culture. Etzioni helped to launch a new "communitarian" discourse among academics and policy makers, including advisors in the

Clinton White House, that helped influence Clinton's rhetoric about a "New Covenant" and greater personal and social responsibility.[14]

Much will depend on the courage of intellectuals, teachers, and clerics, who have to be uncompromising in teaching that the ethos of fast money, careerism, and obsessional self-aggrandizement spells death for society, while also helping Americans articulate their hunger for community and their vision of the common good. Intellectuals will have to overcome the pressures to conform and show, by their personal example as well as their writings and preachings, that "making it" is not the ultimate value. Institutional change will challenge the moral fiber of both teachers and academic administrators. New financial pressures, for example, are making universities ever more dependent on corporate funding, and many elementary schools will soon be operated as profit-making private enterprises. This threatens to turn American education into the chattel of its corporate class, reinforcing the unpublicized, politically correct dogma of mainstream American economic thinking and making it ever more difficult to teach a morality that transcends the market. Education leaders must act now to ensure that schools and universities resist the changes that will compromise their moral mission, insisting on institutional arrangements that prevent the collapse of the pursuit of knowledge into the pursuit of profit. Some promising beginnings have emerged in the tattered public school system in Chicago, where efforts have been made to revive public education through new forms of parental involvement and community control, tentatively shaking up the entrenched bureaucracy and drawing on the fresh energies and ideas of those with the biggest stake in the educational process: parents, teachers, and the kids themselves.

THE SOCIAL MARKET: SOCIOLOGICAL SENSE AND DOLLARS AND CENTS

On June 12, 1991, President Bush, while pondering a new domestic strategy for the 1992 elections, made a stunning public confession that "the free market had failed." To solve domestic problems in the 1980s, "unconventional wisdom turned to the genius of the free market," the president explained. "We began a decade of exceptional economic growth and created 20 million new jobs. And yet, let's face it, many of our streets are still not safe, our schools have lost their edge, and millions still trudge the path of poverty." This remarkable statement, something akin to the pope publicly renouncing Catholicism, was a frank acknowledgement of the incompatibilities between the free market and civil society.

Political pundits and the public rapidly discounted the president's statement because he did not follow it up with any new policy initiatives.

But it was significant not only because of the source of the remark, but because it reflected nagging doubts about the free market that have persisted through much of American history. As Americans have struggled to choose between the materialist dream and the moral dream, they have had to wrestle with the tensions between the free market and community. The market system was an excellent vehicle for delivering the promises of the materialist dream, but as Bush himself finally seemed to recognize, it was far less effective in preserving the moral fiber of society. In periods when the moral dream comes more strongly to the fore, such as the 1930s and 1960s, Americans have pioneered economic models such as the New Deal and the Great Society, that depart from free-market scripture.

When Bush delivered his speech on free-market failure, he said that there was a "better way," suggesting that to tackle the urgent problems on the home front required new economic thinking. Unfortunately, virtually the only innovative economic policies in his administration came from those zealots who seek to have the market take over everything from the public schools to police protection. Some advocated such innovations as a "free market in babies," which could help resolve the abortion debate by making it economically feasible for (especially poor) mothers to carry their babies to term and then sell them.

Such radical extensions of the market model, exemplified by some publicized cases of surrogate parenting, help to highlight the ways in which the free market violates civil society. Surrogate mother Mary Beth Whitehead sued to get her baby back, feeling she was wilding against her own humanity by selling her infant. In the pure free market, as Gary Becker, one of its leading intellectual advocates, proposes, the cash nexus governs all human behavior, including relations between teachers and students, men and women, parents and children. One does not have to be a fan of Karl Marx to recognize that such commodification of life undermines the trust, love, and morality that sustains civil society.[15]

In the wake of Communism's collapse, the Bush and Clinton administrations tried to export a free-market revolution abroad rather than find prosocial economic alternatives at home. But the Eastern Europeans are paying more attention to their fellow Europeans, especially the Germans, who long ago renounced the free-market model and embraced what they now call "the social market." Under this model, Germans have not only prospered economically, but, like the Japanese, have preserved a civil society and have maintained, until the stresses of reunification caused a recent explosion of attacks on immigrants, an impressive immunity from the wilding epidemic. As Helmut Giesecke, head of the foreign trade department in the Association of German Chambers of Industry and Commerce, asks, "Do you see people on the street here? Are they without cars? They have decent food, housing and clothes, and their children are well-educated." He is polite enough not to mention that the murder rate in his country is barely one-tenth that in America, although this will come as no surprise to most American tourists, who feel safer on the streets of Frankfurt or Bonn than Detroit or New York.[16]

This is the legacy of a century of European efforts to build an alternative with a social conscience to the free market. The Swedes, Danes, Austrians, and Germans recognize that they are not playing Adam Smith's game. "We are not operating a marketplace economy," admits German industrialist Giesecke, but rather a "social marketplace economy [that] guarantees food, shelter, schooling, and medical attention to every person, not as welfare but as human rights." Government, labor, and business work together to reconcile prosperity with social justice. German business has supported this program, according to Giesecke, because "this social network really works," leading to a well-educated, healthy, and motivated work force whose productivity keeps increasing.[17]

Perhaps ultimately the Germans support the social infrastructure because they know firsthand the horrific consequences when society totally breaks down. They have experienced a Germany gone completely wild, and many recognize that it could happen again. The greater internal homogeneity of Germany, Austria, Sweden, and other European "social market" societies also allows them to feel a greater connection to others and savor the sense of family so powerful in Japan. Even as European cultures grow more individualistic and consumerist, their social marketplace economies may prevent a descent into wilding.

The development of an American social market could be one of the most potent remedies for the wilding epidemic. It would provide a way to reconcile economic growth and justice, and to help solve America's social problems by building on its own deepest value: democracy.

The social market is the economic recipe for a civil society, but the Western-European version is not the one Americans are likely to embrace. The European model is a universal welfare state, in which the government shelters groups unprotected by the market, responds to the medical, housing, and social needs of the population that the market neglects, and comprehensively regulates business to ensure social responsibility. But American history, as well as its current fiscal crisis, argues against the likelihood that Americans, barring another Great Depression, will look solely to the state; although there is a crucial role for government to play in stopping the wilding epidemic, it can only be a catalyst, not the central player.

The key to a social market system is not big government but new institutions, whether public or private, that rectify the tendency of our current market economy to write social costs and benefits out of the equation. The

American free market responds mainly to the desires of the individual actor—whether a person or corporation—and is largely indifferent to the spillover effects that transactions may have on the rest of society. When a factory decides to pollute, the social cost of bad air and ensuing discomfort or respiratory disease is what economists call an *externality,* a real cost, but one that the owner can ignore, because it is society rather than the factory that pays the ultimate bill. In the pure free-market model, there is no economic incentive for the individual to help society nor any market disincentive to be antisocial; the market simply does not discriminate, operating with so-called benign neglect. As such neglect accumulates, with the market turning a blind eye to the millions of externalities that affect society every day, benign neglect becomes catastrophic social blindness and civil society is placed in jeopardy.

A social market corrects such social blindness by writing social costs and benefits back into the equation. It is a market that seeks to internalize the externalities, and thus become socially responsible, by giving social stakeholders a voice in corporate decisions and by devising strategies to guarantee that economic wilders will pay the cost of their sociopathic behavior (and, conversely, that the good citizen will receive his or her just rewards). One way to do this is to rely on government, which can compel pro-social choices through legislation or induce them through tax incentives, as when the state enforces worker health and safety standards or gives tax credits to factories installing antipollution devices. But there is another approach, one more appealing to Americans wary of government and committed to democracy, that involves redesigning economic institutions to be better equipped to exercise social responsibility on their own initiative. One such approach involves new corporate ownership and participation arrangements, in which workers and local citizens gain a voice and can speak up for the needs of the larger community. The Germans, although relying primarily on government, also have invented a "co-determination" system, which requires that every industrial enterprise with more than 500 workers select half its governing board of trustees from among its own employees. This has been successful for over forty years, contributing not only to the German economic boom, but to a civil industrial society in which ordinary workers have been able to ensure that their health and safety are protected, their grievances addressed, and their jobs protected by investment strategies that prioritize domestic employment as well as overseas profit. Co-determination is a version of economic democracy that works.

In a series of seminal books, sociologist Severyn Bruyn describes the many down-to-earth ways, some already highly developed in America, to fashion a self-regulating social market; that is, one that works to dissuade economic wilding and preserve civil society without resorting to big government.

Numerous forms of worker ownership and participation, including cooperatives and employee stock ownership plans (ESOPs), in which employees own
a piece or all of their companies, can help compel the company to treat its
employees fairly and practice workplace democracy. The cooperative, as its
name implies, has the potential to turn the workplace itself into a civil society,
because everyone within it has equal rights and self-interest is more closely
wedded to the collective interest than in a conventional firm. Another inno-
vation involves corporate social charters that bind businesses to serve desig-
nated social missions, as in the case of community credit unions that are
structured to reinvest in the community and offer low-interest loans to poorer
residents. Land trusts, modern versions of the colonial concept of the com-
mons, can remove property from the commercial market and legally ensure
that it is used to serve community needs. A new field of social accounting can
help take stock of the social costs and benefits of corporate decisions. Social
capital, such as the more than $3 trillion in American pension funds, one of
the largest and still growing pots of money in the world, can be used to invest
in affordable housing and community economic development. The new practice of social investing could be the first step in turning the stock market into
what sociologist Ritchie Lowry calls "good money," where investors seek a
profit but also a social return on their money. "Social screens"—report cards
on companies compiled by outside analysts—now tell investors which corporations are economic wilders and which are responsible citizens. Companies
seeking to attract the funds of millions of social investors have to demonstrate
not only what they are doing for the bottom line, but what they are doing for
their communities.[18]

America has not yet built a main highway toward this version of the
social market, but it is already carving out many smaller roads in that direction. There are now over 10,000 American ESOPs, including huge companies such as United Airlines, Avis Rent-a Car, and Weirton Steel, and there is
evidence that they are more responsive to their employees and their customers. Studies show that worker-owners are more productive and deliver
higher quality, with Avis now number one in ratings of customer satisfaction. Hundreds of ESOPs and cooperatives, including large worker-owned
factories, practice sophisticated forms of workplace democracy. They are
proving effective in job creation and retention, and are responsible for saving hundreds of jobs during the epidemic of factory closings in the last
decade. According to polls, including one by Peter Hart, economic democracy makes sense to most Americans; approximately 70 percent say that they
would welcome the opportunity to work in an employee-owned company.[19]

Employee ownership in the United States has grown fifty-fold since
1974, with employees being the largest shareholders in more than 15 percent of all public companies. The cutting edge is in the Fortune 500, where
by 1990 the percentage of employee ownership was 11.7 percent in Ford,

9.3 percent in Exxon, 10 percent in Texaco, 16 percent in Chevron, 24.5 percent in Procter & Gamble, 18.9 percent in Lockheed, and 14.5 percent in Anheuser-Busch. By 1995, employee ownership was higher than 30 percent in huge companies such as Kroger, McDonnell Douglas, Bethlehem Steel, Rockwell International, Hallmark Cards, Trans World Airlines, U.S. Sugar, and Tandy Corporation. Thirteen percent of the labor force—11 million workers—are employee owners, more than the number of private sector union members. The total value of stock owned by workers in their own companies now exceeds $100 billion.

The thousand American companies with the highest percentage of employee ownership constitute the nucleus of a new social market sector of the economy. Collectively, according to employee ownership scholar Joseph Blasi, they hold 29 percent of the market value, 27 percent of the sales, and 20 percent of the private sector jobs in the American economy. The proliferation of 401K retirement plans, in which workers receive pension benefits in the form of employee stocks, will increase the size and power of this new economic sector. If these companies sustain employee loyalty, high productivity, and robust profits, they will teach a much wider range of American companies and employees about the virtues of both employee ownership and social market values.

By 1985, there were already over 500 land trusts nationwide, which have since helped rehabilitate inner-city neighborhoods as well as preserve rural acreage. Pension funds, such as those of state and municipal employees in California and New York, have already invested hundreds of millions of dollars in affordable housing and community economic development. Sociologist Lowry estimates that American social investors have plowed somewhere between half a trillion and one trillion dollars into "ethical investments," rewarding corporations such as Ben and Jerry's, a highly profitable and socially progressive ice-cream company. The company buys nuts harvested from the threatened Brazilian rain forests and gives almost half the profits to organizations fighting to save the forests; it also keeps a relatively small salary gap between its highest and lowest paid employees, cultivating a spirit of egalitarianism that pays off in happier and more motivated employees.[20]

The political genius of these social market innovations is that they are attractive to liberals, because they promote equality and justice, as well as to conservatives, because they do not require massive government intervention and offer ordinary citizens a greater stake in the marketplace. In the 1970s, Senator Russell Long, a conservative Democrat from Louisiana, was the prime sponsor in the Senate for employee-ownership legislation, and the idea found considerable support in the Reagan White House as a strategy for building "people's capitalism." Liberal activists in universities, unions, and local communities also fight for employee ownership, as a way to save jobs and increase workers' control.

Any idea that can draw such enthusiastic support from both sides of the political spectrum has the potential to be instituted on a large scale. At the same time, however, most of the more radical social market innovations have been resisted by powerful forces, as in the case of banks systematically denying credit to cooperatives. Mainstream businesses and politicians have also worked to water down innovations such as ESOPs to keep them from turning real decision-making power over to workers. Nonetheless, both political parties, and particularly those Democrats in 1996 and beyond who seek real solutions to America's wilding crisis, should hone the idea of the social market as a new public philosophy and the basis of a new legislative agenda.

Although government is not the prime mover in this emerging social market, it has helped midwife the new system and will have to nurture it further if a new market order is to grow and become preservative of civil society. Government has to set up the legislative framework for corporate social charters, ESOPs, and worker cooperatives, establish the legal safeguards and guidelines for social investment of pension funds, provide encouragement through loans and tax credits for employee ownership and community-development funds, and help oversee and underwrite the entire new economic nexus. Its regulatory role will remain powerful for many years and will never disappear, for, as I suggest below, many public interests can be guaranteed only by the state. The government will not give the marching orders or own the means of production as it does under communism or socialism; the social market is still a market system, infused with Confucian sensibilities.

There is special urgency now regarding children. One of every four American children lives in poverty, and public policy in the Gingrich era threatens to guarantee that the next generation will mature into uninhibited wilders. As civil society unravels, children are the most vulnerable group, being totally dependent on the love, moral guidance, and social spending that are casualties of the wilding culture. The state cannot raise and socialize children, but one of its highest priorities should be to help finance and save the institutions, including the family and schools, that can do the job. These are now in such desperate condition that further benign neglect is unacceptable; moreover, sensible and economical family and educational strategies have already been articulated by numerous national commissions and children's advocates such as the Children's Defense Fund. The Fund argues that it would only take about $45 billion a year to bail children and families out of poverty, a fraction of what Congress has already appropriated to bail out the S & Ls. None of these programs are utopian and none need to be budget-busters.

The rise of the embryonic social market is part of a second American revolution, this one to ensure economic rights and to save the society liberated by the Revolution 200 years ago. Then, the issue was inventing a political constitution; now it involves rewriting the economic constitution. As in the first Revolution, ordinary citizens will have to struggle against powerful, entrenched forces, the King Georges of contemporary America who are more dedicated to their own privileges than to saving civil society in America.

A NEW BILL OF RIGHTS?
THE POLITICS OF CIVIL SOCIETY

America's romance with individualism and the free market has its virtues, but it has clouded Americans' understanding of what makes society tick. Civil society arises only when individuals develop strong obligations to the larger "us" that can override the perennial, very human preoccupation with the self. Such larger commitments bloom only under special conditions: when the community shows that it cares so deeply for each of its members that each, in turn, fully understands his or her debt to society and seeks to pay it back in full.

The Japanese and Europeans, in their very different ways, seem to appreciate this deal, or contract, that preserves civil society. Japanese corporations smother the Japanese worker in a cocoon of secure employment, health benefits, housing, and other social necessities that make it almost impossible for workers to imagine life outside of the group. Through their expansive welfare states, the Europeans deliver their own bushel of benefits and entitlements that the citizen recognizes as indispensable to personal survival and happiness. Both systems possess their own serious problems, and are partially eroding in the face of global economic pressures, but succeed in creating the allegiance to the larger community that breeds immunity to the wilding epidemic.

Each civil society has to find its own way of inspiring its members' devotion, but all must deliver those rock-bottom necessities essential to the pursuit of life, liberty, and happiness. These include a minimal level of personal safety, food, shelter, and a livelihood. Social orphans deprived of these essentials are unable to fulfill any larger obligation to society, for their existence is entirely consumed by the brutish struggle for personal survival.

This leads to the idea of *social citizenship*, an extension of the familiar but narrower concept of political citizenship. The rights to health care, housing, and a job can be seen as social rights, parallel to our political rights to vote and to free speech enshrined in our constitution. Political rights apply to all citizens automatically, because they are the precondition of democracy as a system. Similarly, social rights should be extended automatically to everyone, for they are the precondition of civil society's survival.

The Japanese deliver such social rights through a paternalistic, corporate, extended family, largely private, whereas the Europeans do it through the welfare state. America will have to find its own way. Ideally, the emerging institutions of the social market would, in the long run, provide a local, democratic, and non-statist solution. One possibility is an American version of the success achieved by Mondragon, a remarkable complex of over 100 industrial cooperatives in the Basque region of Spain. Mondragon has suc- ceeded during the past forty years in guaranteeing job security, housing, health care, and education to its members with scarcely any help from the state. Workers in the cooperatives have created cooperative schools, hospitals, insurance companies, and banks that offer robust social security from birth to death. The Mondragon complex, which is the largest manufacturer of durable goods in Spain and employs thousands of worker-owners, has never permanently laid off a worker, reproducing the equivalent of the Japanese system of lifetime employment, while also inventing new cooperatives in one of the most impressive programs of job creation in the world.

Whether an American social market could evolve in such a direction is purely speculative, but clearly there are ways to provide social rights that are realistic, democratic, and do not require big government. America is the only major industrialized country not to offer health care as a social right to all its citizens. In Germany and other European countries, the federal government is involved in collecting taxes to support national health care, but allows provincial councils and local communities to administer their own programs. Clinton's failure to deliver national health-care reform partly reflected his inability to persuade the public that his plan was not a recipe for big government.

Although government is not the preferred agent, it is the guarantor of last resort. When people are homeless, starving, or jobless, civil society has failed, and a wilding virus is activated. It is not silly idealism or bleeding-heart liberalism, but a conservative and prudent defense of the social order that requires public action.

For this reason, legal scholars such as Columbia University law profes-sor Louis Henkin are pointing to "genetic defects" in our Bill of Rights that constitutionally guarantee political but not social citizenship rights. Chief Justice William Rehnquist, in a 1989 Supreme Court decision, argued that the Constitution confers "no affirmative right to governmental aid, even when such aid may be necessary to secure life." This leads constitutional attorney Paul Savoy, former dean of the John F. Kennedy University School of Law, to point out that "our civil rights and civil liberties are rights in the negative sense" and "do not include affirmative obligations on government. We do not have a constitutional right," Savoy observes, "to have the state provide us with health care, or give us shelter if we are homeless, or prevent a child from being beaten or from starving to death." A coalition of unions, environmentalists, and community groups has responded by calling for a second Bill of Rights that would entitle all citizens to the elementary social rights of shelter, food, and health care.[21]

Social rights are not a free ride for the population, for with them come demanding social obligations. Citizenship is an intimate dance of rights and obligations, and social citizens need to embrace enthusiastically the moral obligations that come with their new entitlements. This means not only willingly paying the taxes required to keep civil society healthy, but also devoting time and effort, as I detail below, to community-building at work, in the neighborhood, and in the country at large.

The problem with the Left is that it demands rights without spelling out the obligations that have to accompany them; the problem with the Right is that it expects obligations to be fulfilled without ceding social rights in return. Both positions are absurd, because rights and obligations are flip sides of civil society's coin of the realm. We need a new politics that marries the Left's moral passion for rights with the Right's sober recognition of duty.

DEFENDING OUR LIVES: GETTING FROM HERE TO THERE

But what do we do now? Americans are a pragmatic people and want down-to-earth answers. Although there is no recipe or magic formula, we can act now to stop the wilding epidemic. If we want to survive with our humanity intact, we have no alternative.

Since wilding can destroy society, we are all fighting to stay alive. Obviously, if we each felt we had a desperate illness, we would mobilize ourselves to act immediately, to save ourselves. But since wilding is a societal crisis and not a biological illness, individuals can feel a deceptive immunity. It is possible to feel healthy, have fun, and enjoy life as society begins to come undone.

But as the epidemic spreads, everyone will increasingly feel at risk. The personal meaning of the wilding crisis is that we each have to spend more and more time simply defending our lives, defending our property, defending our livelihood, defending our health, defending our physical safety, defending our ego. This imposes a terrible burden on the individual, and it can easily fuel the "me" mentality at the heart of the problem, but it also unlocks the riddle of what to do. Not only will the illusion of immunity diminish, but the wisdom of dealing with the underlying disease and not just the symptoms will become more apparent.

One can start defending one's life, as Albert Brook's film comedy of that title suggests, either wisely or foolishly. The shortsighted approach involves trying to save oneself by abandoning everyone else, exemplified by the suburbanites who cocoon themselves within homes wired with the latest security technology and who refuse to pay taxes to support the center city. Robert Reich suggests that such a "politics of secession" is sweeping upper-middle-class America. If so, it is a blind and morally unsustainable choice, for it creates short-term symptomatic relief while worsening the disease.

Because the disease is social, so too must be the cure. As the social infrastructure begins to ulcerate and bleed, the rational long-term way to defend one's life is to help repair the damaged societal tissue, whether it be potholes in the road, hungry people sleeping on grates, or sociopathic competitiveness at the office. Doing the right thing, then, is defending one's life by cooperating to build up community strength and bolster personal and collective resistance. This requires no saintly sacrifice for the common good, but tough-minded and clear-eyed assessment of where the threat lies. When facing a wilding threat, the first question to ask is, "What in myself or my social environment is creating this threat?" Once that question is answered, the next is, "What can I do about it?" Some cases will require purely personal change, falling back on all one's psychological and moral strength, as well as love and support from family, friends, or mentors, to counter wilding impulses within oneself or susceptibility to wilding influence in the environment. Most cases will also require acting for some form of social change to extirpate the external poison, whether at work, in the neighborhood, or in the White House, typically achievable only with the help of others.

Fortunately, the wisdom of social action is obvious in a huge variety of circumstances, and Americans are already responding, especially where their own health is involved. When kids in Woburn, Massachusetts, were getting sick because of toxic chemicals, parents got together to clean up the toxic dump and hold the wilding factory accountable. In the 1990s, Americans are recognizing that staying healthy has become a political action project requiring a massive environmental clean-up, and they are not waiting for lackadaisical governments to take the lead. "People are recognizing they can in fact control their environment," Hal Hiemstra, a Washington environmental activist notes. "They're starting to say, 'we've had it.'" The *Boston Globe* reports that "an environmental wake-up call [is] being sounded nationwide by communities alarmed by the federal government's inertia and inspired by their own sense of power to reshape the landscape." These activists are not only defending their lives but, the *Globe* observes, "are local heroes on planetary matters."[22]

Heroes of a different sort are the residents of suburban communities around Minneapolis, who swam against the tide and rejected the politics of secession, the suburban wilding that has helped push Bridgeport, Connecticut, into Chapter Eleven bankruptcy and left New York City and hundreds of other cities teetering on the brink. The Minnesota suburbs joined with Minneapolis in the mid-1980s and formed a regional pact "whereby any community enjoying 40 percent more than the average growth of the region in any given year would have to share with the other signers of the pact." Such apparent sacrifice for the larger good is just plain common sense, because if the city center failed, it would bring the surrounding communities down with it. The great irony, as John Shannon of the Urban Institute notes, "is that Minneapolis is now enjoying boom times and must pay out to the suburbs." A modern Aesop's fable, it shows how cooperation for the common good is, indeed, a form of enlightened self-interest.[23]

We can begin to cure the wilding sickness by doing more of what we have always done well and doing it better: taking responsibility for our lives through civic participation. Tocqueville was amazed at the richness of America's democracy; its dense web of voluntary associations and democratic town meetings made it unique. "The free institutions which the inhabitants of the United States possess, and the political rights of which they make so much use," Tocqueville explains, "remind every citizen, and in a thousand ways, that he lives in society." In other words, democracy, and more democracy, is the best antidote for wilding and the most nourishing food for the social infrastructure.

Americans have become apathetic and indifferent to national politics, but we still retain our propensity to join together in what Tocqueville called "an immense assemblage of associations." One researcher suggests that there are now over 500,000 self-help groups in the United States with over 15 million members; many, whether alcoholics, abused children, battered spouses, or codependents, are casualties of the wilding epidemic who, by joining with others, are taking enlightened first steps toward not only recovering personally but rebuilding civil society. The same can be said of the millions of others involved in volunteer efforts and political activism at local or higher levels.

President Clinton has said that his favorite achievement was his national service program, which enlisted thousands of young people for work on community programs for the poor, elderly, disabled, and disadvantaged, in exchange for help in getting a college education. Community service has become, in fact, a saving remnant of the 1990s, and Clinton's program is the best example of his "New Covenant," which holds that everyone is entitled to health care, education, and other social rights, but should pay their debt back through a generous life of social responsibility. Millions of Americans recognize that giving back can be both fun and morally compelling, and are serving their communities in movements to help the homeless, feed the hungry, care for AIDS patients, tutor the illiterate, protect the environment, and help organize America's workers and poor people. Many recognize that in addition to individual volunteers, we need sustained social movements that can provide the voice and muscle for ordinary citizens against the power of giant, greedy corporations and unresponsive government. This will require most of all the resurrection of a labor movement that speaks for social justice and economic democracy.

In a recent study, the Kettering Institute of Dayton, Ohio, concluded that Americans' indifference to national politics reflects less pure selfishness or apathy than despair about leaders and the absence of real choices. America desperately needs a new generation of political leaders who will tell the truth about the wilding crisis and articulate a new moral vision. But because no such leaders are now in view, the burden falls on the rest of us, where it ultimately belongs. It remains to be seen whether Americans will find in themselves the emotional and moral strength to forge a new collective dream.

NOTES

1. Alan Wolfe, *Whose Keeper? Social Science and Moral Obligation* (Berkeley: University of California Press, 1989).
2. Alexis de Tocqueville, *Democracy in America,* Vol. II (Cambridge: Sever and Francis, 1863), pp. 119–20, 121, 123.
3. Ibid., p. 128.
4. Ibid., p. 129.
5. Constance L. Hays, "Fall Kills Woman Trying to Help a Friend's Child," *New York Times,* May 15, 1991, p. B3.
6. Robert Preer, "Volunteers Plug Cash Gap in the Suburbs," *Boston Globe,* June 9, 1991, pp. 1, 8.
7. Kathleen Teltsch, "Nowadays, Robin Hood Gets the Rich to Give to the Poor," *New York Times,* June 3, 1991, p. B1.
8. Virginia Ann Hodgkinson and Murray S. Weitzman, *Dimensions of the Independent Sector* (Washington D.C.: Independent Sector, 1989), pp. 7–9.
9. James Combs, *Polpop: Politics and Popular Culture in America* (Bowling Green: Green University Popular Press, 1984), p. 29.
10. Ibid., p. 34.
11. Phillips, *Politics of Rich and Poor* (New York: Random House, 1990), Chapter 1.
12. James Reston, "A Persistent American Yearning," *New York Times Magazine,* June 16, 1991, p. 45.
13. Michio Morishima, *Why Has Japan Succeeded?* (Cambridge: Cambridge University Press, 1982), p. 3.
14. Amitai Etzioni, *The Spirit of Community* (New York: Crown, 1994).

15. For an excellent discussion of the structural incompatibilities between the "free market" and civil society see Alan Wolfe, *Whose Keeper?* pp. 31ff.

16. "Consensus Fuels Ascent of Europe," *Boston Globe,* May 13, 1990, p. 19.

17. Ibid.

18. Severyn Bruyn, *A Future for the American Economy* (Stanford: Stanford University Press, 1991). See also Bruyn, *The Field of Social Investment* (Cambridge: Cambridge University Press, 1987), and Bruyn and James Meehan, *Beyond the Market and the State* (Philadelphia: Temple University Press, 1985). See also Ritchie Lowry, *Good Money* (New York: W.W. Norton, 1991).

19. Bruyn, *Future for the American Economy.* op. cit.

20. Lowry, op. cit.

21. Paul Savoy, "Time for a Second Bill of Rights," *The Nation,* June 17, 1991, p. 815–16.

22. Larry Tye, "Local Heroes on Planetary Matters," *Boston Globe,* June 22, 1991, p. 3.

23. Renee Loth, "Small Cities, Big Problems," *Boston Globe,* June 23, 1991, pp. A25, A28.

(Acknowledgments continued)

James Alan Fox and Jack Levin, excerpts from "Inside the Mind of Charles Stuart," *Boston Magazine* (April 1990). Copyright © 1990 by Boston Magazine, Inc., a subsidiary of METROCORP. Reprinted with the permission of *Boston Magazine.*

Kathleen Hughes and David Jefferson, excerpts from "Why Would Brothers Who Had Everything Murder Their Parents?" *The Wall Street Journal* (March 20, 1990). Copyright © 1990 by Dow Jones & Company, Inc. Reprinted with the permission of *The Wall Street Journal.*

[Approximately 46 words from personal communication by Noam Chomsky with the author, 1991.] CREDIT: Reprinted with the permission of Noam Chomsky.

Connie Bruck, excerpts from *The Predator's Ball* (New York: Penguin, 1988). Copyright © 1988 by Connie Bruck. Reprinted with the permission of Simon & Schuster, Inc. and Penguin Books USA.

Susan Trausch, excerpts from "The Generous Greed Machine," *Boston Globe* (March 4, 1990). Copyright © 1990 by the Globe Newspaper Company. Reprinted with the permission of *The Boston Globe.*

Rob Polner, excerpts from "A Real Education in the New York City School System," *In These Times* (April 11–17, 1990). Reprinted with the permission of *In These Times,* a biweekly news magazine published in Chicago.

Excerpts from "Warning: The Standard of Living is Slipping," *Business Week* (April 20, 1987). Copyright © 1987 by McGraw-Hill, Inc. Reprinted with the permission of *Business Week.*

Phillipe Bourgois, excerpts from *The New York Times* article. Reprinted with the permission of the author.

Craig Wolf, excerpts from "Ten Teen-Age Girls Held in Upper Broadway Pinprick Attacks," *The New York Times* (November 8, 1989). Copyright © 1989 by The New York Times Company. Reprinted with the permission of *The New York Times.*

Dirk Johnson, excerpts from "In U.S. Parks, Some Seek Retreat, But Find Crime," *The New York Times* (August 21, 1990). Copyright © 1990 by The New York Times Company. Reprinted with the permission of *The New York Times.*

Tom Ashbrook, excerpts from "A View From the East," *The Boston Globe Sunday Magazine* (February 19, 1989). Copyright © 1989 by the Globe Newspaper Company. Reprinted with the permission of *The Boston Globe.*

Phillipe Bourgois, "Just Another Night on Crack Street" *The New York Times* magazine, pages 148–150, April 20, 1987. Copyright © 1987 by The New York Times Company. Reprinted by permission.

Index

About the Author

Charles Derber is professor of sociology at Boston College and director of its graduate program in social economy and social justice. A prolific writer and speaker on American society, he has become a leading commentator on economic and cultural individualism, and has advanced influential new communitarian ideas melding the sociology of Durkheim and Marx. His books include *The Pursuit of Attention: Power and Individualism in Everyday Life* (Oxford); *Professionals as Workers: Mental Labor in Advanced Capitalism* (G.K. Hall); *Power in the Highest Degree: Professionals and the Rise of a New Mandarin Order* (Oxford); *The nuclear Seduction: Why the Nuclear Arms Race Doesn't Matter—and What Does* (University of California), and *What's Left" Radical Politics in the Post-Comunist Era* (University of Massachusetts).

In addition to his scholarly writing, Derber espouses a public sociology that brings sociological perspectives on key social and political issues to a general audience. He has played an important role in the public debate about a new communitarian economics and politics. His political and cultural essays appear in *The Boston Globe, The Utne Reader, Science, Tikkun Magazine, The Responsive Community,* and *In These Times.* He appears frequently on radio and television to talk about his books and contemporary political, economic, and social issues.